Mycenae paranaenses

Koninklijke Nederlandse Akademie van Wetenschappen
Verhandelingen, Afd. Natuurkunde, Tweede Reeks, deel 97

Mycenae paranaenses

R.A. Maas Geesteranus and
A.A.R. de Meijer

North-Holland, Amsterdam/Oxford/New York/Tokyo, 1997

Royal Netherlands Academy of Arts and Sciences
P.O. Box 19121, 1000 GC Amsterdam, the Netherlands

Authors' adresses:
R.A. Maas Geesteranus
Rijksherbarium
P.O. Box 9514
2300 RA Leiden
The Netherlands

A.A.R. de Meijer
Sociedade de Pesquisa em Vida
Selvagem e Educação Ambiental
Cx.P. 305 80.001–970 Curitiba
Brazil

ISBN 0-444-85817-2

CONTENTS

PART I

PART II

PART III

PART 1

Fig. A. The States of Brazil (Arq. Biol. Tecnol. 35: 623. 1992).

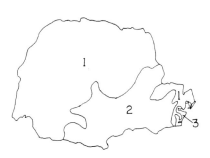

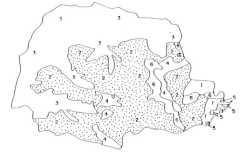

Fig. B. Climatic regions in the State of Paraná

1. Wet subtropical mesothermic with hot summers.
2. Wet subtropical mesothermic with mild summers.
3. Very wet tropical.

Fig. C. Vegetational areas of Paraná
1. Dense ombrophilous forest.
2. Mixed ombrophilous forest.
3. Seasonal semi-deciduous forest.
4. Graminoid-woody savanna.
5. Pioneer formations areas.
6. Ecological tension areas.

3

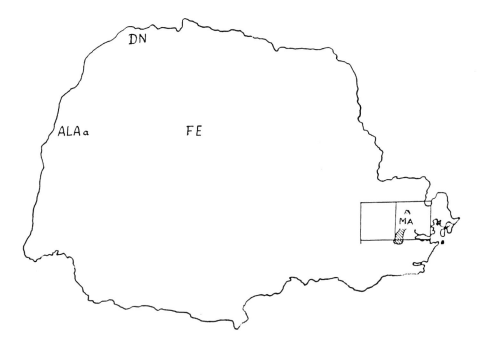

Fig. D. Study areas in the central and northwestern parts of Paraná.

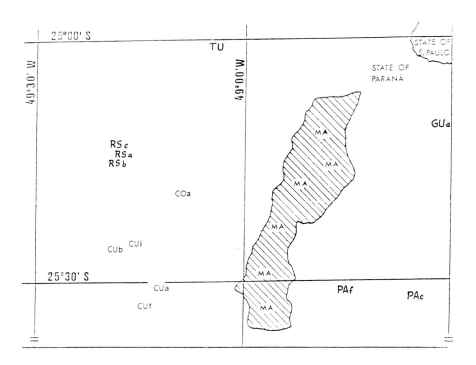

Fig. E. Study areas in and around Curitiba.

Over 250 species of *Mycena* have been described from the South American area. Keys to these species are either non-existent or lacking important detail. To try to name a species from this region, therefore, may be a hazardous enterprise, and when the second author suggested that his recent collections, gathered between 1979 and 1996, from the State of Paraná (Brazil) be identified and the results published, the first author hesitated. He thought of the many South American species described by Singer and his type specimens deposited in various herbaria. He also remembered the advice of a colleague, familiar with South American conditions, not to underestimate the obstacles to be surmounted before permission is granted for the loan of type specimens. He further recalled to mind other cases where reexamination of old types yielded distressingly little microscopic information. With these considerations in mind, it was decided to start the present project, but on the understanding that, unless unavoidable, type specimens would be left alone.

From the outset, both authors realized that their undertaking would be not only one of unknown magnitude, but also one not exempt of difficulties, omissions and possible errors.

PHYSIOGRAPHY OF THE REGION

The State of Paraná is one of the southern states of Brazil, lying mainly south of the Tropic of Capricorn, bounded to the east by the Atlantic Ocean, and covering an area of nearly 200,000 square kilometers. Topographically, it consists of a narrow coastal zone, separated by a mountain range called Serra do Mar from three successive plateaus sloping down to the west.

Paraná is divided into three climatic regions (Fig. B). Region 1, by far the largest, is wet subtropical mesothermic with hot summers and rare frosts in winter, rainfall in the summer and absence of a dry season. Average temperatures range from over 22°C in summer to over 18°C in winter. Region 2 is wet subtropical mesothermic with mild summers, rare frosts in winter and absence of a dry season. Average temperatures are below 22°C in summer and below 18°C in winter. Region 3 is very wet tropical, without frosts. Average temperatures rise above 22°C in the hot months and higher than 18°C in the colder months.

The average annual precipitation varies from 1200 mm in the northern regions to 4000 mm in the cloud forest of the mountains.

The soil in most parts of Paraná is acid, with the exception of a narrow calcareous zone north of Curitiba. This region has long since been denuded of its primary forest, and nowadays abounds with lime-kilns, although some small and isolated patches of secondary forest still remain.

It has been estimated that 85 per cent of the surface of Paraná was originally covered by native forest (Fig. C), three per cent of which remains at present, predominantly situated in three major areas. These are (1) the Iguazu National Park (Brazil's oldest national park) with seasonal semi-deciduous submontane forest; (2) the Serra do Mar mountain area with dense om-brophilous forest (ranging from lowland forest to high mountain forest; (3) the coastal plainland in and around Guaraqueçaba bay, with dense om-brophilous lowland forest, restinga forest (restinga being the Brazilian term for vegetation on marine sands) and mangrove. Of the mixed ombrophilous montane forest only very small 'islands' remain, while the mixed om-brophilous high mountain forest, occurring above 1000 m, is very limited in its extent, as it always has been. In certain parts of Paraná, extensive natural graminoid savannas are to be found with streams which are bordered by gallery forest, while the flood-plains of the larger rivers are partially covered by seasonal semi-deciduous alluvial forest.

The devastation of the original forest must be attributed to the large-scale extraction of native timber species and, more particularly, to the demands of agriculture (cattle raising and growing of coffee, soybeans, cotton, corn, sugar-cane, rice, wheat). Locally, reforestation occurs with exotic *Pinus* and *Eucalyptus* and native *Mimosa scabrella* Benth. in the temperate climate zone, and with *Eucalyptus* only in the tropical area. While large tracts of land have thus been claimed, *Pteridium aquilinum* (L.) Kühn. frequently invades areas where the original vegetation has been destroyed.

LOCALITIES VISITED BY THE SECOND AUTHOR

Most of the collecting sites mentioned under the species are situated in and around Curitiba, the capital of Paraná and 8th largest city of Brazil. The names used for the vegetational formations follow the terminology proposed by Veloso and Goés-Filho (1982) who based their classification on that given by UNESCO (1973).

Most of the localities thus far visited cover an approximately rectangular area of some 5800 square kilometers, which is less than three per cent of the total area of Paraná. Considering the enormous area to be explored and the difficulties to be reckoned with in travelling with public transport (the second author has no other choice) it should be clear that it may take some time before the whole of the State of Paraná will be covered.

DISTRIBUTION AND NUMERICAL ABUNDANCE

Ryvarden and Johansen (1980: 8) stated that 'a surprisingly large number of the tropical polypores are pantropical' and 'No one should be surprised to learn that a species collected in Bolivia could next time be recorded from Java.'

Thus far, this does not seem applicable to the species of *Mycena* of Paraná. It is noteworthy that none of the newly described species from the South American area by Dennis (1951–1970), Singer (1951–1982) or Pegler (1983), from East Africa by Pegler (1977), from Madagascar by Métrod (1949), from Malaysia by Corner (1995) and from Papua New Guinea by Maas Geesteranus and Horak (1995) have as yet been recognized in Paraná. But it should not be excluded that continued exploration may change the situation.

Among the Agaricales collected by the second author in Paraná, the genus with by far the greatest number of species is *Entoloma* (c. 74 species), followed by *Mycena* and *Marasmius* (each with 60 odd species), numbers which are not likely to remain unchanged, however.

The collector of *Mycena* species in Paraná is often confronted with the problem of what to do with two or three tiny basidiomes growing in each other's vicinity. The question that naturally arises is whether they are conspecific and whether it is worth taking them. For, what is left of the dried material after microscopic investigation would most probably make an unacceptably poor herbarium specimen. On the other hand, one may not have a second chance.

It is this problem that must have induced Corner (1972: 122) to write: 'It is unsatisfactory to describe species from single gatherings, but this is the fate of the mycologist in the tropics . . . [but] it is his duty to assist in indicating what there is to be found.'

In the case of the Mycenas from Paraná, the first author frequently felt compelled to reject collections because of scarcity of material.

Hedger and Gitay (Hedger *et al.*, 1995: 148) recorded that the 'agaric litter decomposers' in the rainforests of Ecuador are 'numerically dominated by small species such as *Mycena* spp. in Sect. *Sacchariferae*.' The situation would seem to be much the same in Paraná.

SOUTH AMERICAN MYCENAS IN LITERATURE

Numerous taxa of higher fungi collected within the South American territory have been described in a considerable number of publications, but very few of the latter contained descriptions of Mycenas. Authors whose concern also included species of *Mycena* are the following: [J.F.] C. Montagne (1854, 1856), C. Spegazzini (1887–1925), N. Patouillard and A. Gaillard (1888), N. Patouillard (1891), J. Rick (1919–1961), R.W.G. Dennis (1951–1970), R. Singer (1955–1986), J. Raithelhuber (1972–1987), E. Horak (1978), D.N. Pegler (1983), D.J. Lodge (1988), D.E. Desjardin (1994).

MATERIALS AND METHODS

The second author described the fresh material with the aid of a hand-lens (a dissecting microscope being an unaffordable luxury), and took care to record the colours by using the colour-codes of Kornerup and Wanscher's Handbook of colour (1978). In the beginning he also provided the microscopic details, but abandoned this practice because the sacrifice of a whole specimen proved too much for gatherings which generally were scanty and consisted of small specimens.

Drying methods which initially met with little success were much improved later on. It is not high temperature that is essential but, instead, the rapid dissipation of the warm air. Keeping the specimens dry was effectuated by wrapping them in tissue paper and placing them, protective matchboxes and all, in plastic bags. Infection by moulds, in the beginning the cause of serious losses, could largely be eliminated by sparingly adding small fragments of moth-balls to the material.

The macroscopic descriptions published in this work are adapted from those furnished by the second author, complemented with observations by the first author on the dried specimens under the dissecting microscope. The microscopic details are almost exclusively based on reexamination of rehydrated fragments. Spore measurements, which exclude the apiculus, have as a rule been taken from spores from the apical portion of the stipe or from rehydrated hymenium fragments mounted in ammoniacal Congo red. The spore form is expressed by the length/width rations (average Q). The habitus drawings have been executed after the most suitable dried specimens.

Before the work proper of identifying the Brazilian collections could be started, keys had been constructed to all South American *Mycena* species, even to those for which certain authors (e.g. Dennis, Pegler, Raithelhuber) had already provided their own keys. All keys are in the first author's possession and solely meant for personal use, with the exception of the key to Singer's species which is appended at the end of this work.

Holotype material, indicated by a serial number followed by a capital L, is preserved at the Rijksherbarium, Leiden. Isotypes, duplicate specimens and copies of notes and drawings are deposited at the Herbario, Museu Bôtanica Municipal (MBM), Curitiba.

ACKNOWLEDGEMENTS

Colleagues of the second author's at the Sociedade de Pesquisa em Vida Selvagem e Educação Ambiental (SPVS) and the Associação de Defesa e Educação Ambiental (ADEA) are sincerely thanked for providing accommodation and working facilities.

Dr D. Jean Lodge (Center for Forest Mycology Research, Palmer, Puerto Rico, U.S.A.) kindly sent a copy of Singer's notes on *Mycena tucumanensis*, a species mentioned in the fourth edition of the 'Agaricales' but never validly published. Her help is gratefully acknowledged.

P<small>ART</small> II

MYCENA (Pers.) ROUSSEL

Agaricus [sect.] *Mycena* Pers., Tent. Fung. Suppl.: 69. 1797. – *Agaricus* sect. *Mycena* Pers., Syn. meth. Fung.: XVI, 375. 1801. – *Mycena* (Pers.) Roussel, Flore Calvados, ed. 2: 64. 1806. – Type species: *Agaricus galericulatus* Scop.

Basidiomata very small to large, of mycenoid, omphalinoid or, more rarely, collybioid habit. Pileus conical, convex or campanulate, with the surface glabrous, pruinose, puberulous, granular or floccose, covered with a gelatinous pellicle or not, in one section covered with a universal veil. Lamellae free, adnexed, adnate and ascending or decurrent and arcuate, tender to elastic-tough. Stipe mostly central, hollow, fragile to elastic-tough or cartilaginous with the surface glabrous, pruinose or puberulous, dry or lubricous when moist or covered with a gelatinous layer and viscid, insititious or attached to the substratum by fibrils, or springing from a basal disc or a basal patch of radiating fibrils.

Basidia generally clavate, 2- or 4-spored, with or without clamps. Spore print whitish, never dark. Spores pip-shaped, almost cylindrical or globose, smooth, amyloid or inamyloid. Cheilocystidia nearly always present, variously shaped, clamped or not, smooth, branched or covered with excrescences, with hyaline or coloured contents. Pleurocystidia numerous to absent, with hyaline or coloured contents. Lamellar trama vinescent in Melzer's reagent or not. Pileipellis (a) a cutis or an ixocutis of repent, smooth or variously diverticulate hyphae, with infrequent terminal cells or profusely covered with mostly globose terminal cells (acanthocysts), or (b) hymeniform (in section *Roridae*). Universal veil (in section *Sacchariferae*) made up of acanthocysts and/or variously ornamented cherocytes. Hypoderm consisting of parallel hyphae with much inflated cells. Hyphae of the cortical layer of the stipe smooth or diverticulate, clamped or not, covered with gelatinous matter or not. Caulocystidia frequent, variously shaped.

Lignicolous, folicolous or humicolous.

KEY TO THE SECTIONS

Key 1.

1. Spores amyloid, albeit sometimes weakly. *Lamellar trama not brownish vinescent in Melzer's reagent*, at the most pale brownish.
  2. Pileus white-powdered, covered with globose, thin-walled, spinulose cells:
    . . . . *M. pistacea* (sect. Sacchariferae)
  2. Pileus differently characterized.
    3. Pileus dry. Lamellae 8–18 reaching the stipe. Cheilocystidia not fusiform.
      4. Cheilocystidia clavate, apically covered with much inflated excrescences:
      . . . . 27. sect. *Nodosae*
      4. Cheilocystidia lageniform, smooth: . . . . 30. sect. *Diversae*
    3. Pileus viscid. Lamellae 18–35 reaching the stipe. Cheilocystidia fusiform, those near the margin of the pileus with narrow, branched necks: . . . . 28. sect. *Exornatae*
1. Spores either amyloid and lamellar trama as a rule vinescent in Melzer's reagent, or spores inamyloid: . . . . Key 2

11

Key 2.

5. Spores inamyloid.
  6. Cheilocystidia smooth.
    7. Lamellar trama vinescent in Melzer's reagent. Pileus very dark purplish brown:
    . . . . .22. sect. *Calodontes*, subsect. *Violacellae*
    7. Lamellar trama not vinescent in Melzer's reagent. Pileus more brightly coloured.
      8. Pileus red, orange or pale yellow. Cheilocystidia generally subfusiform to sublageni-
      form, apically not broadly rounded: . . . . .23. sect. *Adonideae*
      8. Pileus pale yellow or whitish. Cheilocystidia generally cylindrical, apically usually
      broadly rounded: . . . . 26. sect. *Hiemales*
  6. Cheilocystidia ornamented.
    9. Cheilocystidia cylindrical, entirely and fairly densely covered with cylindrical ex-
    crescences: . . . . 25. sect. *Notabiles*
    9. Cheilocysitidia clavate, apically covered with not very numerous, somewhat inflated ex-
    crescences: . . . . 24. sect. *Granuliferae*
5. Spores amyloid: . . . . Key 3

Key 3.

10. Pileus viscid or lubricous when moist, or again, appearing dry but under the microscope
  covered with a gelatinous layer.
  11. Lamellar edge concolorous with the sides to white or orange-yellow.
    12. Stipe viscid.
      13. Lamellar edge viscid; cheilocystidia embedded in gelatinous matter.
        14. Cheilocystidia branched and diverticulate: . . . . 16. sect. *Fuliginellae*
        14. Cheilocystidia smooth or with an occasional excrescence:
        . . . . 19. sect. *Caespitosae*
      13. Lamellar edge not viscid; cheilocystidia not embedded in gelatinous matter.
        15. Terminal cells of the hyphae of the cortical layer of the stipe (or caulocys-
        tidia) much branched: . . . . 17. sect. *Insignes*
        15. Terminal cells smooth: . . . . 18. sect. *Euspeireae*
    12. Stipe not viscid.
      16. Cheilocystidia largely embedded in gelatinous matter, slender-stalked, apically
      much branched. Pleurocystidia present: . . . . 12. sect. *Indutae*
      16. Cheilocystidia not embedded in gelatinous matter, usually short-stalked to al-
      most sessile, apically covered with coarse excrescences. Pleurocystidia absent:
      . . . . .29. sect. *Adornatae*
  11. Lamellae white to pale grey-brown with very dark brown edge. Cheilocystidia somewhat
  branched and covered with coarse excrescences: . . . . 9. sect. *Infuscatae*
10. Pileus dry, not covered with a gelatinous layer: . . . . Key 4

Key 4.

17. Stipe viscid.
  18. Cheilocystidia densely covered with cylindrical excrescences. Pileipellis a cutis of repent,
  radiately aligned hyphae: . . . . 6. sect. *Aspratiles*
  18. Cheilocystidia smooth. Pileipellis hymeniform, made up of erect, clavate, smooth cells:
  . . . . 20. sect. *Roridae*
17. Stipe not viscid: . . . . Key 5

Key 5.

19. Lamellar edge darker than the sides and of a different colour.

12

20. Hyphae of the cortical layer of the stipe smooth or sparsely covered with excrescences. Cheilocystidia slender.
    21. Lamellae densely intervenose. Cheilocystidia apically usually furcate. Pleurocystidia present, smooth. Hyphae of the pileipellis smooth: . . . . 7. sect. *Dactylinae*
    21. Lamellae not intervenose. Cheilocystidia clavate, not apically furcate. Pleurocystidia absent. Hyphae of the pileipellis sparsely covered with obtuse excrescences:
    . . . . 13. sect. *Saniosae*
20. Hyphae of the cortical layer of the stipe densely covered with coarse, rounded excrescences. Cheilocystidia squat: . . . . 15. sect. *Nigrescentes*
19. Lamellar edge concolorous with the sides or paler to whitish: . . . . Key 6

Key 6.

22. Hyphae of the pileipellis covered with loose acanthocysts: . . . . 1. sect. *Sacchariferae*
22. Pileipellis devoid of acanthocysts: . . . . Key 7

Key 7.

23. Hyphae of the pileipellis smooth or with few, scattered excrescences.
    24. Spores pip-shaped.
        25. Cheilocystidia smooth.
            26. Odour raphanoid: . . . . 22. sect. *Calodontes*
            26. Odour not raphanoid: . . . . part of 10. sect. *Fragilipedes*
        25. Cheilocystidia covered with not numerous but usually rather coarse excrescences:
        . . . . part of 10. sect. *Fragilipedes*
    24. Spores globose: . . . . part of 2. sect. *Supinae*
23. Hyphae of the pileipellis (mostly densely) diverticulate or producing pileocystidia: . Key 8

Key 8.

27. Stipe not exuding a red drop when bruised or cut.
    28. Spores pip-shaped.
        29. Cheilocystidia smooth or apically covered with a few excrescences.
            30. Stipe springing from a basal patch of radiating fibrils.
                31. Pileus and at least lower part of the stipe dark brown.
                    32. Cheilocystidia clavate, ornamented: . . . . 27. sect. *Nodosae*
                    32. Cheilocystidia fusiform, smooth: . . . . 11. sect. *Obductae*
                31. Pileus pale yellow, stipe pale yellow or pale orange: . . 5. sect. *Carolinenses*
            30. Stipe not springing from a basal patch.
                33. Basidiomata purple throughout: . . . . 21. sect. *Cerasinae*
                33. Basidiomata differently coloured: . . . . 10. sect. *Fragilipedes*
        29. Cheilocystidia apically more or less branched or covered with fairly numerous excrescences.
            34. Stipe springing from a basal patch of radiating fibrils.
                35. Hyphae of the pileipellis densely covered with warts or cylindrical excrescences.
                    36. Hyphae of the pileipellis simple. Caulocystidia simple, broad:
                    . . . . 8. sect. *Polyadelphia*
                    36. Hyphae of the pileipellis branched. Caulocystidia (solid hairs excluded) branched, narrow: . . . . 5. sect. *Carolinenses*
                35. Hyphae of the pileipellis covered with fairly coarse excrescences, but not very densely: . . . . 4. sect. *Sejunctae*
        34. Stipe not springing from a basal patch of radiating fibrils.

13

1. MYCENA section SACCHARIFERAE Kühn. ex Sing.

Mycena [sect.] *Sacchariferae* Kühn., Genre *Mycena*: 159, 205. 1938 [not val. publ.: no Latin descr.); Sing. in Annls mycol. **41**: 137. 1943 (formally accepted as section; not val. publ.: no Latin descr.); Kühn. ex Sing. in Sydowia **15**: 65. 1962. – Holotype: *Mycena tenerrima* (Berk.) Quél.

For further synonymy, see Maas Geesteranus (1983: 403) and Desjardin (1995: 8).

Basidiomata small. Pileus covered (in its primordial stage) with a universal veil forming spines or floccose granules, losing the veil with age and exposing a dry to somewhat viscid, minutely pulverulent surface, variously coloured in shades of yellowish or greyish. Context very thin. Odour not distinctive or not recorded. Lamellae generally present, tender, ascending, adnate to free, ventricose, white with concolorous edge. Stipe hollow, fragile, dry, puberulous to pilose, white, springing from a basal disc or not.

Basidia 2-spored or 4-spored, broadly clavate, with or without clamps. Spores globose to pip-shaped, smooth, amyloid. Cheilocystidia clavate to subglobose or lageniform to fusiform with a slender neck, more or less densely covered with warts or cylindrical excrescences, more rarely smooth, rarely absent. Pleurocystidia absent. Lamellar trama vinescent in Melzer's reagent. Pileipellis a cutis with acanthocyst terminal cells or, at the centre of the pileus, a subhymeniform layer of acanthocysts which are globose, thin-walled, densely covered with warts or cylindrical excrescences. Universal veil made up of variously shaped, thick-walled, in part coarsely spinulose cells. Hyphae of the cortical layer of the stipe smooth. Caulocystidia covered with warts or cylindrical excrescences, rarely smooth.

Growing on vegetable debris.

KEY TO THE SPECIES

1. Surface of the primordium or the disc of the young pileus or the disc at the base of the stipe bearing cherocytes.
　　2. Cherocytes with thick-walled to solid, smooth spines.
　　　　3. Cheilocystidia covered with comparatively few excrescences.
　　　　　　4. Cheilocystidia with narrowed base, apically covered with excrescences 1.8–3.5 × 0.9 μm.
　　　　　　　　5. Spores 8.1–9.0 × 5.4–6.3 μm (Q = 1.6). Cheilocystidia 18–24 μm long, with excrescences 1.8–3.5 μm long: . . . . *M. impexa*
　　　　　　　　5. Spores 8.9–10.7(–11.6) × 4.4–5.4 μm (Q = 2.1). Cheilocystidia 10.5–16 μm long, with excrescences c. 1.8 μm long: . . . . *M. paula*
　　　　　　4. Cheilocystidia almost sessile, apically covered with excrescences 0.5–0.9 × 0.5 μm:
　　　　　　. . . . . *M. propinqua*

14

3. Cheilocystidia covered with very numerous excrescences 0.9–1.3 × 0.5 μm: . *M. excelsa*
2. Cherocytes with moderately thick-walled, spinulose spines.
    6. Stipe with somewhat bulbous base. Spores (6–)7.2–8.1 μm long. Cheilocystidia short-stalked: .... *M. atrox*
    6. Stipe springing from a basal disc. Spores 9.4–10.7(–11.6) μm long. Cheilocystidia frequently long-stalked: .... *M. chloroxantha*
1. Surface of the primordium or the disc of the young pileus devoid of cherocytes.
    7. Pileus white, whitish or pale grey to pale grey-brown, without grey-green tints. Stipe springing from a basal disc or a white-powdered basal patch. Basidia 4-spored. Spores up to 10 μm long.
        8. Caulocystidia gradually tapering towards their apices, smooth: .... *M. adscendens*
        8. Caulocystidia with much swollen apices, densely covered with short excrescences: .... *M. dissimilis*
    7. Pileus grey, grey-greenish between the striae. Stipe not springing from a basal disc or patch, densely tomentose. Basidia (1–)2(–3)-spored. Spores 12–15 μm long: .... *M. pistacea*

Mycena cf. adscendens (Lasch) Maas G. – Fig. 1 (1–3)

Agaricus adscendens Lasch in Linnaea **4**: 536. 1829. – *Mycena adscendens* (Lasch) Maas G. in Proc. K. Ned. Akad. Wet. **84**: 211. 1981. – Type locality: Germany, province Brandenburg.
    For further synonymy, see Maas Geesteranus, l.c.
    For a full description, see Maas Geesteranus (1983: 404).

Basidiome solitary. Primordia absent. Pileus dried less than 1 mm across, convex, whitish. Lamellae 10 forming a pseudocollarium. Stipe broken, white, with the base lacking.

Basidia immature, 10–11.5 × 6.5 μm. Spores few seen, 8.1–10.2 × 5.0–5.4 μm (Q = 2.0), pip-shaped, smooth, amyloid. Cheilocystidia c. 14.5 × 9 μm, obpyriform, covered with evenly spaced, cylindrical excrescences 0.9–1.8 × 0.5 μm. Lamellar trama brownish vinescent in Melzer's reagent. Hyphae of the pileipellis c. 4.5 μm wide, densely spinulose. Acanthocysts 14.5–20 × 11–18 μm, globose, thin-walled, densely covered with evenly spaced, cylindrical excrescences 0.9–2.5 × 0.5 μm. Caulocystidia not observed.

Material examined: '23 April 1995 / Paraná: Curitiba, Parque Municipal do Iguaçu, Zoológico / A.A.R. de Meijer, no number / on dead leaves of *Araucaria angustifolia* in mixed ombrophilous forest, 900 m alt.' (notes and drawings only, No. 990.200–168; L; MBM 188486).

The single specimen partly described above was detected among a mixed collection of small greyish and whitish agarics. The analysis did not yield sufficient details to be quite certain about the identity of the species, but some characters seem to point to *M. adscendens*: 1) the lamellae adhered to each other to form a pseudocollarium; 2) the size of the mature spores compared to the size of the (admittedly very young) basidia seen suggests that the latter would have grown out to become two-spored; 3) the size of the mature spores corresponds well with that of the spores of *M. adscendens*. One difficulty remains, however. All cheilocystidia were of the kind as illustrated in Fig. 1(2), and there were none with a conspicuous, elongated neck.

Unfortunately, the few remains left after the (somewhat clumsily executed) investigation proved no longer fit for preservation.

Mycena atrox* Maas G. and de Meijer, *spec. nov.* – Fig. 1 (4–8)

Basidiomata dispersa. Pileus usque ad 8 mm latus, e campanulato-convexo plano-convexus, siccus, esulcatus, striatus, totus floccoso-farinosus, pallide griseus. Caro tenuis. Lamellae c. 18 stipitem attingentes, molles, adscendentes, ventricosae, usque ad 1.3 mm latae, adnexae, albae, margine convexae, concolores. Stipes c. 40 × 1–1.7 mm, cavus, fragilis, aequalis, cylindraceus, siccus, levis, totus albo-pubescens, albus, basi subbulbosus, albo-tomentosus.
Basidia 12–15 × 8–10 μm, clavata, 4-sporigera, efibulata. Sporae (6–)7.2–8.1 × 4.3–5.4 μm, inaequilateraliter ellipsoideae, leves, amyloideae. Cheilocystidia 11–16 × 8–11 μm, clavata, pyriformia, efibulata, surculis cylindraceis, rectis, 2–4.5 × 1 μm praedita. Pleurocystidia nulla. Trama lamellarum iodi ope tenuiter vinescens. Hyphae pileipellis 4.5–5.5 μm latae, dense verrucosae. Acanthocystides 27–30 × 14.5–22.5 μm, globosae vel ellipsoideae, dense verrucosae. Velum universale e cherocytibus 36–45 × 30–35 μm, subglobosis, dense diverticulatis, 2–4 surculis 20–150 × 3–11 μm, crasse-tunicatis pro parteque spinulosis instructis. Hyphae stipitis corticales leves. Caulocystidia 125 × 10–12 μm, cylindracea, tenuitunicata, dense verrucosa. Lignicola.
Holotypus: A.A.R. de Meijer cu-a 258d (No. 988.233–006; L); notulae: mbm 188493.

Basidiomata scattered. Pileus up to 8 mm across, at first campanulate-convex, then plano-convex, dry, not sulcate, translucent-striate, entirely floccose-mealy, the centre and striae very pale grey, between the striae whitish. Context thin. Lamellae c. 18 reaching the stipe, tender, ascending, ventricose, up to 1.3 mm broad, adnexed, white, with convex, concolorous edge. Stipe c. 40 × 1–1.7 mm, hollow, fragile, equal, terete, dry, smooth, entirely white-pubescent, white, the base somewhat bulbous, white-tomentose.

Basidia (none seen mature) 12–15 × 8–10 μm, clavate, 4-spored, clampless. Spores (6–)7.2–8.1 × 4.3–5.4 μm (Q = 1.7), pip-shaped, smooth, amyloid. Cheilocystidia 11–16 × 8–11 μm, forming a sterile band (lamellar edge homogeneous), clavate, pyriform, clampless, short-stalked, not very densely covered with evenly spaced, cylindrical, simple, straight excrescences 2–4.5 × 1 μm. Pleurocystidia absent. Lamellar trama weakly vinescent in Melzer's reagent. Pileipellis a cutis of repent, radiately aligned hyphae which are 4.5–5.5 μm wide, densely covered with warts. Acanthocysts (at the pileus disc) 27–30 × 14.5–22.5 μm, globose to ellipsoid, thin-walled, densely covered with wart-like excrescences 0.5–1 × 0.5 μm. Velum universale made up of clusters of cherocytes which are 36–45 × 30–35 μm, subglobose, fairly thick-walled, densely covered with wart-like to cylindrical, simple, straight excrescences 0.9–4.5 × 1 μm, and bearing 2–4 very coarse spines; the latter 20–150 × 3–11 μm, fairly thick-walled, coarsely spinulose in the lower part, generally smooth in the apical part. Hyphae of the cortical layer of the stipe hardly discernable but certainly smooth. Caulocystidia numerous but only one distinctly visible, 125 × 10–12 μm, thin-walled, densely covered with fine warts < 0.5 × < 0.5 μm.

---

*Etymologie: atrox, fearsome, in reference to the thorny spines of the cherocytes.

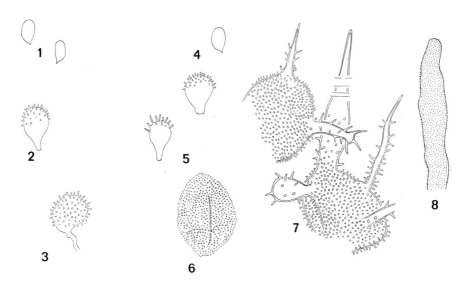

Fig. 1 (1–3) *Mycena* cf *adscendens* (no number). – 1. Spores. – 2. Cheilocystidium. – 3. Acanthocyst. (4–8) *Mycena atrox* (de Meijer cua-258d). – 4. Spores. – 5. Cheilocystidia. – 6. Acanthocyst. – 7. Cherocytes. – 8. Caulocystidium. All figs., × 700.

On dead wood of a dicotyledonous tree in seasonal semideciduous alluvial forest, 870 m alt.

Holotype: '*Mycena atrox* Maas G. and de Meijer / 3 April 1980 / Paraná: Curitiba, Uberaba Distr., Reserva Biológica Cambuí / A.A.R. de Meijer cua-258d' (No. 988.233–006; L); notes and drawings: мвм 188493.

Unfortunately, the two specimens of the type proved to be in poor condition, as a result of which the description is somewhat incomplete. Going by the coarse and partly thorny but smooth-tipped spines emanating from the cherocytes, one could think of a close ally of *Mycena chloroxantha* Sing. but there are some differences. The type variety of this species and var. *appalachienensis* described by Desjardin (1995: 22, 24) possess a yellow or greenish yellow pileus, their spores are slightly larger, their caulocystidia are definitely more coarsely ornamented, especially at the apex, and both taxa occur on twigs or leaves.

MYCENA CHLOROXANTHA Sing. – Fig. 2

Mycena chloroxantha Sing. in Cryptogamie (Mycol.) **4**: 114. 1983. – Holotype (not seen): Singer B 10836 (INPA).

Basidiomata scattered. Primordium 0.7 mm across, hemispherical, white, densely covered with short, stiff, white hairs (the cherocytes). Pileus 2–7 mm across, up to 3 mm high, campanulate, dry, translucent-striate, at first evenly pale yellow (2A3), gradually darkening, becoming olive-grey (2D3), more rarely grey (2D1), between the striae pale yellow or more rarely turning pale grey (2B1), the whole thickly covered with pale yellow flues which readily fall off when touched. Context very thin. Odour absent. Lamellae 11–13 reaching the stipe, tender, ascending, ventricose, c. 0.5 mm broad, narrowly adnate to almost free, at first white, then pale grey (2B1), rarely darker grey (2D1), with convex white edge. Stipe 15–50 × 0.1–0.4 mm, fistulose, fragile, equal for the greater part, terete, dry, smooth, entirely white-pubescent, white-hairy near the base, springing from a small, fluffy-hairy, white basal disc.

Basidia (none seen mature) 13.5–18 × 8–11.5 μm, clavate to ellipsoid, short-stalked, clampless, with 4 incipient sterigmata. Spores 9.4–10.7(–11.6) × 4.5–5.4 μm (Q = 2.6), pip-shaped to almost cylindrical, smooth, amyloid. Cheilocystidia 14.5–22.5 × 6.5–10 μm, locally forming a sterile band, clavate, clampless, generally long-stalked, apically covered with comparatively few, evenly spaced, cylindrical, simple, straight excrescences 1.5–2.5 × 0.5–0.9 μm. Pleurocystidia absent. Lamellar trama brownish vinescent in Melzer's reagent. Pileipellis a cutis of few, repent, radiately aligned hyphae which are 3.5–6.5 μm wide, densely covered with fine excrescences, and terminated by inflated cells 12.5–22.5 μm wide. Hypoderm made up of parallel hyphae with inflated cells up to 25 μm wide. Acanthocysts (at the pileus disc) 18–27 × 16–22.5 μm, globose to subglobose, thin-walled, densely covered with fine excrescences 0.9–1.5 × 0.5 μm. Velum universale disappeared from the pi-

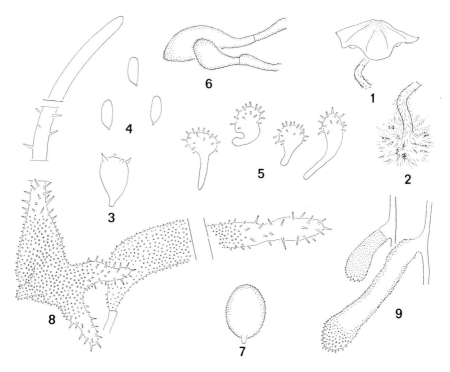

Fig. 2 (1–9) *Mycena chloroxantha* (de Meijer PAf–3079). – 1. Habitus. – 2. Basal part of the stipe. – 3. Immature basidium. – 4. Spores. – 5. Cheilocystidia. – 6. Terminal cells of hyphae of the pileipellis. – 7. Acanthocyst. – 8. Cherocytes. – 9. Caulocystidia.
Fig. 1, × 5; fig. 2, × 10; all others, × 700.

leus. Cherocytes, taken from the basal disc, consisting of a swollen main body, from which issue up to 3 shorter spines and 1 very long spine. Main body (15–35 μm broad) and shorter spines (up to c. 30 μm long) moderately thick-walled, densely covered with fine excrescences which become much longer towards the apices of the spines. The long spine (–360 × 6–10 μm) moderately thick-walled, near its base densely covered with fine excrescences which soon change to long, acute spinulae 1.5–7 × 0.9–1.5 μm, and often leave the spine glabrous till its end. Hyphae of the cortical layer of the stipe 1.5–2.5 μm wide, clampless, smooth. Caulocystidia –300 (and possibly longer) × 7–22 μm, mostly cylindrical, thin-walled, densely covered with fine excrescences 0.5–0.9 × 0.5 μm which are longer at the apex.

On dead leaves of a dicotyledonous tree in dense ombrophilous forest, 5–70 m alt.

Material examined: '*Mycena chloroxantha* Sing. / 22 June 1995 / Paraná: Paranaguá, Saquarema / A.A.R. de Meijer PAf-3079' (No. 991.343–695; L); duplicate: MBM.

The greying pilei of the present material indicate that collection 3079 belongs to var. *chloroxantha*. Desjardin (1995: 24) noted that the basal disc contained cherocytes as well as caulocystidium-like cystidia. In order to leave the basal discs of collection 3079 as far as possible intact, a search for these caulo-cystidia was omitted.

Mycena dissimilis* Maas G. and de Meijer, *spec. nov.* – Fig. 3

Basidiomata dispersa. Pileus 1.5–4 mm latus, 0.7–3 mm altus, campanulatus vel convexus, siccus, haud sulcatus, vix striatus, minute pulverulentus, albus. Caro pertenuis, odore indistincto. Lamellae 10–12 stipitem attingentes, molles, adscendentes, ventricosae, c. 0.3 mm latae, adnatae, albae, margine convexae, concolores. Stipes 10–17 × 0.2 mm, cavus, fragilis, aequalis, cylindraceus, siccus, levis, minute puberulus, albus, e disco basali minuto natus.

Basidia 11.5–14.5 × 10–11 μm, subglobosa, 4-sporigera, efibulata. Sporae 8.1–9.8 × 4.5–6.3 μm, inaequilateraliter ellipsoideae, leves, amyloideae. Cheilocystidia 15–23 × 11–13.5 μm, globosa, efibulata, surculis cylindraceis, rectis 0.9–1.5 × 0.5 μm instructa. Pleurocystidia nulla. Trama lamellarum iodi ope brunneovinescens. Hyphae pileipellis c. 5 μm latae, dense diverticulatae. Acanthocystides 23–30 × 19–28 μm, globosae, dense spinulosae. Hyphae stipitis corticales 1.8–2.5 μm latae, leves. Caulocystidia 50–80 × 7–23 μm, clavata vel raro subcylindracea, dense spinulosa.

Corticola.

Holotypus: A.A.R. de Meijer CUb-2927 (No. 991.343–712; L); notulae: MBM 188511.

Basidiomata scattered. Primordia absent. Pileus 1.5–4 mm across, 0.7–3 mm high, campanulate to convex, dry, not sulcate, hardly striate, minutely pulverulent, white. Context very thin. Odour indistinct. Lamellae 10–12 reaching the stipe, tender, ascending, more or less ventricose, c. 0.3 mm broad, adnate, white, with convex to straight, concolorous edge. Stipe 10–17 × 0.2

---

*Etymology: dissimilis, different, in reference to the caulocystidia which are different from those of the other members of the section.

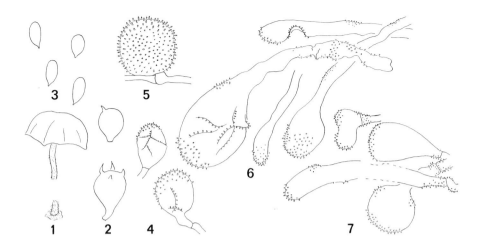

Fig. 3 (1–7) *Mycena dissimilis* (de Meijer CUB-2927). – 1. Habitus and basal part of the stipe. – 2. Basidia. – 3. Spores. – 4. Cheilocystidia. – 5. Acanthocyst. – 6. Caulocystidia. – 7. Caulocystidia at the base of the stipe.
Fig. 1, × 10; all others, × 700.

mm, hollow, fragile, equal, terete, dry, smooth, minutely puberulous, white, springing from a very small, white-powdered patch c. 0.3 mm across.

Basidia 11.5–14.5 × 10–11 μm, subglobose to obpyriform, 4-spored, clampless, with sterigmata c. 4.5 μm long. Spores 8.1–9.8 × 4.5–6.3 μm (Q = 2.0), pip-shaped, smooth, amyloid. Cheilocystidia not numerous, 15–23 × 11–13.5 μm, globose, subglobose or spheropedunculate, clampless, densely covered with evenly spaced, cylindrical, simple, straight excrescences 0.9–1.5 × 0.5 μm. Pleurocystidia absent. Lamellar trama brownish vinescent in Melzer's reagent. Pileipellis a narrow cutis of repent, radiately aligned hyphae which are c. 5 μm wide and densely spinulose. Acanthocysts 23–30 × 19–28 μm, globose, thin-walled, densely covered with evenly spaced, cylindrical, simple, straight excrescences 0.9–2.5 × 0.5 μm. Cherocytes absent. Hyphae of the cortical layer of the stipe 1.8–2.5 μm wide, clampless, smooth. Caulocystidia 50–80 (total length) × 7–23 μm, clavate to subglobose and long-stalked or subcylindrical with little inflated apex, densely spinulose all over; caulocystidia at the base of the stipe similar.

On the decayed trunk of a dicotyledonous tree in mixed ombrophilous forest, 900 m alt.

Holotype: '*Mycena dissimilis* Maas G. and de Meijer / 14 Nov. 1994 / Paraná: Curitiba, Santo Inácio Distr., Parque Barigui / A.A.R. de Meijer CUB-2927' (No. 991.343–712); notes and drawings: MBM 188511.

The feature that separates *Mycena dissimilis* from all other members of the section thus far described is the strikingly swollen apex of the caulocystidia, but some attention should nevertheless be given to *M. depilata* Sing. (1989: 72). Desjardin (1995: 47, fig. 63) depicted the caulocystidia of the type material of that species with swollen apices, while Singer described the species as being entirely white, with the stipe springing from a very small disc. *Mycena depilata*, however, differs from *M. dissimilis* in having almost free lamellae, narrower cheilocystidia (6–8 μm), short-stalked to almost sessile caulocystidia.

Mycena excelsa* Maas G. and de Meijer, *spec. nov.* – Fig. 4

Basidiomata dispersa. Pileus 0.5–3 mm latus, usque ad 1.5 mm altus, primo semiglobosus, spinulosus, albus, postea e convexo applanatus, siccus, subsulcatus, striatus, pruinosus, albogriseus, centro griseus. Caro pertenuis, odore indistincto. Lamellae 11–12 stipitem attingentes, molles, adscendentes, ventricosae, usque ad 0.5 mm latae, subliberae, albae, margine convexae, concolores. Stipes 5–18 × 0.2 mm, cavus, fragilis, aequalis, cylindraceus, siccus, levis, totus pubescens, albus, basi disco c. 0.5 mm lato substrato affixus.

Basidia 14–15 × 8–10 μm, late clavata, 2?-sporigera, efibulata. Sporae 7.3–9.2(–10.7) × 4.5–5.4(–6.3) μm, inaequilateraliter ellipsoideae, leves, amyloideae. Cheilocystidia 23–27 × 9–13.5 μm, clavata, surculis cylindraceis, rectis 0.9–1.3 × 0.5 μm instructa. Pleurocystidia nulla. Trama lamellarum iodi ope brunneovinescens. Hyphae pileipellis 6.5–8 μm latae, efibulatae, dense diverticulatae. Acanthocystides 13.5–30 × 11–23 μm, globosae vel clavatae, dense diverticulatae. Velum universale e cherocytibus crasse-tunicatis 20–67 × 20–45 μm, spiniferis atque pustulis instructis. Hyphae stipitis corticales 1.8–2.7 μm latae, efibulatae, leves. Caulocystidia –200 (vel ultra?) × 5.5–8 μm, cylindracea, dense diverticulata.

Ramulicola.

Holotypus: A.A.R. de Meijer CUB-2925 (No. 991.343–768; L); notulae: MBM 188514.

Basidiomata scattered. Pileus 0.5–3 mm across, up to 1.5 mm high, in the primordial stage semiglobose, densely covered with minute, obtuse-tipped spines, white, later convex and somewhat flattening with age, dry, shallowly sulcate, translucent-striate, pruinose, the striae very pale greyish, the centre grey, between the striae white. Context very thin. Odour indistinct, taste not recorded. Lamellae 11–12 reaching the stipe, tender, ascending, ventricose, up to 0.5 mm broad, free to very narrowly adnate, white, with convex, concolorous edge. Stipe 5–18 × 0.2 mm, hollow, fragile, equal, terete or slightly narrowed upwards, dry, smooth, pubescent all over, white, springing from a small, somewhat costate, semitransparent basal patch c. 0.5 mm across.

Basidia (none seen mature) 14–15 × 8–10 μm, broadly clavate, 2?-spored, clampless. Spores 7.3–9.2(–10.7) × 4.5–5.4(–6.3) μm (Q = 1.9), pip-shaped, smooth, amyloid. Cheilocystidia 23–27 × 9–13.5 μm, occurring mixed with the basidia (lamellar edge heterogeneous), clavate, densely covered over much of their surface with evenly spaced, cylindrical, simple, straight excrescences 0.9–1.3 × 0.5 μm. Pleurocystidia absent. Lamellar trama strongly brownish vinescent in Melzer's reagent. Pileipellis a cutis of repent, radiately aligned hyphae which are 6.5–8 μm wide, clampless, densely covered with cylindrical, simple, straight excrescences 0.9 × 0.5 μm. The pileipellis covered with (i) numerous acanthocysts (which cause the pruinosity of the mature pileus surface) and (ii) cherocytes which cause the densely spinulose aspect of the primordium. Acanthocysts 13.5–30 × 11–23 μm, globose or broadly clavate,

*Etymology: excelsus, excellent, so named because of the impressive cherocytes.

21

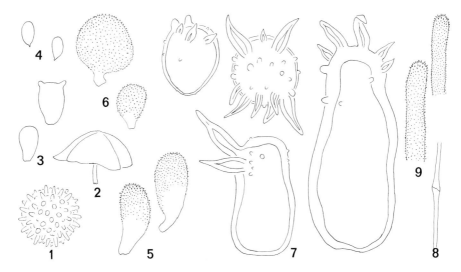

Fig. 4 (1–9) *Mycena excelsa* (de Meijer CUb-2925). – 1. Primordium, seen from above. – 2. Pileus. – 3. Immature basidia. – 4. Spores. – 5. Cheilocystidia. – 6. Acanthocysts. – 7. Cherocytes. – 8. Hypha of the cortical layer of the stipe. – 9. Caulocystidia.
Fig. 1, × 30; fig. 2, × 10; all others, × 700.

thin-walled, densely covered with evenly spaced, cylindrical, simple, straight excrescences 0.9–1.3 × 0.5 µm. Cherocytes solitary (or arranged in chains of two?) 20–67 × 20–45 µm, globose, ellipsoid or subcylindrical, very thick-walled (1.8–4.5 µm), covered with few to several, thick-walled, smooth, mostly acute spines 3.5–22.5 × 3.5–6.5 µm, as well as with few, wart-like, obtuse excrescences 1.3–2.5 × 0.9–1.8 µm. Hyphae of the cortical layer of the stipe 1.8–2.7 µm wide, clampless, smooth. Caulocystidia –200 (or possibly more) × 5.5–8 µm, cylindrical, thin-walled, densely covered with cylindrical, simple, straight excrescences 0.9–1.3 × 0.5 µm.

On decayed twigs of a dicotyledonous tree in mixed ombrophilous forest, 900 m alt.

Holotype: '*Mycena excelsa* Maas G. and de Meijer / 14 Nov. 1994 / Paraná: Curitiba, Santo Inácio Distr., Parque Barigui / A.A.R. de Meijer CUb-2925' (No. 991.343–768; L); notes and drawings: MBM 188514.

Mycena impexa* Maas G. and de Meijer, *spec. nov.* – Fig. 5 (1–9) and 6 (1–3)

Basidiomata dispersa. Pileus 4–6 mm latus, 2–3 mm altus, primo late ellipsoideus, albus, dense elementis veli universalis vulgo curvatis, pallide flavis, –0.5 × –0.1 mm obtectus, postea convexus vel campanulatus, siccus, sulcatus, striatus, minute puberulus vel pulverulentus, albus, centro striisque tamen pallide griseoflavis. Caro pertenuis, alba, odore nullo. Lamellae 16–17 stipitem attingentes, molles, adscendentes, ventricosae, usque ad 0.8 mm latae, adnexae, albae, margine convexae, concolores. Stipes 10–22 × 0.2–0.3 mm, cavus, fragilis, aequalis, cylindraceus, siccus, levis, minute puberulus, albus, an radicans?

*Etymology: impexus, unkempt, referring to the disorderly growth of the velar elements covering the primordium.

22

Basidia c. 16 × 11 μm, subglobosa, vel ellipsoidea, 4-sporigera, efibulata, sterigmatibus 4.5 μm longis praedita. Sporae 8.1–9.0 × 5.4–6.3 μm, inaequilateraliter ellipsoideae, leves, tenuiter amyloideae. Cheilocystidia 18–24 × 7–9 μm, clavata, efibulata, surculis cylindraceis, rectis 1.8–3.5 × 0.9 μm instructa. Pleurocystidia nulla. Trama lamellarum iodi ope tenuiter brunneovinescens. Hyphae pileipellis 2.7–5.5 μm latae, efibulatae, dense diverticulatae, cellulae terminales –40 × 9–15 μm. Acanthocystides 16–36 × 13.5–28 μm, globosae, dense diverticulatae. Velum universale e cherocytibus crasse-tunicatis spinuliferisque formatum, superioribus 30–40 × 18–40 μm. Hyphae stipitis corticales c. 1.5 μm latae, leves. Caulocystidia 35–>150 × 12.5–27 μm, cylindracea vel subclavata, dense diverticulata.

Corticola.

Holotypus: A.A.R. de Meijer coa-2890 (No. 990.200–079; L); isotypus: mbm 188526.

Basidiomata scattered. Pileus 4–6 mm across, 2–3 mm high, in the primordial stage broadly ellipsoid, white, covered with a universal veil consisting of separate, cylindrical, usually curved, pale yellow (2A2–2A3) structures –0.5 × 0.1 mm; later convex to campanulate, dry, sulcate, translucent-striate, minutely puberulous or pulverulent, white but with pale yellowish grey (3B2) centre and striae. Context very thin, white. Odour absent, taste not recorded. Lamellae 16–17 reaching the stipe, tender, ascending,

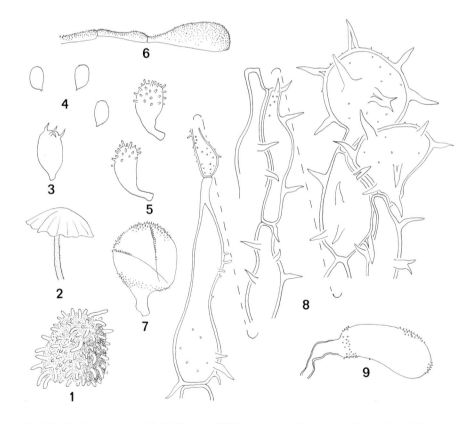

Fig. 5 (1–9) *Mycena impexa* (de Meijer coa-2890). – 1. Primordium. – 2. Habitus. – 3. Basidium. – 4. Spores. – 5. Cheilocystidia. – 6. Part of a hypha of the pileipellis and terminal cell. – 7. Acanthocysts. – 8. Cherocytes. – 9. Caulocystidia.
Fig. 1, × 10; fig. 2, × 5; all others, × 700.

ventricose, up to 0.8 mm broad, adnexed, white, with convex, concolorous edge. Stipe 10–22 × 0.2–0.3 mm, hollow, fragile, equal, terete, dry, smooth, minutely puberulous, white, rooting?

Basidia (none seen mature) c. 16 × 11 μm, subglobose to ellipsoid, 4-spored, clampless, with sterigmata 4.5 μm long. Spores 8.1–9.0 × 5.4–6.3 μm (Q = 1.6), pip-shaped, smooth, weakly amyloid. Cheilocystidia 18–24 × 7–9 μm, forming a sterile band (lamellar edge homogeneous), clavate, clampless, rather sparsely covered with evenly spaced, cylindrical, simple, straight excrescences 1.8–3.5 × 0.8 μm. Pleurocystidia absent. Lamellar trama faintly brownish vinescent in Melzer's reagent. Pileipellis a cutis of repent, radiately aligned hyphae which are 2.7–5.5 μm wide, densely covered with short, cylindrical excrescences 0.9 × 0.5 μm, terminated by more or less inflated terminal cells –40 × 9–15 μm, and also giving rise to numerous acanthocysts, the whole overlaid by the allantoid velar structures which consist of detersile bundles of catenulate cherocytes. Acanthocysts 16–36 × 13.5–28 μm, globose, short- to long-stalked, some originating (as it seems) from deeper layers under the pileipellis, thin-walled, densely covered with short, cylindrical excrescences 0.9–2 × 0.5–0.9 μm. Cherocytes arranged in elongate bundles, those at the base of the bundle subcylindrical or sub-lageniform and wavy in outline, those at the top 30–40 × 18–40 μm, globose, thick-walled (1.8–2.5 μm), covered with scattered (5–7), thick-walled to massive, acute, glabrous spines 5.5–13.5 × 2.5–3.5 μm, as well as with a few warts or small cylindrical excrescences. Hyphae of the cortical layer of the stipe c. 1.5 μm wide, smooth. Caulocystidia 35– > 150 × 12.5–27 μm, cylindrical to subclavate, densely covered with short, cylindrical excrescences 0.9–2 × 0.5–0.9 μm.

On much decayed bark of a branch of a dicotyledonous tree in mixed ombrophilous forest, 900 m alt.

Holotype: 'Mycena impexa Maas G. and de Meijer / 18 May 1994 / Paraná: Colombo, EMBRAPA-Florestal, native forest / A.A.R. de Meijer COA-2890' (No. 990.200–079; L); isotype: MBM 188526.

Additional material: '17 Nov. 1994 / Paraná: Morretes, Parque Marumbi, near road BR-277 / A.A.R. de Meijer MA-2940, on dead twigs of a dicotyledonous tree in dense ombrophilous forest, 850 m alt.' (No. 991.343–723; L); duplicate: MBM 188527.

A very close ally of *Mycena impexa* is *M. spinosissima* (Sing.) Desjardin (1995: 15). Although the differences between the two species are clear enough, it is unfortunate that some can be observed only if primordia are present. The differences are tabulated below.

	cheilocystidia	velar structures (called spines by Desjardin)	warts or small cylindrical excrescences covering the cherocytes
M. impexa	rather sparsely covered with excrescences which are 1.8–3.5 μm long	up to 0.5 mm long; cylindrical; curved	few to very few
M. spinosissima	densely covered with excrescences which are 0.5–1.5 μm long	up to 2 mm long; conical to pyramidal	numerous

Mycena paula* Maas G. and de Meijer, *spec. nov.* – Fig. 6 (4–11)

Basidiomata dispersa. Pileus 0.8–2.2 mm latus, usque ad 1 mm altus, primo convexus vel plano-conicus, minute puberulus, postea hemisphaericus vel convexus, siccus, sulcatus, striatus, minute pulverulentus, vulgo albus. Caro pertenuis, odore nullo. Lamellae 8–10 stipitem attingentes, molles, adscendentes, ventricosae, c. 0.4 mm latae, adnexae, albae, margine convexae, concolores. Stipes 4–7 × 0.1–0.2 mm, cavus, fragilis, aequalis, cylindraceus, siccus, levis, minute puberulus, albus, basi fibrillis radiantibus, albis substrato affixus.

Basidia c. 13.5–15 × 10.5–11.5 μm, subglobosa, 4-sporigera, efibulata. Sporae 8.9–10.7(–11.6) × 4.4–5.4 μm, subcylindraceae, leves, amyloideae. Cheilocystidia 10.5–16 × 4.5–9 μm, clavata, efibulata, surculis cylindraceis, rectis c. 1.8 × 0.9 μm munita. Pleurocystidia nulla. Trama lamellarum iodi ope brunneovinescens. Hyphae pileipellis 3.5–9 μm latae, efibulatae, dense diverticulatae. Acanthocystides 14.5–22.5 × 11.5–22.5 μm, globosae, dense diverticulatae. Velum universale e cherocytibus crasse-tunicatis, sparse diverticulatis formatum, superioribus 27–36 × 15–36 μm, spinuliferis. Hyphae stipitis corticales 1.5–3.5 μm latae, leves. Caulocystidia 35–>150 × 5.5–9 μm, cylindracea, dense diverticulata.

Corticola.

Holotypus: A.A.R. de Meijer COA-2891 (No. 990.200–080; L); isotypus: MBM 190332.

Basidiomata scattered. Pileus 0.8–2.2 mm across, up to 1 mm high, in the primordial stage convex or shallowly conical, densely and minutely puberulous, later hemispherical to convex, dried often centrally depressed, dry, shallowly sulcate, translucent-striate, minutely pulverulent, white or, more rarely, with faintest pale yellow shade towards the centre. Context very thin. Odour absent, taste not recorded. Lamellae 8–10 reaching the stipe, tender, ascending, ventricose, c. 0.4 mm broad, narrowly adnate to adnexed, white, with convex, concolorous edge. Stipe 4–7 × 0.1–0.2 mm, hollow, fragile, equal, terete, dry, smooth, minutely puberulous, white, springing from a very small patch of radiating, white fibrils, which is not always equally well discernible.

Basidia (none seen mature) c. 13.5–15 × 10.5–11.5 μm, more or less globose, a few seen with four incipient sterigmata, clampless. Spores 8.9–10.7 (–11.6) × 4.4–5.4 μm (Q = 2.4), elongated pip-shaped, smooth, amyloid. Cheilocystidia scarce, hardly discernible, 10.5–16 × 4.5–9 μm, occurring mixed with the basidia (lamellar edge heterogeneous), clavate, clampless, not very densely covered with evenly spaced, cylindrical, simple, straight ex-

*Etymology: paulus, small.

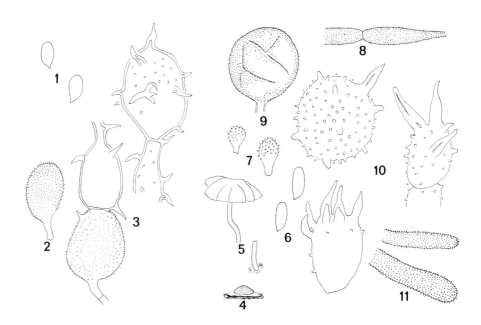

Fig. 6 (1–3) *Mycena impexa* (de Meijer MA-2940). – 1. Spores. – 2. Acanthocyst. – 3. Cherocytes.
(4–11) *Mycena paula* (de Meijer COA-2891). – 4. Primordium. – 5. Habitus and basal part of the
stipe. – 6. Spores. – 7. Cheilocystidia. – 8. Fragment of a hypha of the pileipellis. – 9. Acanthocyst. –
10. Cherocytes, one seen from above. – 11. Caulocystidia. Figs. 4–5, × 10; all others, × 700.

crescences, c. 1.8 × 0.9 μm. Pleurocystidia absent. Lamellar trama somewhat
brownish vinescent in Melzer's reagent. Pileipellis a very narrow cutis of
repent, radiately aligned hyphae which are 3.5–9 μm wide, densely covered
with short, cylindrical excrescences 0.9–1.5 × 0.9 μm. The pileipellis covered
with (i) numerous acanthocysts and (ii) cherocytes which in the primordial
stage cause the densely puberulous aspect. Acanthocysts 14.5–22.5 × 11.5–
22.5 μm, globose, thin-walled, densely covered with small excrescences 0.9–
1.5 × 0.9 μm. Cherocytes arranged in chains (the length of which has not
been ascertained), those at the top of the chains 27–36 × 15–36 μm, ellipsoid
to globose, thick-walled, covered with one to several, thick-walled to massive,
smooth, acute spines 10–20(–24) × 4.5–7 μm, as well as with more or less
numerous, obtuse excrescences 1.8–4.5 × 1.8–3.5 μm. Hyphae of the cortical
layer of the stipe 1.5–3.5 μm wide, smooth. Caulocystidia 35–>150 × 5.5–
9 μm, cylindrical, thin-walled, densely covered with short, cylindrical excrescences 0.9–1.5 × 0.9 μm.

On decayed twigs of a dicotyledonous tree in mixed ombrophilous forest,
900 m alt.

Holotype: '*Mycena paula* Maas G. and de Meijer / 18 May 1994 / Paraná:
Colombo, EMBRAPA-Florestal, native forest / A.A.R. de Meijer COA-2891' (No.
990.200–080; L); isotype: MBM 190332.

The extremely small size of the dried specimens made investigation a difficult undertaking and the result is a description that leaves a few things to be desired.

Mycena pistacea* Maas G. and de Meijer, *spec. nov.* – Fig. 7

Basidiomata dispersa. Pileus 5–8 mm latus, usque ad 8 mm altus, campanulatus, siccus, sulcatus, striatus, albopulverulentus, centro striisque griseis, inter strias griseoviridis. Caro pertenuis, odore nullo. Lamellae 16? stipitem attingentes, molles, adscendentes, ventricosae, < 1 mm latae, liberae, pallide griseae, margine convexae, concolores. Stipes c. 35 × 0.7 mm, cavus, fragilis, aequalis, cylindraceus, siccus, levis, totus pubescens, albus, basi tomentosus.

Basidia c. 22.5 × 10–11.5 μm, clavata, (1–)2(–3)-sporigera, efibulata, sterigmatibus 6.5–9 μm longis instructa. Sporae 11.6–15.2 × 5.4–7.2 μm, inaequilateraliter ellipsoideae, leves, amyloideae. Cheilocystidia 11.5–18 × 6.5–10 μm, clavata, subfusiformia, efibulata, surculis cylindraceis, simplicibus vel furcatis 1.5–8 × 0.9 μm munita. Pleurocystidia nulla. Trama lamellarum iodi ope haud vinescens. Hyphae pileipellis 6.5–9 μm latae, efibulatae, dense diverticulatae. Acanthocystides 20–55 × 10–40 μm, clavatae vel ellipsoideae, dense diverticulatae. Cherocytes nullae. Hyphae stipitis corticales leves. Caulocystidia 27- > 300 × 20–30 μm, cylindracea, dense diverticulata.

Lignicola.

Holotypus: A.A.R. de Meijer CUa-448b (No. 990.200–273; L); notulae: MBM 190335.

Basidiomata scattered. Pileus 5–8 mm across, up to 8 mm high, campanulate, dry, sulcate, translucent-striate, white-powdered, centre and striae grey (1D2), between the striae fairly pale greyish green (1B3). Context very thin. Odour absent. Lamellae 16? reaching the stipe, tender, ascending, ventricose, < 1 mm broad, free, very pale grey (between 1A1 and 1B1), with convex, concolorous edge. Stipe c. 35 × 0.7 mm, hollow, fragile, equal, terete, dry, smooth, pubescent all over, white, the base densely white-tomentose.

Basidia (not mature) c. 22.5 × 10–11.5 μm, clavate, 2-spored, but also 1- and 3-spored, clampless, with sterigmata 6.5–9 μm long. Spores 11.6–15.2 × 5.4–7.2 μm (Q = 2.0), the larger ones probably shed by 1-spored basidia, pip-shaped, smooth, amyloid. Cheilocystidia 11.5–18 × 6.5–10 μm, locally forming a short sterile band, mostly occurring mixed with basidia, clavate to subfusiform, clampless, covered with more or less evenly spaced, fairly coarse, cylindrical, simple or furcate, mostly straight excrescences 1.5–8 × 0.9 μm. Pleurocystidia absent. Lamellar trama not vinescent in Melzer's reagent. Pileipellis a cutis of repent, radiately aligned hyphae which are 6.5–9 μm wide, densely covered with wart-like excrescences 0.5 × 0.5 μm. Acanthocysts 20–55 × 10–40 μm, clavate to ellipsoid, thin-walled, densely covered with wart-like excrescences 0.5 × 0.5 μm, with colourless contents. Cherocytes absent. Hypoderm made up of hyphae with inflated cells. Hyphae of the cortical layer of the stipe smooth. Caulocystidia 27– > 300 × 20–30 μm, cylindrical, thin-walled, densely covered with wart-like and, apically, short, cylindrical excrescences 0.9–3.5 × 0.5–0.9 μm.

On decayed wood of a dicotyledonous tree in seasonal semi-deciduous alluvial forest, 870 m alt.

Holotype: '*Mycena pistacea* Maas G. and de Meijer / 24 May 1980 /

---

*Etymology: pistaceus, greenish, referring to the greyish-greenish colour of the pileus.

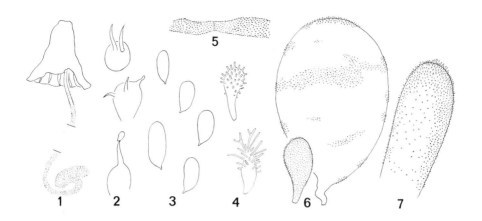

Fig. 7 (1–7) *Mycena pistacea* (de Meijer cua-448b). – 1. Habitus. – 2. Basidia. – 3. Spores. – 4. Cheilocystidia. – 5. Fragment of a hypha of the pileipellis. – 6. Acanthocysts. – 7. Caulocystidium. Fig. 1, × 3; all others, × 700.

Paraná: Curitiba, Uberaba Distr., Reserva Biológica Cambuí / A.A.R. de Meijer cua-448b' (No. 990.200–273; L); notes and drawings: мвм 190335.

The type material, although scanty, now fragmented and in rather poor condition, yielded sufficient information for a description. It is to be expected, however, that with further finds changes in both the macro- and microscopic data may be necessary.

The shape of the pileus, its white-furfuraceous surface, the two-spored basidia, the verrucose hyphae of the pileipellis, and the lack of cherocytes suggest some close relationship between *M. pistacea* and *M. alphitophora* (Berk.) Sacc. The latter species differs from *M. pistacea* among other features in its differently coloured pileus, presence of a basal disc, and much shorter spores (8.1–9.6 µm).

Mycena propinqua* Maas G. and de Meijer, *spec. nov.* – Fig. 8

Basidiomata dispersa. Primordium c. 1 mm latum, hemisphaericum, album pallide flavo-tinctum, elementis veli universalis –0.5 × –0.1 mm dense obtectum. Pileus 1.5–4 mm latus, usque ad 2 mm altus, e hemisphaerico campanulatus vel planoconvexus, siccus, levis vel sulcatus, striatus, minute pulverulentus, glabrescens, hygrophanus, albus, centro striisque pallide griseis. Caro pertenuis, alba, odore nullo. Lamellae 9–13 stipitem attingentes, molles, adscendentes, ventricosae, usque ad 0.5 mm latae, anguste adnatae, albae, margine concolores. Stipes 10–35 × 0.2–0.6 mm, cavus, fragilis, aequalis, cylindraceus, siccus, levis, puberulus vel pubescens, albus, basi bulbosus.

Basidia 13.5–15 × 8–10 µm, subclavata vel ellipsoidea, 4-sporigera, efibulata. Sporae 8.1–9.8 × (4.0–)4.6–5.2 µm, inaequilateraliter ellipsoideae, leves, tenuiter amyloideae. Cheilocystidia 11–24 × 8–13.5 µm, subclavata vel ellipsoidea, plerumque sessilia, efibulata, surculis cylindraceis, rectis 0.5–1.5 × 0.5 µm instructa. Pleurocystidia nulla. Trama lamellarum iodi ope brunneovi-

*Etymology: propinquus, related, in reference to the primordia which resemble those of *Mycena impexa*, suggesting relationship.

28

nescens. Hyphae pileipellis 2.7–3.6 μm latae, efibulatae, diverticulatae. Acanthocystides 14.5–24 × 11–22.5 μm, globosae, dense diverticulatae. Velum universale e cherocytibus crasse-tunicatis formatum, superioribus spinuliferis 23–40 × 13.5–27 μm. Hyphae stipitis corticales 1.5–2.5 μm latae, leves. Caulocystidia –300 (vel ultra) × 4.5–11 μm, cylindracea, dense diverticulata.

Foliicola.

Holotypus: A.A.R. de Meijer RSC–3131 (No. 991.343–744; L); isotypus: MBM 190336.

Basidiomata scattered. Primordium c. 1 mm across, hemispherical, densely covered with cylindrical elements of the universal veil 0.5 × 0.1 mm, white very faintly tinged yellow. Pileus 1.5–4 mm across, up to 2 mm high, hemispherical, then campanulate to planoconvex, dry, smooth to sulcate, translucent-striate, minutely pulverulent, glabrescent, hygrophanous, the centre and striae pale grey, between the striae white. Context very thin, white. Odour absent. Lamellae 9–13 reaching the stipe, tender, ascending, ventricose, up to 0.5 mm broad, narrowly adnate, white with concolorous edge. Stipe 10–35 × 0.2–0.6 mm, hollow, fragile, equal, terete, dry, smooth, puberulous to pubescent, white, attached to the substratum by a bulbous base.

Basidia (immature) 13.5–15 × 8–10 μm, subclavate or ellipsoid, with four incipient sterigmata, clampless. Spores 8.1–9.8 × (4.0–)4.6–5.2 μm (Q = 2.0), pip-shaped, smooth, weakly amyloid. Cheilocystidia 11–24 × 8–13.5 μm, locally somewhat crowded but not forming a sterile band, subclavate to ellipsoid, very short-stalked to (mostly) sessile, clampless, apically covered with not very numerous, barely visible, cylindrical, straight excrescences 0.5–1.5 × 0.5 μm. Pleurocystidia absent. Lamellar trama brownish vinescent in Melzer's reagent. Pileipellis a cutis of fairly scarce, repent, radiately aligned hyphae which are 2.7–3.6 μm wide, clampless, not very densely covered with short, cylindrical excrescences 0.9 × 0.5 μm. Acanthocysts 14.5–24 × 11–22.5 μm, globose, sessile to short-stalked, thin-walled, densely covered with short, cylindrical excrescences 0.5–1.5 × 0.5 μm. Cherocytes arranged in chains, those at the top of the chain 23–40 × 13.5–27 μm, broadly ellipsoid or globose to subclavate, thick-walled (2 μm), covered with 2–7, scattered, coarse, somewhat curved, thick-walled or solid, acute spines 5–12 × 2–3.5 μm, as well as with a number of warts and small excrescences; those farther down the chain 22.5–55 × 15–22.5 μm, ellipsoid and with fewer warts or smooth. Hyphae of the cortical layer of the stipe 2.5 μm wide, smooth. Caulocystidia –300 (or more) × 4.5–11 μm, cylindrical, densely covered with excrescences 0.5–0.9 × 0.5 μm, at the tip with excrescences 0.9–1.5 × 0.9 μm.

Found on dead leaves of a single, unidentified dicotyledonous tree in mixed ombrophilous forest, 900 m alt.

Holotype: 'Mycena propinqua Maas G. and de Meijer / 10 July 1995 / Paraná: Rio Branco do Sul, near cemetery / A.A.R. de Meijer RSC-3131' (No. 991.343–744; L); isotype: MBM 190336.

Additional material: '28 Dec. 1994 / Paraná: Morretes, Parque Marumbi, Estação Marumbo / A.A.R. de Meijer MA-2998, on decayed dicotyledonous

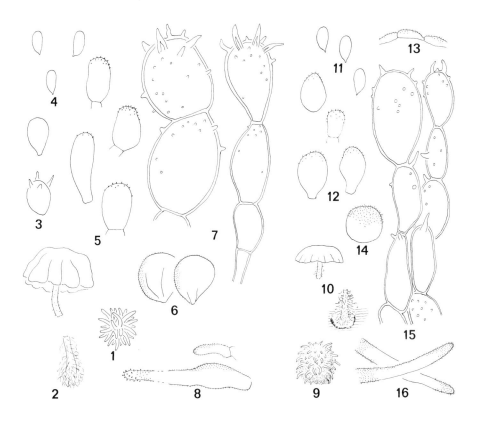

Fig. 8 (1–8) *Mycena propinqua* (de Meijer RSC-3131). – 1. Primordium. – 2. Habitus and basal part of the stipe. – 3. Basidia. – 4. Spores. – 5. Cheilocystidia. – 6. Acanthocysts. – 7. Cherocytes. – 8. Caulocystidia.

(9–16) *Mycena propinqua* (de Meijer MA-2998). – 9. Primordium. – 10. Habitus and basal part of the stipe. – 11. Spores. – 12. Cheilocystidia. – 13. Fragment of a hypha of the pileipellis. – 14. Acanthocyst. – 15. Cherocytes. – 16. Caulocystidia.

(Figs. 1–2, 9–10, × 10; all others, × 700.

leaves in dense ombrophilous forest, 450 m alt.' (No. 991.343–648; L); notulae: MBM 190337.

Mycena spinosissima (Sing.) Desjardin (1995: 15) and *M. heteracantha* (Sing.) Desjardin (1995: 18) are two further species whose primordia are covered with velar elements very much resembling those of *M. propinqua*. From the former species, *M. propinqua* can be told by the sessile cheilocystidia with apically far fewer spinulae, by the far less ornamented to glabrous cherocytes in the proximal part of the chain, and by the bulbous base of the stipe. From *M. heteracantha*, the present species can be separated by the completely different construction of what Desjardin calls the 'conic spines' of the universal veil. The narrowed base of the cheilocystidia in *M. heteracantha* is a further difference.

2. Mycena sect. Supinae Konr. and Maubl.

Mycena sect. *Supinae* Konr. and Maubl., Ic. sel. Fung. **6**: 274. 1934. – Lectotype: *Mycena supina* (Fr.) Gillet.

For further synonymy, see Maas Geesteranus, 1984: 139.

Basidiomata small to medium-sized. Pileus pruinose or puberulous to minutely flocculose, glabrescent, variously coloured. Context thin. Odour insignificant or none. Lamellae tender, rarely ascending, usually horizontal to arcuate, broadly adnate, more or less concolorous with the pileus, pallescent, with the edge generally paler to whitish. Stipe pruinose or puberulous to floccose, glabrescent, the base covered with white fibrils.

Basidia 4-spored or 2-spored, clamped when 4-spored. Spores globose to subglobose, smooth, amyloid. Cheilocystidia clavate to irregularly shaped, covered with variously shaped excrescences. Pleurocystidia absent or scarce. Lamellar trama vinescent in Melzer's reagent. Hyphae of the pileipellis covered with warts or cylindrical excrescences, rarely smooth. Hyphae of the cortical layer of the stipe diverticulate.

Corticolous.

Mycena fera and *M. globulispora* are placed in this section with some doubt. Although they fit the section's description in having arcuate lamellae, globose spores and ornamented cheilocystidia, hyphae of the pileipellis and caulocystidia, they differ widely from the section's members of the Northern Temperate zone by the strikingly coarse excrescences of the cheilocystidia as well as of the hyphae of the pileipellis and the cortical layer of the stipe.

The third species, *Mycena recessa*, is equally unusual in that its hyphae of the cortical layer of the stipe are smooth. Apparently, the distinguishing features applicable to North Temperate sections of *Mycena* must be expected to show considerable variation in more southern regions.

KEY TO THE SPECIES

1. Spores 8.9–10.7 μm broad. Cheilocystidia with coarse to very coarse excrescences.
   2. Cheilocystidia with very coarse, branched or furcate excrescences 13–24 μm long. Hyphae of the cortical layer of the stipe largely smooth: . . . . *M. fera*
   2. Cheilocystidia with simple excrescences 2.5–4.5 μm long. Hyphae of the cortical layer of the stipe covered with coarse excrescences: . . . . *M. globulispora*
1. Spores 4.5–5.5 μm broad. Cheilocystidia with small, simple excrescences 1–2 μm long:
  . . . . *M. recessa*

Mycena fera* Maas G. and de Meijer, *spec. nov.* – Fig. 9

Basidiomata dispersa. Pileus 8–11 mm latus, 5–8 mm altus, campanulatus, interdum subumbilicatus, siccus, levis, striatus, subtomentosus, griseobrunneus. Caro tenuis, odore nullo. Lamellae 7–10 stipitem attingentes, molles, arcuatae, c. 2 mm latae, late adnatae, dente de-

*Etymology: ferus, rough, wild, referring to the wild aspect of the cheilocystidia and the hyphae of the pileipellis.

currentes, griseo-albae, margine concavo, albo. Stipes 15–30 × 0.8–1 mm, cavus, fragilis, aequalis, cylindraceus, siccus, levis, apice minute pruinosus, albus, basi fibrillis sparsis munitus.

Basidia 24–30 × 12.5–15 μm, clavata, 4-sporigera, fibulata, sterigmatibus c. 6.5 μm longis
praedita. Sporae 11.2–12.5 × 9.5–10.7 μm, globosae vel subglobosae, leves, amyloideae. Cheilocystidia 22.5–34 × 12.5–17 μm, clavata, fibulata, apice surculis crassis 13.5–24 × 2.5–10 μm
instructa. Pleurocystidia nulla. Trama lamellarum iodi ope brunneovinescens. Hyphae pileipellis
2.5–4.5 μm latae, fibulatae, crasse diverticulatae. Hyphae stipitis corticales 2.5 μm latae, fibulatae, pro majore parte leves, cellulae terminales 3.5–9 μm latae, diverticulatae.

Ramicola.

Holotypus: A.A.R. de Meijer cub-2581 (No. 988.233–009; L); notulae: мвм 188517.

Basidiomata scattered. Pileus 8–11 mm across, 5–8 mm high, campanulate,
at times slightly umbilicate, dry, smooth, striate up to the centre, minutely
tomentose, greyish brown. Context thin. Odour absent. Lamellae 7–10
reaching the stipe, tender, arcuate, c. 2 mm broad, broadly adnate, decurrent
with a short tooth, greyish white, the edge concave, white. Stipe 15–30 ×
0.8–1 mm, hollow, fragile, equal, terete, dry, smooth, apically minutely
pruinose, white, shiny, the base pale yellowish, sparsely covered with short
fibrils.

Basidia 24–30 × 12.5–15 μm, clavate, 4-spored, clamped, with plump
sterigmata c. 6.5 μm long. Spores 11.2–12.5 × 9.5–10.7 μm (Q = 1.2), globose to subglobose, smooth, amyloid. Cheilocystidia 22.5–34 × 12.5–17 μm,

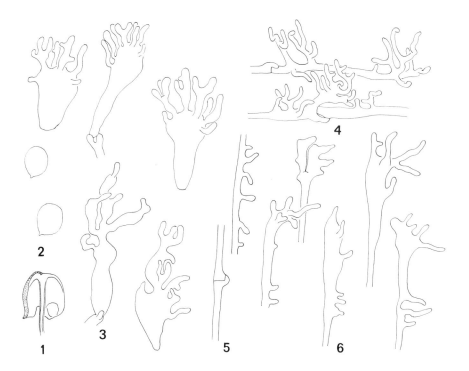

Fig. 9 (1–6) *Mycena fera* (de Meijer cub-2581). – 1. Habitus. – 2. Spores. – 3. Cheilocystidia. – 4.
Hyphae of the pileipellis. – 5. Hyphae of the cortical layer of the stipe. – 6. Terminal cells.
Fig. 1, × 2; all others, × 700.

forming a sterile band (lamellar edge homogeneous), clavate, clamped, sessile to fairly long-stalked, apically covered with comparatively few but very coarse, subcylindrical or variously shaped, simple to furcate or branched excrescences 13.5–24 × 2.5–10 µm. Pleurocystidia absent. Lamellar trama brownish vinescent in Melzer's reagent. Pileipellis a cutis of repent, radiately aligned hyphae which are 2.5–4.5 µm wide, clamped, somewhat sparsely covered with coarse, cylindrical, generally much branched, curved to tortuous excrescences 6.5–27 × 1.8–5.5 µm. Hypoderm consisting of parallel, thin-walled hyphae up to c. 25 µm broad. Hyphae of the cortical layer of the stipe 2.5 µm wide, clamped, smooth for the greater part but towards the terminal cells occasionally covered with fairly coarse, cylindrical, mostly simple excrescences 3–5.5 × 2 µm, the terminal cells (caulocystidia) to be found near the apex of the stipe, 3.5–9 µm wide, sometimes furcate, covered with few but coarse, generally cylindrical, simple to somewhat branched excrescences 2.5–14.5 × 1.5–4.5 µm.

Growing on a decayed branch of a dicotyledonous tree in mixed ombrophilous forest, 900 m alt.

Holotype: 'Mycena fera Maas G. and de Meijer / 21 March 1993 / Paraná: Curitiba, Santo Inácio Distr., Parque Barigui / A.A.R. de Meijer CUB-2581' (No. 988.233–009; L); notes and drawings: MBM 188517.

Singer described from the South American realm four species which he placed in section *Mycena* subsection *Corticolae* Kühn., one of the synonyms of section *Supinae*. These species are *M. hypsizyga* Sing. (1969: 122), *M. abieticola* Sing. (1973: 37), *M. melinocephala* Sing. (1973: 43), and *M. costaricensis* Sing. (1982: 41). *Mycena costaricensis, M. hypsizyga,* and *M. melinocephala* are easily distinct from *M. fera* on account of the cheilocystidial excrescences which are described as setae or setuliform and are said not to exceed 6 µm in length. *Mycena abieticola* can be separated from *M. fera* by the colour of the pileus ('alutaceo-ochraceo') and of the stipe ('centro pilei concolori'), the apparently 2-spored, clampless basidia, and the setulose appendages of both cheilocystidia and hyphae of the pileipellis.

Mycena globulispora* Maas G. and de Meijer, *spec. nov.* – Fig. 10

Basidiomata dispersa. Pileus 5–11 mm latus, 4–6 mm altus, hemisphaericus, siccus, subsulcatus, totus albo-pruinosus, griseobrunneus. Caro 0.8 mm lata, alba, odore nullo. Lamellae 9–11 stipitem attingentes, molles, arcuatae, usque ad 3.5 mm latae, late adnatae, dente decurrentes, griseobrunneae, margine concavo, albo. Stipes 13–15 × 1.2–1.5 mm, cavus, fragilis, aequalis, cylindraceus, siccus, levis, totus pruinosus, albus, basi fibrillis crassis albis substrato affixus.

Basidia 30–40 × 11.5–13.5 µm, clavata, 4-sporigera, fibulata, sterigmatibus 9–10 µm longis instructa. Sporae 9.8–10.7 × 8.9–10.3 µm, globosae, leves, amyloideae. Cheilocystidia 22.5–40 × 7–21 µm, clavata vel late ellipsoidea, fibulata, sessilia, surculis 2.5–4.5 × 1.8–3.5 µm praedita. Pleurocystidia sparsa, similia. Trama lamellarum iodi ope brunneovinescens. Hyphae pileipellis 2.5–7 µm latae, fibulatae, leves, cellulae terminales inflatae atque crasse diverticulatae. Hyphae

*Etymology: globulispora, globose-spored.

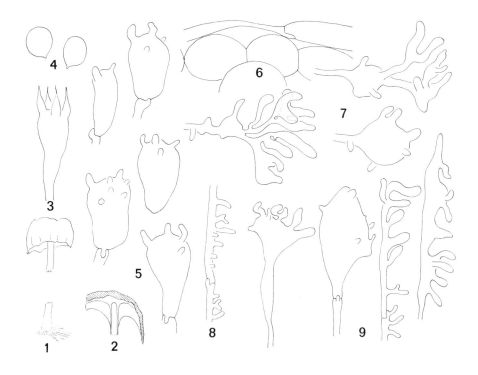

Fig. 10 (1–9) *Mycena globulispora* (de Meijer MA-2910). – 1. Habitus and basal part of the stipe. – 2. Section of the pileus. – 3. Basidium. – 4. Spores. – 5. Cheilocystidia. – 6. Hypha of the pileipellis. – 7. Terminal cells of hyphae of the pileipellis. – 8. Hypha of the cortical layer of the stipe. – 9. Terminal cells of hyphae of the cortical layer of the stipe. (1–2, × 2; all others, × 700.

stipitis corticales 2.7–4.5 µm latae, fibulatae, crasse diverticulatae, cellulae terminales 70–90 × 2.5–20 µm, crasse diverticulatae.

Corticola.

Holotypus: A.A.R. de Meijer MA-2910 (No. 990.200–154; L); isotypus: MBM 188523.

Basidiomata scattered. Pileus 5–11 mm across, 4–6 mm high, hemispherical, dry, somewhat irregularly sulcate, translucent-striate?, entirely white-pruinose, dark grey-brown (7E3). Context up to 0.8 mm broad, white. Taste mild, odour absent. Lamellae 9–11 reaching the stipe, tender, arcuate, up to 3.5 mm broad, broadly adnate, decurrent with a tooth, fairly dark brownish grey (7D2), the edge concave, white. Stipe 13–15 × 1.2–1.5 mm, hollow, fragile, equal, terete, dry, smooth, entirely white-pruinose, white, the base attached to the substratum by coarse, white fibrils.

Basidia 30–40 × 11.5–13.5 µm, fairly slender-clavate, 4-spored, clamped, with plump sterigmata 9–10 µm long. Spores 9.8–10.7 × 8.9–10.3 µm (Q = 1.2), globose, smooth, amyloid. Cheilocystidia 22.5–40 × 7–21 µm, forming a sterile band (lamellar edge homogeneous), broadly clavate to broadly ellipsoid, clamped, sessile, apically covered with few, unevenly spaced, coarse, simple, straight or curved, cylindrical excrescences 2.5–4.5 × 1.8–3.5 µm. Pleurocystidia scarce, similar. Lamellar trama brownish vinescent in Melzer's

34

reagent. Pileipellis a cutis made up of one or two repent, radiately aligned hyphae (directly overlying the pileal trama) which are 2.5–7 µm wide, clamped, smooth, with variously inflated terminal cells (– 60 × – 20 µm), covered with coarse to very coarse, simple to branched excrescences. Context of the pileus made up of unusually large, ellipsoid to globose cells up to 70 µm wide. Hyphae of the cortical layer of the stipe 2.7–4.5 µm wide, clamped, covered with coarse, cylindrical, simple to furcate excrescences 1.8 – 8 × 1.8–3.5 µm, the terminal cells (caulocystidia) 70–90 × 2.5–20 µm, apically hardly broadened to very much so and covered with few to numerous, fairly small to very coarse excrescences.

On dead bark (1 m above the ground) of a living dicotyledonous tree in dense ombrophilous forest, 300 m alt.

Holotype: '*Mycena globulispora* Maas G. and de Meijer / 12 June 1994 / Paraná: Morretes, Parque Marumbi near Nhundiaquara River / A.A.R. de Meijer MA 2910' (No. 990.200–154; L); isotype: MBM 188523.

A species which has a hemispherical pileus, 8–9 arcuate-decurrent lamellae and globose spores of about the same size in common with *M. globulispora* is *Mycena singeri* described by Lodge (1988: 111) from Puerto Rico, West Indies. Some other characters, of the latter, however, such as a red edge to the lamella, lobed or branched cheilocystidia, and pileocystidia and caulocystidia with reddish brown intracellular pigment readily show the two species to be different from each other and not even members of the same section. *Mycena singeri* was not assigned to any section of *Mycena*.

Mycena globulispora deviates from most other members of the section in that its cheilocystidia have fewer as well as coarser excrescences than is the general rule, while its hyphae of the pileipellis are smooth. The basal patch of radiating fibrils which attach the stipe to the substratum is also unusual.

The specific epithet *globulispora* should not be confused with *Mycena globispora* Kühn., which is a synonym of *Mycena clavularis* (Batsch: Fr.) Sacc. (Maas Geesteranus, 1983: 416).

Mycena recessa* Maas G. and de Meijer, *spec. nov.* – Fig. 11

Basidiomata dispersa. Pileus 2.3–3 mm latus, 2 mm altus, hemisphaericus, siccus, sulcatus striatusque, totus albo-pruinosus, griseus. Caro tenuissima, odore indistincto. Lamellae 7–8 stipitem attingentes, molles, arcuatae, usque ad 1 mm latae, adnatae, subdecurrentes, albae, margine concolore. Stipes 2.5–3 × 0.2 mm, cavus, curvatus, fragilis, aequalis, cylindraceus, siccus, levis, totus pruinosus, albus, basi subincrassatus, fibrillis tenuibus brevibusque substrato affixus.

Basidia c. 20 × 6.5–7 µm, clavata, 2?-sporigera, fibulata, sterigmatibus c. 4.5 µm longis praedita. Sporae 6.3–7.2 × 4.6–5.5 µm, subglobosae, leves, amyloideae. Cheilocystidia 18–23 × 11–11.5 µm, clavata, fibulata, surculis sparsis 1–2 × 1–2 µm munita. Pleurocystidia haud observata. Trama lamellarum iodi ope brunneovinescens. Hyphae pileipellis 1.8–2.7 µm latae, fibulatae, diverticulatae, cellulis terminalibus diverticulatis instructae. Hyphae stipitis corticales 2.7 µm latae, fibulatae, parietibus subincrassatis praeditae, caulocystidia ellipsoidea 16–36 × 10–22.5 µm, diverticulata.

*Etymology: recessus, hidden from view (because of its small size and colour).

Bambusicola.
Holotypus: A.A.R. de Meijer MA-2942 (No. 990.200–042; L); notulae: MBM 190344.

Basidiomata scattered. Pileus 2.3–3 mm across, 2 mm high, hemispherical, dry, sulcate, translucent-striate, entirely white-pruinose, the centre and striae grey with a slight brownish shade (6D2), whitish between the striae. Context very thin. Taste not recorded, odour indistinct. Lamellae 7–8 reaching the stipe, tender, arcuate, up to 1 mm broad, broadly adnate, decurrent with a short tooth, pure white, with concave, concolorous edge. Stipe 2.5–3 × 0.2 mm, hollow, curved, fragile, equal, terete, dry, smooth, entirely pruinose, pure white, the base somewhat broadened and attached to the substratum by very short, fine, white fibrils.

Basidia (mostly immature) c. 20 × 6.5–7 μm, clavate, two seen with two sterigmata, a few more with one large sterigma, clamped, sterigmata c. 4.5 μm long. Spores (mature?) 6.3–7.2 × 4.6–5.5 μm (Q = 1.3), subglobose, smooth, amyloid. Cheilocystidia 18–23 × 11–11.5 μm, clavate, clamped, apically covered with fairly few, simple, cylindrical excrescences 1–2 × 1–2 μm. Pleurocystidia not observed. Lamellar trama brownish vinescent in Melzer's reagent. Pileipellis a cutis made up of radiately aligned hyphae which are 1.8–2.7 μm wide, clamped, much branched, the branches densely covered with simple, cylindrical, straight excrescences 1.8–5.5 × 1–2 μm, the terminal cells globose, clavate, ellipsoid, 13.5–36 × 6.5–18 μm, equally covered with simple, cylindrical, straight or somewhat curved excrescences. Hypoderm made up of hyphae with inflated cells. Hyphae of the cortical layer of the stipe 2.7 μm wide, clamped, with smooth, somewhat thickened cell-walls, the caulocystidia mostly ellipsoid, but also globose or clavate, 16–36 × 10–22.5 μm, somewhat sparsely covered with simple, cylindrical excrescences 1–2.5 × 1–2 μm.

On a decayed bamboo twig in dense ombrophilous forest, 850 m alt.

Holotype: 'Mycena recessa Maas G. and de Meijer / 17 Nov. 1994 / Paraná: Morretes, Parque Marumbi, near road BR-277 / A.A.R. de Meijer MA-2942' (No. 990.200–042; L); notes and drawings: MBM 190344.

Although no more than three basidiomata of the present species could be found and one and a half had to be sacrificed for analysis, it was decided to retain the remainder for the holotype and give a formal description. Unfortunately, the hymenial details are not as complete as is desirable, but there should be no difficulty recognizing the species.

Mycena recessa deviates from most other members of the section because of the smooth hyphae of the stipe cortex.

Singer (Singer and Gomez, 1982: 41) described another member of section *Supinae* which he called *Mycena costaricensis* and which, like *M. recessa*, has a dark pileus and a white stipe, and lacks pleurocystidia. The difference between the two species is that the pileus of his species is said to become umbilicate on drying, while the lamellae are grey towards the base, the stipe is 'glabro vel subglabro,' the cheilocystidia are covered with much longer excrescences (5–6 μm; 1–2 μm in *M. recessa*), and the epicutis is described as gelatinous.

The association of *Mycena recessa* with bamboo brings to mind that Berkeley (apud Cooke, 1890: 54) described an *Agaricus (Mycena) bambusarum* collected by Mr Kurz at Bogor, Java. In spite of the very brief diagnosis, it is obvious that a species with a large (one inch across) and white pileus, crowded and narrowly adnate lamellae cannot possibly be the same as *M. recessa*.

Murrill (in Proc. Fla. Acad. Sci. 7: 124. ('1944') 1945; not seen) described a *Mycena bambusicola* which he later (p. 127) recognized to be not a *Mycena*, and transferred to *Bolbitius*. The correctness of this transfer was confirmed by Watling and Gregory (1981: 68).

3. MYCENA section FILIPEDES (Fr.) Quél.

Agaricus [sect.] *Filipedes* Fr., Epicr. Syst. mycol.: 111. 1838 ('*Filopedes*'); Cooke, Handb. Br. Fungi 1: 70. 1871 ('Filopedes', formally accepted as section). – *Mycena* [sect.] *Filipedes* (Fr.) Quél., in Mém. Soc. Emul. Montbél. II 5: 106. 1872 ('*Filopedes*'). – *Mycena* [subsect.?] *Filipedes* (Fr.) Kühn., Genre *Mycena*: 161, 279. 1938. – *Mycena* subsect. *Filipedes* (Fr.) Métrod in Prodr. Flore mycol. Madagasc. 3: 20, 21, 33. 1949. – Lectotype (Maas Geesteranus, 1980: 99): *Mycena filopes* (Bull.: Fr.) Kummer.

For further synonymy, see Maas Geesteranus, 1984: 413.

Basidiomata very small to fairly large. Pileus at first pruinose (but pruinosity probably often remaining unobserved), glabrescent, typically dry, but at times becoming slightly viscid, variously coloured. Context thin. Odour very variable, none or fragrant to spicy, raphanoid to chemical or disagreeable, in some species of iodoform on drying out. Taste none, indistinctive or disagreeable. Lamellae tender, ascending, narrowly adnate or somewhat emar-

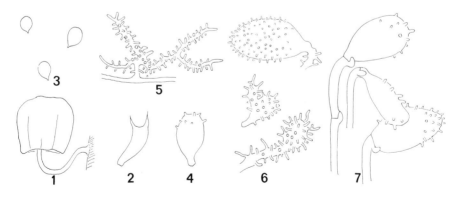

Fig. 11 (1–7) *Mycena recessa* (de Meijer MA-2942). – 1. Habitus. – 2. Basidium. – 3. Spores. – 4. Cheilocystidium. – 5. Hypha of the pileipellis. – 6. Terminal cells of hyphae of the pileipellis. – 7. Caulocystidia.
Fig. 1, × 10; all others, × 700.

ginate, sometimes decurrent with a small tooth, narrow to more or less ventricose, variously coloured, whitish, brownish, olivaceous, greenish, in some species turning pink with age, with the edge convex, concolorous with or paler than the sides or greenish to citrine. Stipe usually elongated and narrow, fragile to fairly firm, hollow, pruinose to minutely puberulous (mostly only visible at the apex), glabrescent, not viscid, generally concolorous with the pileus, in some species tinged bluish or violaceous but fading to brownish with age, at the base covered with coarse fibrils.

Basidia 4-spored or 2-spored, clavate, mostly clamped. Spores pip-shaped, smooth, amyloid. Cheilocystidia stipitate or sessile, mostly regularly shaped and clavate but also obovoid to obpyriform, generally covered with evenly spaced, cylindrical excrescences. Pleurocystidia if present similar. Hyphae of the pileipellis and the cortical layer of the stipe diverticulate (perhaps those of *M. peyerimhoffii* excepted).

Growing among vegetable debris in deciduous and coniferous woods, corticolous on living trees, or among grass and low herbs in the coastal dunes with no apparent association with trees.

Mycena scotina* Maas G. and de Meijer, *spec. nov.* – Fig. 12

Basidioma solitarium. Pileus 8 mm latus, 3 mm altus, subcampanulatus, haud sulcatus, siccus, minute albo-pruinosus, atrobrunneus. Caro tenuis, alba, odore nullo. Lamellae 12 stipitem attingentes, molles, adscendentes, c. 1 mm latae, adnatae, dente decurrentes, albae griseo-tinctae, margine convexae, concolores. Stipes 20 × 0.4 mm, cavus, fragilis, aequalis, cylindraceus, siccus, levis, glaber videtur, superne albus, inferne obscure griseobrunneus, basi fibrillis crassis albisque munitus.

Basidia c. 18 × 6.5 μm, subclavata, 2-sporigera, efibulata. Sporae 9.0–9.4 × 5.4–5.6 μm, inaequilateraliter ellipsoideae, leves, amyloideae. Cheilocystidia 15–45 × 9–27, ellipsoidea, clavata, spheropedunculata, efibulata, surculis cylindraceis, simplicibus, rectis 1.8–4.5 × 0.9–1.3 μm munita. Pleurocystidia nulla. Trama lamellarum iodi ope brunnescens. Hyphae pileipellis 7–11.5 μm latae, efibulatae, diverticulatae. Hyphae stipitis corticales 2.7–4.5 μm latae, efibulatae, diverticulatae, cellulae terminales 4.5–5.5 μm latae, diverticulatae, rarae.

Lignicola.

Holotypus: A.A.R. de Meijer RS-3027 (No. 990.200–174; L); notulae: MBM 190348.

One single specimen collected. Pileus 8 mm across, 3 mm high, somewhat campanulate, not sulcate, dry, delicately white-pruinose, almost black-brown (8F3). Context thin, white. Odour absent. Lamellae 12 reaching the stipe, tender, ascending, c. 1 mm broad, adnate, decurrent with a short tooth, more or less intervenose, white with a faint, greyish tint, with convex, concolorous edge. Stipe 20 × 0.4 mm, hollow, fragile, equal, terete, dry, smooth, appearing glabrous, whitish at the apex, grey-brown (6D4) farther down, dark greyish brown (7E5) for the greater part, the base covered with coarse, white fibrils.

Basidia (immature) c. 18 × 6.5 μm, subclavate, with two incipient sterigmata, clampless. Spores 9.0–9.4 × 5.4–5.6 μm (Q = 1.8), pip-shaped,

*Etymology: scotinus, latinized form of σκοτεινός, dark, referring to the dark pileus.

38

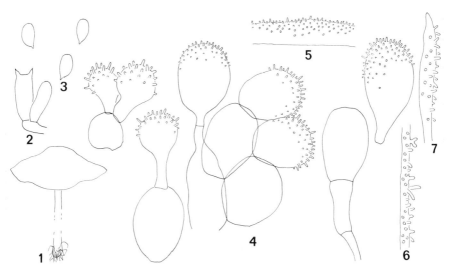

Fig. 12 (1–7) *Mycena scotina* (de Meijer RS-3027). – 1. Habitus. – 2. Basidia. – 3. Spores. – 4. Cheilocystidia and the supporting cells from which they arise. – 5. Hypha of the pileipellis. – 6. Hypha of the cortical layer of the stipe. – 7. Terminal cell.
Fig. 1, × 3; all others, × 700.

smooth, amyloid. Cheilocystidia 15–45 × 9–27 μm, forming a sterile band (lamellar edge homogeneous), ellipsoid, clavate, spheropedunculate, clampless, apically covered with evenly spaced, cylindrical, simple, straight excrescences 1.8–4.5 × 0.9–1.3 μm, arising from short chains of supporting cells which are 13.5–35 × 13.5–22.5 μm, globose to ellipsoid, thin-walled, smooth. Pleurocystidia absent. Lamellar trama rather more brunnescent than vinescent in Melzer's reagent. Pileipellis a cutis made up of radiately aligned hyphae which are 7–11.5 μm wide, clampless, covered with short cylindrical excrescences 0.9–2.7 × 0.9 μm. Hypoderm made up of hyphae with inflated cells up to 25 μm wide. Hyphae of the cortical layer of the stipe 2.7–4.5 μm wide, clampless, covered with cylindrical, mostly simple and generally straight excrescences 2.2–7.2 × 1.8–2.5 μm, terminal cells rare, 4.5–5.5 μm wide, diverticulate.

On decayed stump of a dicotyledonous tree in secondary mixed ombrophilous forest, 900 m alt.

Holotype: '*Mycena scotina* Maas G. and de Meijer / 11 Feb. 1995 / Paraná: Rio Branco do Sul, Areias Distr., / A.A.R. de Meijer RS-3027' (No. 990.200–174; L); notes and drawings: MBM 190348.

This species is a member of section *Filipedes* but an unusual one in that the cheilocystidia arise from short chains of smooth supporting cells. Scantiness of the material precluded further investigation to see whether it is these cells or the hyphae of the lamellar trama which are filled with darkish pigment.

4. MYCENA sect. **Sejunctae** Maas G. and de Meijer, *sect. nov.*

Basidiomata parva. Pileus pruinosus, e cinereo albus. Caro tenuis. Lamellae molles, anguste adnatae, albae, margine concolore. Stipes fragilis, sparse puberulus, supra albus, e disco basali fibrilloso natus.

Basidia clavata, fibulata. Sporae vulgo subcylindraceae, leves, amyloideae. Cheilocystidia clavata, ellipsoidea, fibulata, apice surculis cylindraceis munita. Pleurocystidia haud observata. Trama lamellarum iodi ope brunneovinescens. Hyphae pileipellis fibulatae, diverticulatae. Hyphae stipitis corticales fibulatae, leves. Caulocystidia levia.

Foliicola.

Species typica: *Mycena sejuncta.*

This section is possibly best placed near section *Filipedes* (Fr.) Quél. (Maas Geesteranus, 1984: 413) from which it differs in subcylindrical spores and smooth hyphae of both the pileipellis and the stipe cortex (section *Filipedes* has pip-shaped spores and diverticulate surface hyphae of both pileus and stipe).

Mycena sejuncta* Maas G. and de Meijer, *spec. nov.* – Fig. 13

Basidiomata dispersa. Pileus 1.5–4 mm latus, convexus, siccus, subsulcatus, striatus, pruinosus, e pallido griseo-albus. Caro tenuis, alba, odore nullo. Lamellae 9–14 stipitem attingentes, molles, adscendentes, usque ad 1 mm latae, anguste adnatae vel collariatae, albae, margine concolore. Stipes 6–10 × 0.1–0.3 mm, cavus, fragilis, aequalis, cylindraceus, siccus, levis, minute sparseque puberulus, supra albus, infra pallide griseus, e disco basali 0.4–0.9 mm lato albo-fibrilloso natus.

Basidia 18–21 × 7–8 μm, clavata, 2(–3)-sporigera, fibulata, sterigmatibus 5.5–7 μm longis instructa. Sporae 7.2–8.1 × 3.1–3.6(–4.5) μm, vulgo subcylindraceae, leves, amyloideae. Cheilocystidia 16–23 × 7–13.5 μm, clavata, ellipsoidea, fibulata, apice surculis cylindraceis 1.8–4.5 × 1–1.5 μm munita. Pleurocystidia haud observata. Trama lamellarum iodi ope brunneovinescens. Hyphae pileipellis 2.7–3.5 μm latae, fibulatae, diverticulatae. Hyphae stipitis corticales 2.7 μm latae, fibulatae, leves. Caulocystidia sparsa, clavata 20–27 × 4.5–7 μm.

Foliicola.

Holotypus: A.A.R. de Meijer MA-3000 (No. 990.200–013; L); notulae: MBM 190349.

Basidiomata scattered. Pileus 1.5–4 mm across, hemispherical to convex, dry, shallowly sulcate, translucent-striate, pruinose to minutely puberulous, the centre and striae pale grey with some yellowish-greenish touch (1C3), white between the striae, drying entirely white. Context thin, white. Odour none. Lamellae 9–14 reaching the stipe, tender, ascending, little ventricose, up to 1 mm broad, narrowly adnate or forming a pseudocollarium, white, with hardly convex, concolorous edge. Stipe 6–10 × 0.1–0.3 mm, hollow, fragile, equal for the greater part, terete, dry, smooth, minutely and sparsely puberulous, white above, pale grey (1C1) towards the base, springing from a 0.4–0.9 mm wide, white basal patch made up of fine, radiating fibrils.

Basidia 18–21 × 7–8 μm, clavate, 2-(occasionally 3-)spored, clamped, with 5.5–7 μm long sterigmata. Spores 7.2–8.1 × 3.1–3.6(–4.5) μm (Q = 2.4), almost cylindrical, more rarely pip-shaped, smooth, amyloid. Cheilocystidia 16–23 × 7–13.5 μm, forming a sterile band (lamellar edge homogeneous), clavate, ellipsoid, some fairly long-stalked, clamped, apically covered with

*Etymology: sejunctus, separated (from members of section *Polyadelphia*).

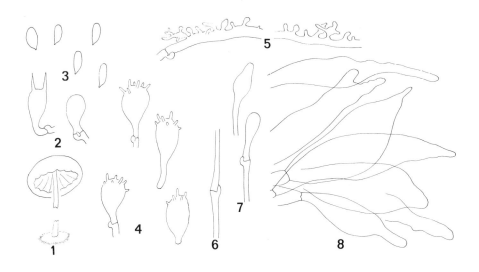

Fig. 13 (1–8) *Mycena sejuncta* (de Meijer MA-3000). – 1. Habitus and basal part of the stipe. – 2. Basidia. – 3. Spores. – 4. Cheilocystidia. – 5. Hyphae of the pileipellis. – 6. Hypha of the cortical layer of the stipe. – 7. Terminal cells of hyphae of the stipe cortex (caulocystidia). – 8. Terminal cells of hyphae of the basal patch.

Fig. 1, × 7.5; all others, × 700.

comparatively few, unevenly spaced, simple, cylindrical, straight excrescences 1.8–4.5 × 1–1.5 μm. Pleurocystidia not observed. Lamellar trama brownish vinescent in Melzer's reagent. Pileipellis a cutis made up of radiately aligned hyphae which are 2.7–3.5 μm wide, clamped, not very densely covered with fairly coarse, simple to more or less branched, cylindrical to swollen, mostly curved excrescences 3.5–11 × 1–4.5 μm. Hypoderm made up of hyphae with inflated cells, some 35 μm wide. Hyphae of the cortical layer of the stipe 2.7 μm wide, clamped, smooth. Caulocystidia (very few seen) clavate, smooth, 20–27 × 4.5–7 μm. Terminal cells of the hyphae of the basal patch fusiform, clampless, 36–90 × 11–23 μm.

On dead leaves of a dicotyledonous tree in dense ombrophilous forest, 450 m alt.

Holotype: '*Mycena sejuncta* Maas G. and de Meijer / 28 Dec. 1994 / Paraná: Morretes, Parque Marumbi, Estação Marumbi / A.A.R. de Meijer MA-3000' (No. 990.200–013; L); notes and drawings: MBM 190349.

In the early stages of the analysis, a number of the characters of the present species (occurrence on dead leaves; a basal patch of radiating fibrils; a small number of lamellae; amyloid spores; clavate cheilocystidia with few, cylindrical excrescences; apparent lack of pleurocystidia) seemed to point to section *Polyadelphia* Sing. ex Maas G. But the hyphae of the pileipellis and the cortical layer of the stipe give a completely different picture, which is sufficient reason to keep *M. sejuncta* separate in a section of its own.

Several features of *Mycena agloea* Sing. (1989: 69) described from Brazil suggest that collection MA-3000 could well represent this species (small, whitish pileus; 13 lamellae reaching the stipe; stipe springing from a basal patch; amyloid spores; apically diverticulate cheilocystidia; diverticulate hyphae of the pileipellis; smooth hyphae of the stipe cortex; occurrence on fallen leaves of a dicotyledonous tree). A few illustrations of *M. agloea*, lacking as usual, would have been a great help, but even without these, Singer's description offers some important points that indicate the difference between the two species (*M. agloea*: pileus whitish, later turning greyish white; basal patch 'manifeste costato'; basidia 4-spored; cheilocystidia with fairly numerous apical excrescences; presence of some pleurocystidia; apparent absence of caulocystidia).

5. MYCENA section CAROLINENSES Maas G.

Mycena stirps *Carolinensis* A.H. Smith, N. Am. Spec. *Mycena*: 40. 1947 (nomen nudum). – *Mycena* section *Carolinenses* Maas G. in Proc. K. Ned. Akad. Wet. (Ser. C) **89**: 95. 1986. – Holotype: *Mycena carolinensis* Smith and Hesler.

Basidiomata medium-sized. Pileus at first puberulous to somewhat villous, glabrescent, more or less viscid but without separable gelatinous pellicle, yellow. Context pliable, whitish. Odour and taste mild. Lamellae tender, arcuate, broadly adnate, yellowish white, with pallid edge. Stipe hollow, puberulous above, covered with scattered, minute tufts farther down, pale yellow to brownish, the base attached to the substratum by a whorl of radiating, stiff, whitish fibrils.

Basidia clavate, 4-spored, clamped. Spores pip-shaped, smooth, amyloid. Cheilocystidia clavate to somewhat fusiform, some few with the apex attenuated to form a neck and thus more or less lageniform, clamped, usually covered with coarse, variously shaped excrescences, more rarely smooth. Pleurocystidia lageniform, clamped, somewhat thick-walled, smooth. Lamellar trama vinescent in Melzer's reagent. Hyphae of the pileipellis clamped, smooth to densely diverticulate. Caulocystidia somewhat incrassate, diverticulate.

Growing on fallen twigs or leaves.

Mycena luteola* Maas G. and de Meijer, *spec. nov.* – Fig. 14

Basidiomata dispersa. Pileus 1.5–4.5 mm latus, usque ad 2 mm altus, campanulatus vel convexus, striatus, glaber ut videtur, siccus, hygrophanus, pallide flavus. Caro tenuis, odore nullo. Lamellae 12–13 stipitem attingentes, molles, adscendentes, usque ad 1 mm latae, ventricosae, late adnatae, dente longe decurrentes, luteo-albae, margine convexae, concolores. Stipes 13–22 × 0.2–0.5 mm, cavus, fragilis, aequalis, cylindraceus, levis, siccus, puberulus, deorsum subpubescens, pallide luteus, sursum pallide aurantiacus, basi fibrillis radiantibus albis substrato affixus.

Basidia 16–20 × 7 μm, clavata, 4-sporigera, fibulata, sterigmatibus 4.5 μm longis praedita. Sporae 7.2–8.1 × (2.8–)3.6–4.5 μm, inaequilateraliter ellipsoideae, leves, amyloideae. Cheilo-

Etymology: luteolus, pale yellow, referring to the colours of the pileus.

cystidia 27–36 × 10–15 μm, clavata, fusiformia, fibulata, apice in collum attenuata vel surculis munita 4.5–18 × 2–4.5 μ. Pleurocystidia exstant, vieta. Trama lamellarum iodi ope brunneovinescens. Hyphae pileipellis 2.5–4.5 μm latae, fibulatae, dense diverticulatae. Hyphae stipitis corticales 1.5 4.5 μm latae, fibulatae, caulocystidiis versiformibus pilisque solidis longis instructae.

Foliicola.

Holotypus: A.A.R. de Meijer PAf-3078 (No. 991.343–785; L); notulae MBM 188531.

Basidiomata scattered. Pileus 1.5–4.5 mm across, up to 2 mm high, campanulate to convex, translucent-striate, appearing glabrous, dry, hygrophanous, the striae fairly pale ochraceous yellow (4A5), the centre and between the striae straw-coloured (3A3–3A4), drying paler. Context very thin. Odour absent. Lamellae 12–13 reaching the stipe, tender, ascending, up to 1 mm broad, ventricose, broadly adnate, long decurrent with a tooth, not intervenose, very pale straw-coloured (2A3), with convex, concolorous edge. Stipe 13–22 × 0.2–0.5 mm, hollow, fragile, equal, terete, smooth, dry, puberulous, short-haired towards the base, pale straw-coloured (3A3), pale orange (5A5) above, the base springing from a patch of radiating, long, white fibrils.

Basidia 16–20 × 7 μm, clavate, 4-spored, clamped, with sterigmata 4.5 μm long. Spores 7.2–8.1 × (2.8–)3.6–4.5 μm (Q = 2.1), pip-shaped, smooth, amyloid. Cheilocystidia 27–36 × 10–15 μm, forming a sterile band (lamellar edge homogeneous), clavate, fusiform, clamped, apically narrowed into a slender neck up to 18 μm long or with 2–3 fairly coarse excrescences 4.5–10 × 2–4.5 μm. Pleurocystidia present, but shrivelled. Lamellar trama brownish vinescent in Melzer's reagent. Pileipellis a cutis of repent, radiately aligned hyphae which are 2.5–4.5 μm wide, clamped, densely covered with warts and simple to much branched, cylindrical excrescences, –9 × 1–3 μm. Hyphae of the cortical layer of the stipe 1.5–4.5 μm wide, clamped, thin-walled, covered with scattered, branched, variously shaped excrescences 2.5–13.5 × 2–

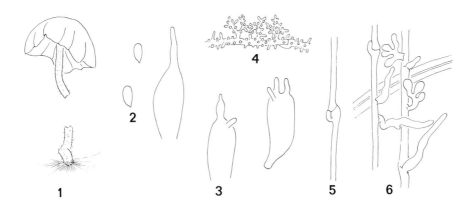

Fig. 14 (1–6) *Mycena luteola* (de Meijer PAf-3078). – 1. Habitus and basal part of the stipe. – 2. Spores. – 3. Cheilocystidia. – 4. Hypha of the pileipellis. – 5. Hypha of the cortical layer of the stipe. – 6. Caulocystidia and thick-walled hair.

Fig. 1, × 10; all others, × 700.

4.5 μm and shorter or longer hairs (both of which are solid), the latter farther down the stipe growing out into very thick-walled (2–3 μm) hairs up to c. 500 μm long and up to 6 μm wide.

Growing on decayed leaves of dicotyledonous trees in dense ombrophilous forest, 20 m alt.

Holotype: '*Mycena luteola* Maas G. and de Meijer / 22 June 1995 / Paraná: Paranaguá, 5 km W of Saquarema / A.A.R. de Meijer PAf-3078' (No. 991.343–785; L); notes and drawings: MBM 188531.

Mycena clivicola Speg. (1926: 118) is a small, corticolous, yellow species, whose meagre description reads somewhat like the one of *M. luteola*. It is certainly necessary to reexamine the type of Spegazzini's species, but for the present *M. clivicola* is taken to differ from *M. luteola* on account of the 'ochroleuco' stipe (partly pale orange in *luteola*); its villose-radicating base (springing from a patch of radiating fibrils in *luteola*); and the rather smaller volume of the cheilocystidia ('18–20 × 8 μm'; 27–36 × 10–15 μm in *luteola*).

A remarkable feature of *M. luteola* is that a number of the hyphae of the context of the stipe just inside the cortical layer are thick-walled with cell-walls of up to 2 μm. These hyphae, not much longer than 100–120 μm and with septa not much narrower (8–9 μm) than the width of the hyphae (12–14 μm), can in no way be compared with the inflated skeletal hyphae which are characteristic of Corner's sarcodimitic construction (1966: 175), but most probably have the same function.

6. MYCENA sect. **Aspratiles** Maas G. and de Meijer, *sect. nov.*

Basidiomata parva. Pileus griseus, marginem versus albus. Caro odore nullo. Lamellae molles, arcuatae, albae, margine concolores. Stipes fragilis, viscidus, superne albus, basi albopuberulus. Basidia clavata, fibulata. Sporae inaequilateraliter ellipsoideae, leves, amyloideae. Cheilocystidia radicantes, cylindracea, crassetunicata, surculis cylindraceis dense instructa. Pleurocystidia similia. Trama lamellarum iodi ope brunneovinescens. Hyphae pileipellis fibulatae, diverticulatae. Hyphae stipitis corticales fibulatae, in materiam gelatinosam immersae, maxima ex parte leves, cellulae terminales diverticulatae, caulocystidia crassetunicata, surculis dense praedita.

Foliicola.

Species typica: *Mycena aspratilis*.

This section might be placed near section *Polyadelphia* Sing. ex Maas G. (1980: 103), but is widely different on account of the thick-walled cheilo- and pleurocystidia.

Mycena aspratilis* Maas G. and de Meijer, *spec. nov.* – Fig. 15

Basidiomata solitaria. Pileus 1.5–5 mm latus, 1–2.8 mm altus, subhemisphaericus vel convexus, centro depressus, siccus, e levi sulcatus, striatus, albus, centro striisque tamen griseis. Caro tenuis, odore nullo. Lamellae 8–12 stipitem attingentes, molles, arcuatae, parum ventricosae, usque ad 1 mm latae, adnatae, longe decurrentes, albae, margine concolores. Stipes 10–35 ×

---

*Etymology: aspratilis, rough, referring to the rough surface of the hyphae of the pileipellis, the cheilocystidia, and the caulocystidia.

0.2–0.7 mm, cavus, fragilis, aequalis, cylindraceus, viscidus, levis, inferne subflavidogriseus, superne albus, basi albo-puberulus, subinsititius.

Basidia c. 27 × 7–9 μm, clavata, 4-sporigera, fibulata. Sporae 7.2–9.0 × 3.1–4.5 μm, inaequilateraliter ellipsoideae, leves, amyloideae. Cheilocystidia 30–36 × 4.5–10 μm, radicantia, cylindracea, crassetunicata, surculis cylindraceis 1.8–2.7 × 0.8–1.3 μm dense instructa. Pleurocystidia sparsa, similia. Trama lamellarum iodi ope brunneovinescens. Hyphae pileipellis 1.8–3.5 μm latae, fibulatae, subgelatinosae, surculis 1.5–5.5 × 1–1.5 μm praeditae. Hyphae stipitis corticales 1–2 μm latae, fibulatae, in materiam gelatinosam immersae, maxima ex parte leves, apicem versus diverticulatae, cellulae terminales diverticulatae, caulocystidia 24–35 × 7–12.5 μm, subglobosa, ellipsoidea vel cylindracea, crassetunicata, surculis cylindraceis 1.8–5.5 × 0.9–1.8 μm munita.

Ad folia putrida.

Holotypus: A.A.R. de Meijer MA-2886 (No. 990.200–077; L); isotypus: MBM 188490.

Basidiomata solitary. Pileus 1.5–5 mm across, 1–2.8 mm high, almost hemispherical to convex, with the centre depressed already from the beginning, appearing dry, at first smooth, then sulcate, translucent-striate, white but the centre and striae fairly pale grey with a touch of yellow (4C2). Context thin, concolorous with the pileus. Odour none, taste mild. Lamellae 8–12 reaching the stipe, tender, arcuate, little ventricose, up to 1 mm broad,

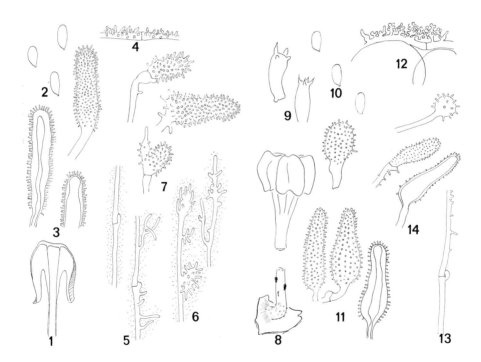

Fig. 15 (1–7) *Mycena aspratilis* (de Meijer MA-2886). – 1. Habitus. – 2. Spores. – 3. Cheilocystidia. – 4. Hypha of the pileipellis. – 5. Hyphae of the cortical layer of the stipe. – 6. Terminal cells and caulocystidia. – 7. Caulocystidia.
(8–14) *Mycena aspratilis* (de Meijer MA-3047). – 8. Habitus and basal part of the stipe. – 9. Basidia. – 10. Spores. – 11. Cheilocystidia. – 12. Hypha of the pileipellis. – 13. Hypha of the cortical layer of the stipe. – 14. Caulocystidia.
Fig. 1, × 8; fig. 8, × 10; all others, × 700.

adnate, far decurrent down the stipe, white, with concolorous edge. Stipe 10–35 × 0.2–0.7 mm, hollow, fragile, equal, terete, covered with a thick, hyaline, slimy layer, smooth, fairly pale grey with a more or less pronounced yellowish touch (4B3–4C3) below, white above, the base subinsititious or surrounded by a thin plaque of gelatinous matter, more or less densely white-puberulous (owing to the presence of thick-walled caulocystidia).

Basidia (none seen mature) c. 27 × 7–9 μm, clavate, with four incipient sterigmata, clamped. Spores (few observed) 7.2–9.0 × 3.1–4.5 μm (Q = 2.2), narrowly pip-shaped, almost cylindrical, smooth, amyloid. Cheilocystidia 30–36 × 4.5–10 μm, deep-seated, forming a sterile band (lamellar edge homogeneous), the protruding part cylindrical, thick-walled (1–2.5 μm), densely covered with cylindrical excrescences 1.8–2.7 × 0.8–1.3 μm. Pleurocystidia scarce, similar. Lamellar trama brownish vinescent in Melzer's reagent. Pileipellis a cutis of repent, radiately aligned hyphae which are 1.8–3.5 μm wide, clamped, apparently becoming more or less gelatinized (in warm, diluted KOH), covered with cylindrical to somewhat irregularly shaped excrescences 1.5–5.5 × 1–1.5 μm. Hypoderm made up of parallel hyphae with inflated cells up to 20 μm wide. Hyphae of the cortical layer of the stipe 1–2 μm wide, clamped, embedded in gelatinous matter (which readily dissolves in diluted KOH), slightly thick-walled, largely smooth but towards their apices more or less sparsely covered with cylindrical, straight to curved, simple to branched excrescences 2.5–13.5 × 1–1.5 μm, the terminal cells covered with similar excrescences; caulocystidia 24–35 × 7–12.5 μm, lateral and terminal, subglobose or ellipsoid to cylindrical, more or less thick-walled, densely covered with evenly spaced, cylindrical excrescences 1.8–5.5 × 0.9–1.8 μm.

On decayed, non-leathery dicotyledonous leaves in dense ombrophilous forest, 900 m alt.

Holotype: '*Mycena aspratilis* Maas G. and de Meijer / 15 May 1994 / Paraná: São José dos Pinhais, Parque Marumbi, along road BR-277, near Rio Pequeno / A.A.R. de Meijer MA-2886' (No. 990.200–077; L); isotype: MBM 188490.

Additional material: '8 May 1994 / Paraná: Colombo, EMBRAPA-Florestal native forest / A.A.R. de Meijer COA-2893 / On dead, non-leathery dicotyledonous leaves in mixed ombrophilous forest, 900 m alt.' (No. 990.200–057; L); notes and drawings: MBM 188491.

'16 March 1995 / Paraná: Quatro Barras, Parque Marumbi, Morro Sete / A.A.R. de Meijer MA-3047 / On dead leaves of consistently the same species of woody plant in dense ombrophilous forest, 1100 m alt.' (No. 990.200–027; L); duplicate: MBM 188492.

One of the striking features of the present species, reminding one of Singer's stirps *Metuloidifera* (1975: 393 and 1986: 410), lies in the deep-seated cheilocystidia. The following table shows that *Mycena aspratilis* is widely different from *M. metuloidifera* Sing. (1969: 116), the type species of the stirps.

	pileus centre depressed	stipe viscid	spore width 5–6.5 μm	cheilocystidia entirely spinulose	caulocystidia present
M. aspratilis	+	+	–	+	+
M. metuloidifera	–	–	+	–	–

The second species of stirps *Metuloidifera, Mycena cystidiosa* (Stevenson) Horak (1971: 417), first described from New Zealand, is much larger than *M. aspratilis,* with a distinctly papillate pileus, apparently non-viscid stipe, 7 μm wide spores, and largely smooth cheilocystidia.

The terminal cells of the hyphae of the stipe cortex, observed in the type material, were not found in collections COA-2893 and MA-3047, but further search was abandoned because of scarcity of the material.

7. MYCENA sect. **Dactylinae** Maas G. and de Meijer, *sect. nov.*

Basidiomata statura media. Pileus glaber, obscure brunneus. Caro tenuis. Lamellae molles, pallidae, margine obscure brunneo. Stipes fragilis, glaber, pileo pallidior.

Basidia clavata, fibulata. Sporae inaequilateraliter ellipsoideae, leves, amyloideae. Cheilocystidia subcylindracea, fibulata, sucum brunneum continentia, apice incrassata, surculis instructa. Pleurocystidia lageniformia, fibulata, levia. Trama lamellarum iodi ope vinescens. Hyphae pileipellis et hyphae stipitis corticales fibulatae, leves.

Lignicola.

Species typica: *Mycena dactylina.*

The one subdivision of *Mycena* which, like sect. *Dactylinae,* has lamellae with the edge much darker than the sides, amyloid spores, smooth pleurocystidia, and smooth hyphae of the pileipellis and the cortical layer of the stipe, is sect. *Calodontes* (Fr. ex Berk.) Quél. subsect. *Marginatae* J.E. Lange (Maas Geesteranus, 1992: 403). There are important differences, however. The cheilocystidia in subsect. *Marginatae* are smooth, the pleurocystidia have coloured contents, terminal cells of the hyphae of the stipe cortex are abundant and conspicuous, and the odour is invariably strong. There is no reason to suppose that sect. *Dactylinae* and subsect. *Marginatae* will be confused.

Section *Dactylinae* would seem to be best placed near section *Cinerellae* Sing. ex Maas G. (1980: 104). The former possesses cheilocystidia with brown contents and smooth hyphae of the pileipellis, the latter has cheilocystidia with colourless contents and diverticulate hyphae of the pileipellis.

Mycena dactylina* Maas G. and de Meijer, *spec. nov.* – Figs. 16 (1–4)

Basidiomata gregaria. Pileus 14–16 mm latus, convexus, siccus, levis, striatus, glaber, atrobrunneus. Caro tenuis, odore nullo. Lamellae c. 15 stipitem attingentes, molles, arcuatae, usque ad 2.5 mm latae, decurrentes, pallide flavidogriseae, margine concavo, obscure brunneo. Stipes 11–15 × 1.2 mm, cavus, fragilis, aequalis, cylindraceus, siccus, levis, glaber, griseobrunneus.

Basidia 20–22.5 × 7–8 μm, clavata, 2-sporigera?, fibulata. Sporae 7.2–7.6 × 4.9–5.4 μm,

---

*Etymology: dactylinus, divided like fingers, referring to the finger-like excrescences of the cheilocystidia.

inaequilateraliter ellipsoideae, leves, amyloideae. Cheilocystidia 16–24 × 3.5–7 μm, sub-cylindracea, fibulata, sucum brunneum continentia, apice incrassata, surculis simplicibus vel furcatis, 3.5–10 × 1.8–55 μm instructa. Pleurocystidia 27–40 × 5.5–7 μm, lageniformia, fibulata, levia. Trama lamellarum iodi ope vinescens. Hyphae pileipellis 1.8–4.5 μm latae, fibulatae, leves. Hyphae stipitis corticales 2.5 μm latae, fibulatae, leves, cellulae terminales non visae.

Ramulicola.

Holotypus: A.A.R. de Meijer MA-2670 (No. 988.233–010; L); isotypus: MBM 188503.

Basidiomata gregarious. Pileus 14–16 mm across, convex, dry, smooth, striate, glabrous, the centre and striae dark brown (6F4), between the striae fairly pale yellowish grey-brown (5C4). Context thin, drying whitish. Odour absent. Lamellae c. 15 reaching the stipe, tender, arcuate, up to 2.5 mm broad, decurrent, minutely and densely intervenose, pale yellowish grey (5B2), the edge concave, dark brown. Stipe 11–15 × 1.2 mm, hollow, fragile, equal, terete, dry, smooth, glabrous, grey-brown (6D4).

Basidia (none seen mature) 20–22.5 × 7–8 μm, clavate, a few observed with two incipient sterigmata, clamped. Spores (few seen and probably immature) 7.2–7.6 × 4.9–5.4 μm (Q = 1.6), pip-shaped, smooth, amyloid. Cheilocystidia 16–24 × 3.5–7 μm, forming a sterile band (lamellar edge homogeneous), subcylindrical clamped, with brown contents, apically somewhat broadened and generally subdivided into two or three heads which are more or less densely covered with simple to furcate, cylindrical to subfusiform excrescences 3.5–10 × 1.8–5.5 μm. Pleurocystidia 27–40 × 5.5–7 μm, predominantly lageniform, clamped, with colourless contents, smooth. Lamellar trama vinescent in Melzer's reagent. Pileipellis a cutis of repent, radiately aligned hyphae which are 1.8–4.5 μm wide, clamped, smooth. Hyphae of hypoderm up to 20 μm wide. Hyphae of the cortical layer of the stipe 2.5 μm wide, clamped, smooth, terminal cells not observed.

Found on decayed twigs of a dicotyledonous tree in dense ombrophilous forest.

Holotype: 'Mycena dactylina Maas G. and de Meijer / 27 April 1993 / Paraná: Marumbi Parque / A.A.R. de Meijer MA-2670' (No. 988.233–010; L); isotype: MBM.

Although the few basidia observed to have incipient sterigmata were two-spored, their size in comparison with the spores suggests that the full-grown basidia could well be four-spored.

Singer (1989: 70) described two new species – M. castaneomarginata and M. castaneostipitata – which have a very dark, glabrous pileus, rather distant and brown-edged lamellae, a glabrous stipe, and spores of about the same size in common with M. dactylina. Singer considered the two species related to each other, which seems unlikely when one reads their descriptions, but they appear to be equally different from M. dactylina on account of their conspicuously diverticulate hyphae of the pileipellis.

Another species with dark-edged lamellae is Mycena anchietana Raith. (1984: 12), a new name proposed for M. sanguinolenta sensu Rick. This species is easily distinguishable from *M. dactylina* by the rather more reddish pileus, the pale reddish sides of the lamellae, the bleeding stipe, and the smooth cheilocystidia.

In the field, *M. dactylina* may be mistaken for a member of section *Rubromarginatae* but it differs widely in its microscopic characters. No species of that section has cheilocystidia of the shape and ornamentation like those of *M. dactylina* and, unlike *M. dactylina*, almost all species have conspicuously diverticulate hyphae of the pileipellis, while all possess easily visible terminal cells to the hyphae of the stipe cortex.

8. MYCENA section POLYADELPHIA Sing. ex Maas G.

Mycena [subsect.?] *Insititiae* Kühn., Genre *Mycena*: 161, 248. 1938 (invalid: later homonym); not *Mycena* [sect.] *Insititiae* (Fr.) Quél., 1872: 109.

Mycena stirps *Polyadelpha* Sing. in Annls mycol. **41**: 138. 1943, in Lilloa **22**: 358. ('1949') 1951; Agar. mod. taxon., 3rd ed.: 390. 1975 (inadmissable term denoting rank). – *Mycena* sect. *Polyadelphia* Sing. ex Maas G. in Persoonia **11**: 103. 1980. – Lectotype (Maas Geesteranus, l.c.): *Mycena polyadelphia*.

For further synonymy, see Maas Geesteranus, 1986: 159.

Basidiomata small to minute. Pileus dry, pruinose to somewhat granular, glabrescent, generally not becoming lubricous when wet, white, pale yellowish brown, pale greyish brown or pink to somewhat purplish or violaceous. Context very thin. Odour and taste indistinctive or absent. Lamellae not numerous, tender, arcuate or ascending, generally decurrent with a tooth, with some shade of the pileus colour or white, the edge concave but with age sometimes becoming convex, white. Stipe fistulose to hollow, pruinose, glabrescent, white or with some shade of the pileus colour, in some species dark at first but soon pallescent, rarely black, insititious or attached to the substratum by a whorl of radiating mycelial hyphae or strands of hyphae, the base in many cases conspicuously puberulous.

Basidia 2-spored (infrequent) and clampless or 4-spored and (generally) clamped. Spores pip-shaped, almost cylindrical or subglobose, amyloid. Cheilocystidia usually clavate, clampless (basidia 2-spored) or clamped, more or less densely covered with evenly, more rarely unevenly, spaced, generally cylindrical and straight, usually simple excrescences. Pleurocystidia absent. Lamellar trama (as far as known) vinescent in Melzer's reagent. Hyphae of the pileipellis and of the cortical layer of the stipe (as far as investigated) more or less densely diverticulate. Inflated and diverticulate caulocystidia present at the base of the stipe in several species.

Growing on fallen, decaying leaves of deciduous trees, herbaceous stems, or fronds and rhizomes of ferns.

KEY TO THE SPECIES

1. Stipe insititious. Cheilocystidia with coarse excrescences. Hyphae of the cortical layer of the stipe clamped. Growing on leaves of a dicotyledonous tree: . . . . *M. elongata*
1. Stipe springing from a basal patch of radiating fibrils. Cheilocystidia with fine excrescences.

Hyphae of the cortical layer of the stipe clampless. Growing on leaves of *Araucaria angustifolia*: . . . .*M. tuberifera*

Mycena elongata* Maas G. and de Meijer, *spec. nov.* – Fig. 16 (5–10)

Basidiomata dispersa. Pileus 2–2.5 mm latus, 2 mm altus, campanulatus, centro depressus, striatus, glaber ut videtur, siccus, atrobrunneus. Caro tenuis, odore nullo. Lamellae c. 11 stipitem attingentes, molles, adscendentes, usque ad 1 mm latae, ventricosae, late adnatae, dente longe decurrentes, haud intervenosae, albae, margine convexae, concolores. Stipes 28–35 × c. 0.3 mm, cavus, fragilis, aequalis, cylindraceus, levis, siccus, minute puberulus, pallide flavus, apice albus, basi insititius, flavobrunneus, albo-pilosus.

Basidia immatura, c. 18 × 8 µm, clavata. Sporae 10.1–10.7 × 4.5–4.7 µm, subcylindraceae, leves, forte amyloideae. Cheilocystidia 17–21.5 × 7–13.5 µm, clavata, subpyriformia, fibulata, surculis crassis 3.5–14 × 1.5–4.5 µm munita. Pleurocystidia nulla. Trama lamellarum iodi ope brunneovinescens. Hyphae pileipellis 1.5–4.5 µm latae, fibulatae, verrucis dense praeditae, cellulae terminales globosae, diverticulatae. Hyphae stipitis corticales 2.5–3.5 µm latae, fibulatae, magna ex parte leves, caulocystidia 27–65 × 8–22 × 2.5–3.5 µm, lageniformia, fibulata, levia.

Foliicola.

Holotypus: A.A.R. de Meijer RSC-3133 (No. 991.343–771; L); notulae: MBM 188513.

Basidiomata scattered. Pileus 2–2.5 mm across, 2 mm high, campanulate, centrally depressed, translucent-striate, appearing glabrous, dry, very dark brown (5F4), much paler between the striae. Context very thin. Odour absent. Lamellae c. 11 reaching the stipe, tender, ascending, up to 1 mm broad, ventricose, broadly adnate, far decurrent with a tooth, not intervenose, white, with convex, white edge. Stipe 28–35 × c. 0.3 mm, hollow, fragile, equal, terete, smooth, dry, minutely puberulous all over, pale yellow (4A3) for the greater part, white above, the base c. 0.5 mm broad, insititious, yellowish brown, densely covered with short, white hairs.

Basidia (immature) c. 18 × 8 µm, clavate, sterigmata not seen. Spores 10.1–10.7 × 4.5–4.7 µm (Q = 2.5), narrowly pip-shaped, almost cylindrical, smooth, strongly amyloid. Cheilocystidia 17–21.5 × 7–13.5 µm, forming a sterile band (lamellar edge homogeneous), clavate, subpyriform, clamped, covered with not very numerous, unevenly spaced, fairly coarse, cylindrical to subclavate excrescences 1–2.5 × 1–1.5 µm, and apically with 1–3 very coarse, variously shaped, simple or furcate excrescences 3.5–14 × 1.5–4.5 µm. Pleurocystidia absent. Lamellar trama brownish vinescent in Melzer's reagent. Pileipellis a cutis of few repent, radiately aligned hyphae which are 1.5–4.5 µm wide and densely covered with warts, the terminal cells 18–26 × 13.5–15 µm, clavate to subglobose, clamped, short-stalked, evenly covered with warts or short cylindrical excrescences 1–2 × 1 µm. Hypoderm made up of parallel hyphae with inflated cells up to 30 µm wide. Hyphae of the cortical layer of the stipe 2.5–3.5 µm wide, clamped, largely smooth, caulocystidia lateral and terminal, 27–65 × 8–22 × 2.5–3.5 µm, lageniform, clamped, smooth.

Growing on a decayed leaf of a dicotyledonous tree in mixed ombrophilous forest, 900 m alt.

*Etymology: elongatus, elongated, referring to the proportionally very long stipe.

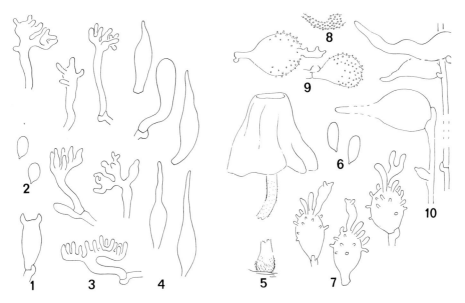

Fig. 16 (1–4) *Mycena dactylina* (de Meijer ᴍᴀ-2670). – 1. Basidium. – 2. Spores. – 3. Cheilocystidia. – 4. Pleurocystidia.

(5–10) *Mycena elongata* (de Meijer ʀꜱᴄ-3133). – 5. Habitus and basal part of the stipe. – 6. Spores. – 7. Cheilocystidia. – 8. Fragment of a hypha of the pileipellis. – 9. Terminal cells of hyphae of the pileipellis. – 10. Caulocystidia.

Fig. 5, × 10; all others, × 700.

Holotype: '*Mycena elongata* Maas G. and de Meijer / 10 July 1995 / Paraná: Rio Branco do Sul, near cemetery / A.A.R. de Meijer ʀꜱᴄ-3133' (No. 991.343–771; L); notes and drawings: ᴍʙᴍ 188513.

There is no doubt that the present species belongs to section *Polyadelphia*, but it is a somewhat unusual member, differing from the Northern Hemisphere members thus far known by the largely smooth hyphae of the stipe cortex and the smooth caulocystidia. Also, the very coarse processes sprouting from the apices of the cheilocystidia of *M. elongata* are unknown in e.g. *Mycena polyadelphia* (Lasch) Kühn. (the type species of the section) and *M. smithiana* Kühn. On the other hand, an ornamentation of the cheilocystidia such as seen in *M. juncicola* (Fr.) Gillet and *M. riparia* Maas G. may be taken as intermediate between the two extremes.

The terminal cells of the hyphae of the pileipellis remind one of the globose, densely warted cells in the pileipellis of species of section *Sacchariferae* which are called acanthocysts. It seems preferable, however, to restrict this term to the *Sacchariferae,* a section which differs from the *Polyadelphia* in the presence of a universal veil.

Singer (1989: 81) described a *Mycena micromelaena* from Brazil which macroscopically is not unlike *M. elongata*. It was said to have a dark, apically somewhat depressed pileus, not more than 3.5 mm across; adnate, somewhat decurrent lamellae; a long, slender, white stipe; and it was found on fallen leaves of a dicotyledonous tree. Its spores, moreover, appear to be of about the same size as those of *M. elongata* and amyloid. The two species can be separated as follows. In *M. micromelaena*, the stipe is glabrous (puberulous in *elongata*) and it springs from a radiating basal mycelium (the stipe is in-sititious in *elongata*); the cheilocystidia are said to be 'ex integro subtiliter diverticulatis' (apically very coarsely diverticulate in *elongata*); the pleuro-cystidia are identical with the cheilocystidia (absent in *elongata*).

Mycena tuberifera* Maas G. and de Meijer, *spec. nov.* – Fig. 17

Basidiomata dispersa. Pileus 0.5–1.5 mm latus, campanulatus vel convexus, sulcatus, striatus, minute pruinosus, siccus, atrobrunneus. Caro tenuis, odore nullo. Lamellae 7–10 stipitem attingentes, molles, adscendentes, c. 0.5 mm latae, ventricosae, adnatae vel pseudocollarium formantes, haud intervenosae, albae, margine convexae, concolores. Stipes 3–12 × 0.1 mm, cavus, fragilis, aequalis, cylindraceus, levis, siccus, pruinosus, deorsum subpuberulus, albus vel deorsum raro pallide griseobrunneus, e disco basali fibrilloso alboque natus.

Basidia 15–18 × 9–10 μm, ellipsoideae, 4-sporigera. Sporae 8.9–10.3 × 4.5–4.9 μm, in-aequilateraliter ellipsoideae, leves, amyloideae. Cheilocystidia 17–19 × 9–12.5 μm, ellipsoidea vel globosa, surculis 1.5–12 × 1 μm munita. Pleurocystidia nulla. Trama lamellarum iodi ope brunneovinescens. Hyphae pileipellis 3.5–6.5 μm latae, haud fibulatae, verrucis dense praeditae, cellulae terminales clavatae. Hyphae stipitis corticales 1.5–3.5 μm latae, haud fibulatae, magna ex parte leves, sursum caulocystidiis globosis, 13.5–27 × 10–13.5 μm instructae, deorsum pilis –270 × 5–7 μm.

Foliicola.

Holotypus: A.A.R. de Meijer 3061 (No. 991.343–792; L); notulae: MBM 190355.

Basidiomata scattered. Pileus 0.5–1.5 mm across, campanulate to convex, sulcate, translucent-striate, delicately pruinose, dry, very dark brown (7F3), paler, more grey-brown (7D2) towards the margin. Context very thin. Odour absent. Lamellae 7–10 reaching the stipe, tender, ascending, c. 0.5 mm broad, ventricose, adnate to the stipe or forming a pseudocollarium, not intervenose, white, with convex, concolorous edge. Stipe 3–12 × 0.1 mm, hollow, fragile, equal, terete, smooth, dry, more or less pruinose above, more pronouncedly so or even subpuberulous below, white throughout or more rarely brownish grey towards the base, springing from an almost floccose basal patch made up of radiating, white fibrils.

Basidia 15–18 × 9–10 μm, broadly ellipsoid, short-stalked, with 4 incipient sterigmata. Spores 8.9–10.3 × 4.5–4.9 μm (Q = 2.0), pip-shaped, smooth, amyloid. Cheilocystidia 17–19 × 9–12.5 μm, forming a sterile band (lamellar edge homogeneous), broadly ellipsoid to globose, short-stalked, covered with fairly evenly spaced, not very numerous, cylindrical excrescences 1.5–5 × 1 μm and, usually, towards the apex with much longer excrescences up to 12 μm. Pleurocystidia absent. Lamellar trama weakly brownish vinescent in Melzer's reagent. Pileipellis a cutis of repent, radiately aligned hyphae which are 3.5–6.5 μm wide, not clamped, densely covered with warts, the terminal cells (few seen) 11–18 × 10–11 μm, clavate, not clamped, densely covered

*Etymology: tuber, swelling; fero, I carry, referring to the swellings on the hyphae of the cortex of the stipe.

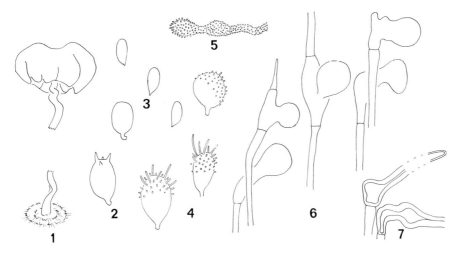

Fig. 17 (1–7) *Mycena tuberifera* (de Meijer cuf-3061). – 1. Habitus and basal part of the stipe. – 2. Basidia. – 3. Spores. – 4. Cheilocystidia. – 5. Hypha of the pileipellis. – 6. Caulocystidia. – 7. Thick-walled hairs near the base of the stipe.
Fig. 1, × 15; all others, × 700.

with warts and (apically) short cylindrical excrescences. Hypoderm made up of parallel hyphae with much inflated cells. Hyphae of the cortical layer of the stipe 1.5–3.5 μm wide, clampless, largely smooth, caulocystidia absent or sparse in the upper part of the stipe, lateral and terminal, 13.5–27 × 10–13.5 μm, globose to clavate, clampless, smooth, with conspicuous lateral swellings, more frequent and some irregularly shaped farther down the stipe, replaced near the base of the stipe by shorter or longer, very thick-walled (1.5–2.5 μm), smooth hairs – 270 × 5–7 μm.

Growing on fallen leaves of *Araucaria angustifolia* in mixed ombrophilous forest, 900 m alt.

Holotype: '*Mycena tuberifera* Maas G. and de Meijer / 23 April 1995 / Paraná: Curitiba, Parque Municipal do Iguaçu, Zoológico / A.A.R. de Meijer cuf-3061' (No. 991.343–793; L); notes and drawings: MBM 190355.

Like *Mycena elongata, M. tuberifera* deviates from all other members of section *Polyadelphia* in that the hyphae of the cortical layer of the stipe are largely smooth. Their caulocystidia, too, are smooth.

It is worth noticing that much of the description of *Mycena mirata* (Peck) Sacc. can be applied to that of the present species. The difference is that *M. mirata*, a member of section *Filipedes* (Fr.) Quél., is corticolous, while the way its stipe is attached to the substratum is different from that in *M. tuberifera*, but this shows the point where two separate sections meet each other.

9. MYCENA sect. **Infuscatae** Maas G. and de Meijer, *sect. nov.*

Basidiomata statura media vel magna. Pileus lubricus, obscurus. Caro odore fungoideo. Lamellae molles, adscendentes, adnatae, margine lateribus obscuriores. Stipes fragilis, lubricus, pruinosus, obscurus, basi fibrillis albis munitus.

Basidia clavata, fibulata. Sporae inaequilateraliter ellipsoideae, leves, amyloideae. Cheilocystidia clavata, longe stipitata, fibulata, in materiam gelatinosam immersa, sucum brunneum continentia, surculis crassis versiformibus praedita. Pleurocystidia nulla. Trama lamellarum iodi ope brunneovinescens. Hyphae pileipellis fibulatae, in materiam gelatinosam immersae, leves. Hyphae stipitis corticales fibulatae, in materiam gelatinosam immersae, leves, cellulae terminales (caulocystidia) crasse diverticulatae.

Lignicola.

Species typica: *Mycena infuscata.*

This section should be placed near section *Rubromarginatae* Sing. ex Maas G. (1980: 106), but deviates on account of its cheilocystidia with dark coloured contents and gelatinous covering.

Mycena infuscata* Maas G. and de Meijer, *spec. nov.* – Fig. 18

Basidiomata dispersa. Pileus 7–35 mm latus, usque ad 12 mm altus, campanulatus vel convexus, papilliger vel obtuse umbonatus, striatus, glaber, lubricus, hygrophanus, atrobrunneus. Caro albidus, odore fungoideo. Lamellae 20 – 24 stipitem attingentes, molles, adscendentes, usque ad 6 mm latae, ventricosae, adnatae, haud intervenosae, albae vel pallide griseobrunneae, margine convexae, atrobrunneae. Stipes 18 – 60 × 1.5–3 mm, cavus, fragilis, aequalis, cylindraceus, levis, pruinosus, siccus ut videtur, griseobrunneus vel obscurior, basi fibrillis albis munitus.

Basidia 25 –30 × 7– 8 μm, clavata, 4-sporigera, fibulata. Sporae 8.1– 9.8 × 5.4 – 6.3 μm, inaequilateraliter ellipsoideae, leves, amyloideae. Cheilocystidia 27–55 × 8 –15 μm, clavata, longe stipitata, fibulata, in materiam gelatinosam immersa, sucum brunneum continentia, surculis crassis versiformibusque praedita. Pleurocystidia nulla. Trama lamellarum iodi ope brunnescens. Hyphae pileipellis 1.8 –3.5 μm latae, fibulatae, leves, in materiam gelatinosam immersae. Hyphae stipitis corticales 1.5 –3.5 μm latae, fibulatae, leves, in materiam gelatinosam immersae, cellulae terminales 3.5 –11.5 μm latae, crasse diverticulatae.

Lignicola.

Holotypus: A.A.R. de Meijer MA-3147a (No. 991.343 –790; L); isotypus: MBM 188528.

Basidiomata scattered. Pileus 7–35 mm across, up to 12 mm high, campanulate to convex, centrally subacute or with central papilla or with obtuse umbo, smooth and translucent-striate when fresh, somewhat sulcate when drying, glabrous, lubricous, hygrophanous, the centre very dark brown (6F5–7F5), the striae dark grey-brown (6E4–7E4), between the striae pale grey slightly tinged orange (6B2), the whole remaining dark when dried. Context whitish. Odour strongly fungoid. Lamellae 20 – 24 reaching the stipe, tender, ascending, up to 6 mm broad, ventricose, adnate, not intervenose, white to pale grey-brown (6C2), with convex, very dark brown (7F4) edge. Stipe 18 – 60 × 1.5 –3 mm, hollow, fragile, equal, terete to compressed, broadened at the base, smooth, pruinose, appearing dry (but originally very probably lubricous), drying shiny, grey-brown to dark brown (6E3–6F3),

*Etymology: infuscatus, darkened, referring to the dark-coloured lamellar edge.

54

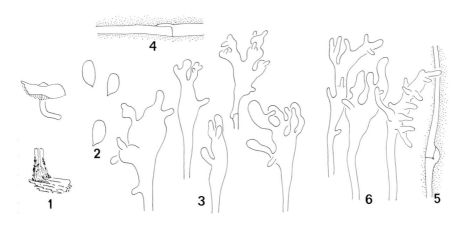

Fig. 18 (1–6) *Mycena infuscata* (de Meijer MA-3147a). – 1. Habitus and basal part of the stipe. – 2. Spores. – 3. Cheilocystidia. – 4. Hypha of the pileipellis. – 5. Hypha of the cortical layer of the stipe. – 6. Caulocystidia.

Fig. 1, × 1/2; all others, × 700.

upwards sometimes paler (6C3–6D3), the base densely covered with white fibrils.

Basidia 25–30 × 7–8 μm, clavate, 4-spored, clamped, with sterigmata c. 5 μm long. Spores 8.1–9.8 × 5.4–6.3 μm (Q = 1.9), pip-shaped, smooth, amyloid. Cheilocystidia 27–55 × 8–15 μm, forming a sterile band (lamellar edge homogeneous), clavate, very long-stalked, clamped, immersed in gelatinous matter, with brownish contents, apically furcate to lobed and covered with coarse, variously shaped excrescences 3.5–18 × 2–7 μm. Pleurocystidia absent. Lamellar trama rather more brownish than vinescent in Melzer's reagent. Pileipellis a cutis of repent, radiately aligned hyphae which are 1.8–3.5 μm wide, clamped, smooth, embedded in gelatinous matter. Hypoderm made up of parallel hyphae with inflated cells up to 30 μm wide. Hyphae of the cortical layer of the stipe 1.5–3.5 μm wide, clamped, smooth, embedded in gelatinous matter, terminal cells (caulocystidia) apically 3.5–11.5 μm wide, clavate, sometimes furcate, covered with coarse excrescences 3.5–13.5 × 1.5–4 μm.

On very decayed trunk of a dicotyledonous tree in mixed ombrophilous forest, 900 m alt.

Holotype: '*Mycena infuscata* Maas G. and de Meijer / 25 July 1995 / Paraná: Piraquara, Mananciais da Serra / A.A.R. de Meijer MA-3147a' (No. 991.343–790; L); isotype: MBM 188528.

A striking feature of the present species is the strongly clammy-viscid feel of the pileus in the fresh condition, but it was also noticed that the pilei dried up quite quickly. The lubricous condition appears to be caused by the presence of a gelatinous layer covering the hyphae of the pileipellis. A similar and very distinct gelatinous layer also covers the hyphae of the cortical layer of the stipe and, although in the field the stipe was found to be dry, it undoubtedly must originally have been lubricous.

It should be noticed that the gelatinous matter which envelopes the cheilocystidia is not of a tough consistence and sometimes even hardly perceptible under the microscope.

A species with viscid or lubricous pileus and stipe, and with long-stalked cheilocystidia could be thought to be a member of section *Euspeireae*, but *M. infuscata* merits a section of its own on account of its cheilocystidia being embedded in gelatinous matter, coarsely ornamented, and filled with brownish sap.

Mycena fuscocystidiata Sing. (1989: 72) is an altogether different species with smaller spores (4.5–7.5 × 3–4 µm), smooth cheilocystidia, and diverticulate hyphae of the pileipellis not embedded in gelatinous matter.

10. MYCENA section FRAGILIPEDES (Fr.) Quél.

Agaricus (sect.) *Fragilipedes* Fr., Epicr. Syst. mycol.: 108. 1838; Cooke Handb. Br. Fungi **1**: 68. 1871 (formally accepted as section). – *Mycena* (sect.) Fragilipedes (Fr.) Quél. in Mém. Soc. Emul. Montbél. II **5**: 105. 1872. – *Mycena* (ser?) *Fragilipedes* (Fr.) Kühn., Genre Mycena: 457. 1938. – *Mycena* groupe *Fragilipedes* (Fr.) Konr. and Maubl., Agar.: 319. 1948 (inadmissable term denoting rank). – Lectotype: *Agaricus alcalinus* Fr. sensu Kühner (1938: 464).

For further synonymy, see Maas Geesteranus, l.c.

Basidiomata fairly small to large. Pileus generally pruinose at first, glabrescent, in some species lubricous when wet, more or less hygrophanous, variously coloured, white, cream, citrine, ochraceous, grey, grey-brown or black, more rarely olivaceous or suffused with a purplish or violaceous tint. Flesh thin. Odour in some cases nitrous or raphanoid, but also indistinctive or absent. Taste raphanoid, mild or absent. Lamellae tender, more rarely somewhat elastic, ascending, ventricose, almost free to adnate, decurrent with a tooth or not, mostly white to greyish or grey-brown, the edge convex, white, in some species olive green to brownish or yellow (but these colours unstable). Stipe hollow, fragile to firm or cartilaginous, pruinose at least above, generally glabrescent farther below, dry or lubricous when wet, variously coloured, white, yellow in various shades, grey, grey-brown to black-brown, in some species with bluish tints when young, the base covered with coarse fibrils, sometimes rooting.

Basidia 2- or 4-spored, without or with clamps. Spores pip-shaped to almost cylindrical, smooth, amyloid. Cheilocystidia usually forming a sterile band, very variably shaped, without or with a clamp, smooth or covered with few but coarse excrescences. Pleurocystidia similar or absent. Lamellar trama generally brownish vinescent in Melzer's reagent. Hyphae of the pileipellis and of the cortical layer of the stipe smooth or diverticulate.

Growing among grass, on humus under trees, on woody debris of deciduous and coniferous trees, or in *Sphagnum* bogs.

Mycena armifera* Maas G. and de Meijer, *spec. nov.* – Fig. 19 (1–5)

Basidiomata solitaria vel dispersa. Pileus 8–22 mm latus, hemisphaericus vel subapplanatus, centro interdum depressus, siccus, levis, striatus, glaber, flavus. Caro tenuis, pileo concolor, odore tenui. Lamellae 11–14 stipitem attingentes, valde intervenosae, molles, adscendentes, 1–2 mm latae, late adnatae, flavae, margine concolores. Stipes 35–50 × 1–3 mm, cavus, fragilis, aequalis, cylindraceus, siccus, levis, glaber, luteus, basi fibrillis albidis munitus.

Basidia 20–22.5 × 5.5–6.5 μm, subclavata, 4-sporigera, fibulata. Sporae 5.5–7 × (2.5–)3–4 μm, inaequilateraliter ellipsoideae, leves, amyloideae. Cheilocystidia 27–52 × 5.5–12.5 × 2.7–5.5 μm, fusiformia vel subcylindracea, fibulata, levia, apice acuta vel obtusa. Pleurocystidia nulla. Trama lamellarum iodi ope brunneovinescens. Hyphae pileipellis 2.5–9 μm latae, fibulatae, leves vel sparse diverticulatae, cellulae terminales plus minusve ramosae. Hyphae stipitis corticales 1.8 μm latae, fibulatae, leves, cellulae terminales nullae.

Humicola.

Holotypus: A.A.R. de Meijer MA-2050 (No. 988.233–082; L); isotypus: MBM 188488.

Basidiomata solitary or scattered. Pileus 8–22 mm across, hemispherical, centrally at times depressed, flattening with age, dry, smooth, striate up to the centre, appearing glabrous, the centre and striae deep yellow (4A8), citrine between the striae (2A8), with dark reddish brown spots in one specimen. Context thin, concolorous with the pileus. Odour more or less spermatic. Hymenophore lamellate-alveolar, made up of radiating lamellae interconnected by 4–8 transverse septa. Lamellae 11–14 reaching the stipe, tender, ascending, 1–2 mm broad, broadly adnate, occasionally decurrent with a short tooth, yellow (4A8), with concolorous edge. Stipe 35–50 × 1–3 mm, hollow, fragile, equal, terete, dry, smooth, glabrous, shiny, citrine (2A8), apically more deeply yellow (4A8), the base covered with fairly few whitish fibrils.

Basidia (none seen mature) 20–22.5 × 5.5–6.5 μm, clavate, with four incipient sterigmata, clamped. Spores (very few observed) 5.5–7 × (2.5–)3–4 μm (Q = 1.8), pip-shaped, smooth, amyloid. Cheilocystidia 27–50 × 5.5–12.5 × 2.7–5.5 μm, forming a very dense sterile band (lamellar edge homogeneous), fusiform to subcylindrical, with yellow intracellular contents,

---

*Etymology: armiferus, armour-bearing, in reference to the lamellar edge which is very densely covered with cheilocystidia.

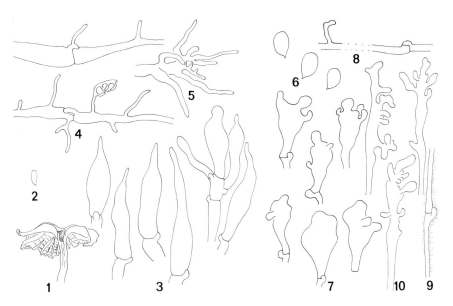

Fig. 19 (1–5) *Mycena armifera* (de Meijer MA-2050). – 1. Habitus. – 2. Spore. – 3. Cheilocystidia. –
4.Hyphae of the pileipellis. – 5. Terminal cell of a hypha of the pileipellis.
(6–10) *Mycena deusta* (de Meijer MA-2667). – 6. Spores. – 7. Cheilocystidia. – 8. Hypha of the pileipellis. – 9. Hypha of the cortical layer of the stipe. – 10. Terminal cells.
Fig. 1, × 2; all others, × 700.

clamped, smooth, apically narrowed to a sharp point or obtuse. Pleurocystidia absent (or perhaps very scarce). Lamellar trama brownish vinescent
in Melzer's reagent. Pileipellis a cutis of repent, radiately aligned hyphae
which are 2.5–9 μm wide, clamped, smooth or very sparsely covered with
usually simple, cylindrical excrescences 5–36 × 1.8–2.5 μm and infrequently
terminated by more or less strongly branched terminal cells. Hypoderm
consisting of parallel hyphae with generally much inflated cells up to 45 μm
wide. Hyphae of the cortical layer of the stipe 1.8 μm wide, clamped, smooth,
terminal cells not observed.

On humus in dense ombrophilous forest, 350 m alt.

Holotype: '*Mycena armifera* Maas G. and de Meijer / 15 Nov. 1991 /
Paraná: Morretes, Parque Marumbi, road near rio dos Padres / A.A.R. de
Meijer MA–2050' (No. 988.233–082; L); isotype: MBM 188488.

Further material examined: '*Mycena armifera* Maas G. and de Meijer / 15
April 1993 / Paraná: same as above / A.A.R. de Meijer MA-2612' (No.
988.233–089; L); duplicate: MBM 188489.

There are not many yellow species in section *Fragilipedes* (Maas Geesteranus,
1992: 352) and no other member of this section has thus far been known to
possess a lamellate-alveolar hymenophore. The combination, therefore, of a
deviating kind of hymenophore and a bright yellow colour which is not
merely restricted to the pileus makes *Mycena armifera* perfectly unique
among the *Fragilipedes*.

The alveolar hymenophore does remind one of the condition in species of the genus *Filoboletus,* but one of the differences is that in no part of the context of *M. armifera* there is any trace of gelatinous matter.

Another feature that requires comment is that the cheilocystidia, at least in the holotype, are strikingly broad-based, whereas in practically all other species of the *Fragilipedes* they are narrow-based. The placement of *M. armifera* in section *Fragilipedes* should therefore be seen as a provisional disposition.

Mycena deusta* Maas G. and de Meijer, *spec. nov.* – Fig. 19 (6–10)

Basidiomata gregaria. Pileus 10–40 mm latus, 7–11 mm altus, campanulatus, siccus, levis, striatus, glaber, centro striisque atrobrunneis. Caro tenuis, odore nullo. Lamellae 19–21 stipitem attingentes, lentae, adscendentes, usque ad 5 mm latae, adnatae, griseobrunneae, margine convexo, pallidiore. Stipes 35–100 × 1–3.5 mm, cavus, fragilis, aequalis, cylindraceus, siccus, levis, apice minute puberulus, deorsum glaber, griseobrunneus, basi fibrillis tenuibus albisque munitus, radicans.

   Basidia 27–29 × 8–9 μm, clavata, 4-sporigera, fibulata, sterigmatibus 6.5 μm longis instructa. Sporae 7.2–9.8 × 5.8–6.5 μm, inaequilateraliter ellipsoideae, leves, amyloideae. Cheilocystidia 22.5–27 × 8–14.5 μm, clavata, fibulata, levia vel surculis crassis 2.5–9 × 1.8–5.5 μm praedita. Pleurocystidia nulla. Trama lamellarum iodi ope subvinescens. Hyphae pileipellis 2.5–4.5 μm latae, fibulatae, leves. Hyphae stipitis corticales 1.8–2.5 μm latae, fibulatae, leves, cellulae terminales 45–80 × 6.5–10 μm, crasse diverticulatae.

   Ad terram termitarum.

   Holotypus: A.A.R. de Meijer MA-2667 (No. 988.233–033; L); isotypus: MBM 188508.

Basidiomata gregarious. Pileus 10–40 mm across, 7–11 mm high, campanulate, smooth, dry (but probably somewhat lubricous when wet), striate, glabrous, the centre and striae very dark brown, almost black-brown (6F3–6F4), between the striae dark grey-brown (6E4). Context thin, white when dry. Odour absent. Lamellae 19–21 reaching the stipe, fairly tough, ascending, up to 5 mm broad, adnate, grey-brown (5D3), with convex, paler edge. Stipe 35–100 × 1–3.5 mm, hollow, fragile, equal, terete, dry (but probably somewhat lubricous when wet), smooth, apically minutely puberulous, glabrous farther below, fairly dark grey-brown throughout (5E4–6E3), the base covered with thin, white fibrils, rooting.

   Basidia 27–29 × 8–9 μm, clavate, 4-spored, clamped, with plump sterigmata 6.5 μm long. Spores 7.2–9.8 × 5.4–6.5 μm (Q = 1.5), pip-shaped, smooth, amyloid. Cheilocystidia 22.5–27 × 8–14.5 μm, forming a sterile band (lamellar edge homogeneous), clavate to pyriform, clamped, thin-walled, easily collapsed, with even to wavy outline near the middle of the lamella, with fairly few but coarse excrescences 2.5–9 × 1.8–5.5 μm near the pileus margin. Pleurocystidia absent. Lamellar trama somewhat vinescent in Melzer's reagent. Pileipellis a cutis of repent, radiately aligned hyphae which are 2.5–4.5 μm wide, clamped, smooth, slightly gelatinizing. Hyphae of the hypoderm up to 30 μm wide. Hyphae of the cortical layer of the stipe 1.8–

*Etymology: deustus, scorched, referring to the dark colour of the pileus.

59

2.5 μm wide, clamped, smooth, gelatinizing, the terminal cells 45–80 × 6.5–10 μm, covered with coarse, simple to branched, clavate to variously shaped excrescences 2–13.5 × 2–5.5 μm.

At the base of a termite hill in dense ombrophilous forest, 900 m alt.

Holotype: '*Mycena deusta* Maas G. and de Meijer / 27 April 1993 / Paraná: Quatro Barras, Parque Marumbi, Estrada da Graciosa, near Taquari River / A.A.R. de Meijer MA-2667' (No. 988.233–033); L); isotype: MBM 188508.

Additional material: '5 April 1995 / Paraná: Colombo, EMBRAPA Florestal / A.A.R. de Meijer COa-3053 / on decayed trunk of a dicotyledonous tree in mixed ombrophilous forest, 900 m alt.' (No. 990.200–194; L); duplicate: MBM 188509.

Dennis (1961: 106) gave a description of a Venezuelan *Mycena* which he believed to be near *M. rubrotincta* A.H. Smith, and several of whose features (smooth, dry, brown pileus; ascending, 2–3 mm broad, adnate lamellae; spores of the same size; thin-walled, irregularly lobed cheilocystidia) remind one of those of *M. deusta*. But there are differences and these are equally numerous. The habit of the Venezuelan fungus is cespitose; the stipe is said to be paler above than below and there is no mention of a root; the cheilocystidia are rather longer; pleurocystidia are present; the hyphae of the pileipellis are very much broader. These differences suffice to separate the two species.

Another species that requires attention is *Mycena tentorium* Raith. (1988: 79), a new name for *M. uracea* of the same author. Raithelhuber first (1985: 39) described *M. uracea* without Latin diagnosis which was later (1986: 22) corrected. Its salient characters are: a black-brown pileus which is viscous when young; at times a rooting stipe; somewhat similarly ornamented cheilocystidia; lacking pleurocystidia. Although the 1985 and 1986 descriptions do not provide much information, it would seem that *M. tentorium* with its lamellae 'etwas gelatinös' and 'angewachsen bis leicht mit Zahn herablaufend' is a different species from *M. deusta*.

The second collection of *M. deusta* – de Meijer COa-3053 – consists of basidiomata apparently long past their prime (cheilocystidia all collapsed), whose lamellae had turned almost white and many of which show a very narrow blackish edge. This dark colour is caused by the dark cell walls of the cheilocystidia.

Mycena modica* Maas G. and de Meijer, *spec. nov.* – Fig. 20 (1–6)

Basidiomata bina. Pileus 32–42 mm latus, applanatus, subacute papilliger, siccus, levis, striatus, glaber, fuligineus, centro atrobrunneus. Caro tenuis, alba, odore indistincto. Lamellae c. 22 stipitem attingentes, intervenosae, molles, adscendentes, ventricosae, usque ad 7 mm latae, an-

*Etymology: modicus, modest, unadorned, in reference to the smooth hyphae of the pileipellis and the simple nature of the cheilocystidia.

guste adnexae, albidae, margine convexae, albae. Stipes 40–55 × 2.5–3 mm, cavus, fragilis, aequalis, cylindraceus, siccus, levis, apice sparse puberulus, deorsum glaber, albidus, infra pallide griseobrunneus, basi usque ad 5 mm latus.

Basidia c. 22.5 × 7–8 μm, clavata, 4-sporigera, fibulata, sterigmatibus 4.5 μm longis instructa. Sporae 7.2–9.8 × 4.0–4.7 μm, inaequilateraliter ellipsoideae, leves, amyloideae. Cheilocystidia 23–60 × 12–15 × 2.5–7 μm, utriformia, subcylindracea vel subconica, fibulata, levia, apice obtusa vel rostrata. Pleurocystidia similia vel lageniformia. Trama lamellarum iodi ope brunneo-vinescens. Hyphae pileipellis 1.8–2.7 μm latae, fibulatae, leves. Hyphae stipitis corticales 1.8–3.5 μm latae, fibulatae, leves, caulocystidia c. 70 × 9–20 μm, versiformia, fibulata, levia.

Lignicola.

Holotypus: A.A.R. de Meijer cua-254c (No. 967. 254–002; L); isotypus: мвм 188534.

Basidiomata in twos. Pileus 32–42 mm across, flattened with a fairly acute papilla, dry, smooth, translucent-striate, glabrous, rather dark brown, the papilla black-brown. Context thin, white. Odour indistinct. Lamellae c. 22 reaching the stipe, dorsally intervenose, tender, ascending, ventricose, up to 7 mm broad, narrowly adnexed, whitish with a pale greyish brown tinge, the edge convex, white. Stipe 40–55 × 2.5–3 mm, hollow, fragile, equal, terete, dry, smooth, apically sparsely puberulous, glabrous farther below, whitish, pale greyish brown below, the base (broken off?) 5 mm broad.

Basidia (possibly not mature) c. 22.5 × 7–8 μm, clavate, 4-spored, clamped, with sterigmata 4.5 μm long. Spores 7.2–9.8 × 4.0–4.7 μm (Q = 1.9), pip-shaped, smooth, amyloid. Cheilocystidia 23–60 × 12–15 × 2.5–7 μm, occurring mixed with basidia (lamellar edge heterogeneous), utriform,

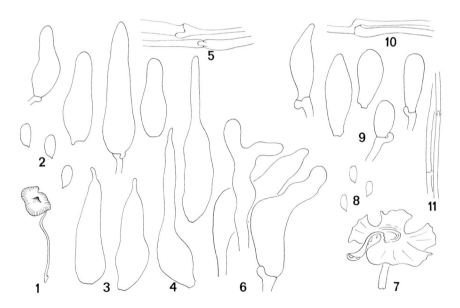

Fig. 20 (1–6) *Mycena modica* (de Meijer cua-254c). 1. – Habitus. – 2. Spores. – 3. Cheilocystidia. – 4. Pleurocystidia. – 5. Hyphae of the pileipellis. – 6. Caulocystidia.
(7–11) *Mycena propria* (de Meijer ma-3102). – 7. Habitus. – 8. Spores. – 9. Cheilocystidia. – 10. Hypha of the pileipelis. – 11. Hyphae of the cortical layer of the stipe.
Fig. 1, × 1/2; fig. 7, × 2; all others, × 700.

subcylindrical or subconical, clamped, smooth, apically obtuse or, less frequently, rostrate. Pleurocystidia similar or more lageniform. Lamellar trama brownish vinescent in Melzer's reagent. Hyphae of the pileipellis 1.8–2.7 µm wide, clamped, smooth. Hyphae of the cortical layer of the stipe 1.8–3.5 µm wide, clamped, smooth, the caulocystidia c. 70 × 9–20 µm, variously shaped, clamped, smooth, very thin-walled.

On dead, horizontal trunk of a dicotyledonous tree in seasonal semi-deciduous alluvial forest, 870 m alt.

Holotype: '*Mycena modica* Maas G. and de Meijer / 11 December 1979 / Paraná: Curitiba, Uberaba Distr., Reserva Biológica Cambuí / A.A.R. de Meijer cua-254c' (No. 988.233–070; L); isotype: мвм 188534.

Mycena propria* Maas G. and de Meijer, *spec. nov.* – Fig. 20 (7–11)

Basidiomata dispersa. Pileus 5–32 mm latus, e convexo planus, siccus, striatus, glaber, aurantiacus. Caro usque ad 0.5 mm lata, pileo concolor, odore fungoideo. Lamellae 14–17 stipitem attingentes, molles, subadscendentes, usque ad 3 mm latae, late adnatae, parum decurrentes, admodum intervenosae, pallide flavae, margine concolore. Stipes 12–70 × 1–2.5 mm, cavus, fragilis, aequalis, cylindraceus, siccus, levis, glaber, pallide flavus, deorsum obscurior, basi 3 mm latus, tomento albo praeditus.

   Basidia c. 22.5 × 6.5 µm, clavata, 4-sporigera, fibulata, sterigmatibus 4.5 µm longis instructa. Sporae 5.4–6.3 × 2.8–3.6 µm, inaequilateraliter ellipsoideae, leves, amyloideae. Cheilocystidia 16–30 × 7–11 µm, clavata, fusiformia, fibulata, levia, tenuitunicata. Pleurocystidia non visa. Trama lamellarum iodi ope vinescens. Hyphae pileipellis 2.7–4.5 µm latae, fibulatae, leves. Hyphae stipitis corticales 1.8–2.5 µm latae, fibulatae, leves, caulocystidia nulla.

   Humicola.

   Holotypus: A.A.R. de Meijer ma-3102 (No. 990.200–160; L); isotypus: мвм 190338.

Basidiomata scattered. Pileus 5–32 mm across, at first convex, flattening with age, dry, smooth to rather uneven, translucent-striate, glabrous, the centre and striae orange (5A7) when young, soon turning somewhat more brownish orange (5B6 or 5C7) to grey-brown (5C4), between the striae pale yellow (3A4–3A5). Context up to 0.5 mm thick, concolorous with the pileus surface. Odour fungoid or raphanoid, taste mild. Lamellae 14–17 reaching the stipe, tender, more or less ascending, up to 3 mm broad, broadly adnate, somewhat decurrent, conspicuously intervenose, pale yellow (3A4–3A5), with straight, concolorous edge. Stipe 12–70 × 1–2.5 mm, hollow, fragile, equal, terete, dry, smooth, glabrous, pale yellow (3A5), more or less brownish orange (5AB6) farther down, the base 3 mm broad, covered with white tomentum.

   Basidia (none seen mature) c. 22.5 × 6.5 µm, clavate, 4-spored, clamped, with sterigmata 4.5 µm long. Spores 5.4–6.3 × 2.8–3.6 µm (Q = 2.1), pip-shaped, smooth, weakly amyloid. Cheilocystidia 16–30 × 7–11 µm, forming a sterile band (lamellar edge homogeneous), clavate, fusiform, clamped, smooth, thin-walled. Pleurocystidia not observed. Lamellar trama strongly vinescent in Melzer's reagent. Pileipellis a cutis of repent hyphae which are

*Etymology: proprius, particular, private, referring to the fact that orange, a rare colour in section *Fragilipedes*, is particular to the present species.

2.7–4.5 μm wide, clamped, smooth. Hypoderm made up of parallel hyphae with inflated cells up to 20 μm wide. Hyphae of the cortical layer of the stipe 1.8–2.5 μm wide, clamped, smooth, terminal cells or caulocystidia not observed.

On decayed leaf litter in dense ombrophilous forest, 20 m alt.

Holotype: 'Mycena propria Maas G. and de Meijer / 29 June 1995 / Paraná: Morretes, Porto de Cima, Parque Marumbi, near Nhundiaquara River / A.A.R. de Meijer MA-3102' (No. 990.200–160; L); isotype: MBM 190338.

Additional material: '5 July 1995 / Paraná: Guaraqueçaba, Potinga / A.A.R. de Meijer GUa-3110, on leaf litter in dense ombrophilous forest, 5 m above sea level' (No. 990.200–118; L); duplicate: MBM 190339.

One may think of *Mycena junquillina* Dennis (1961: 104), another yellow and orange South American species, but Dennis warned that in his species 'no cheilocystida were seen.'

Mycena sabulicola* Maas G. and de Meijer, *spec. nov.* – Fig. 21

Basidiomata dispersa. Pileus 12–14 mm latus, campanulatus, siccus, levis, striatus, glaber, atrobrunneus. Caro tenuis, pileo concolor, odore spermatico. Lamellae c. 20 stipitem attingentes, molles, adscendentes, usque ad 2 mm latae, ventricosae, adnatae, haud intervenosae, pallide griseobrunneae, margine pallidiores vel albidae. Stipes 20–40 × 2 mm, cavus, fragilis, aequalis, cylindraceus, siccus, levis, glaber, pallide griseobrunneus, deorsum obscurior, granulis sabulonis obtectus.

Basidia 30–36 × 7–9 μm, clavata, 4-sporigera, fibulata, sterigmata 7–8 μm longa. Sporae 8.1–9.8 × 5.4–5.8 μm, inaequilateraliter ellipsoideae, leves, amyloideae. Cheilocystidia 35–72 × 7–12.5 μm, clavata vel subcylindracea, fibulata, levia vel apice surculis 1–3 simplicibus vel furcatis munita. Pleurocystidia nulla. Trama lamellarum iodi ope rubrobrunnea. Hyphae pileipellis 2.5–3.5 μm latae, fibulatae, leves. Hyphae stipitis corticales 2.5–3.5 μm latae, fibulatae, leves, paulo gelatinosae, cellulae terminales haud observatae.

In terram sabulosam.

Holotypus: A.A.R. de Meijer CUa-3081 (No. 991.343–756; L); notulae: MBM 190346.

Basidiomata scattered. Pileus 12–14 mm across, campanulate, dry, smooth, translucent-striate, glabrous, the centre and striae black-brown (5F4), between the striae fairly pale grey-brown (5D4), the whole drying paler. Context thin, concolorous with the pileus. Odour spermatic, taste not recorded. Lamellae c. 20 reaching the stipe, tender, ascending, up to 2 mm broad, ventricose, adnate, not intervenose, pale grey-brown (5C3), with convex, paler to whitish edge. Stipe 20–40 × 2 mm, hollow, fragile, equal, terete, dry, smooth, glabrous, very pale grey-brown (5B2) above, much darker grey-brown (5D3) farther below, the base covered with grains of sand.

Basidia 30–36 × 7–9 μm, clavate, 4-spored, clamped, with sterigmata 7–8 μm long. Spores 8.1–9.8 × 5.4–5.8 μm (Q = 1.7), pip-shaped, smooth, amyloid. Cheilocystidia 35–72 × 7–12.5 μm, forming a sterile band (lamellar

---

*Etymology: sabulicola, growing on sand.

63

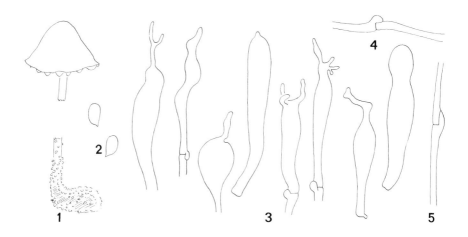

Fig. 21 (1–5) *Mycena sabulicola* (de Meijer CUa-3081). – 1. Habitus and basal part of the stipe. – 2. Spores. – 3. Cheilocystidia. – 4. Hypha of the pileipellis. – 5. Hypha of the cortical layer of the stipe. Fig. 1, × 2.5; all others, × 700.

edge homogeneous), slender-clavate, subcylindrical, clamped, smooth or apically rostrate or with one to three, simple or furcate, coarse excrescences 9–13.5 × 2–4.5 μm. Pleurocystidia absent. Lamellar trama colouring reddish brown in Melzer's reagent. Pileipellis a cutis of repent, radiately aligned hyphae which are 2.5–3.5 μm wide, clamped, smooth. Hypoderm consisting of parallel hyphae with inflated cells up to 35 μm wide. Hyphae of the cortical layer of the stipe 2.5–3.5 μm wide, clamped, smooth, in places tending to gelatinize, terminal cells not observed.

Growing on sandy soil at the edge of a seasonal semi-deciduous alluvial forest, 870 m alt.

Holotype: '*Mycena sabulicola* Maas G. and de Meijer / 26 June 1995 / Paraná: Curitiba, Uberaba Distr., Reserva Biológica Cambuí / A.A.R. de Meijer CUa-3081' (No. 991.343–756; L); notes and drawings: MBM 190346.

The specific epithet has been chosen for obvious reasons but, although the stipes of both specimens of the type collection are severed from their bases, it is clear that the basidiomata must have developed from vegetable debris beneath the sand.

There are two species described from the South American area – *Mycena saxegothaeae* Sing. (1969: 123) and *M. paraboliciformis* Sing. (1969: 134) – with which *M. sabulicola* could be confused. All three are medium-sized, possess a dark pileus, a stipe which is more or less concolorous with the pileus, amyloid spores of approximately the same size, and cheilocystidia with one to several apical outgrowths. The two species described by Singer differ from *M. sabulicola* in that their context is stated to be inodorous (spermatic in *sabulicola*), while the hyphae of the pileipellis are described as diverticulate.

In a former paper, the first author (Maas Geesteranus and Hausknecht, 1995: 53) commented on a small group of species within section *Fragilipedes* which are characterized 'by a greyish to brownish pileus, non-nitrous smelling context, smooth cheilocystidia, and smooth hyphae of both the pileipellis and the stipe cortex, neither of which are embedded in gelatinous matter.' With the exception of its cheilocystidia (many of which are more or less ornamented), *Mycena sabulicola* belongs to this same group which apparently has a steadily growing number of members.

11. Mycena sect. **Obductae** Maas G. and de Meijer, *sect. nov.*

Basidiomata statura media. Pileus siccus, obscure brunneus. Caro odore fungoideo. Lamellae molles, ventricosae, albae, margine concolores. Stipes fragilis, siccus, pileo concolor, superne pallidior, basi fibrillis radiantibus substrato affixus.

Basidia clavata, fibulata. Sporae inaequilateraliter ellipsoideae, leves, amyloideae. Cheilocystidia subfusiformia, fibulata, levia. Pleurocystidia similia, nonnulla guttulis repleta. Trama lamellarum iodi ope vinescens. Hyphae pileipellis fibulatae, ramosae, diverticulatae. Hyphae stipitis corticales fibulatae, leves, cellulae terminales (caulocystidia) leves vel diverticulatae, apicibus ramosis.

Foliicola.

Species typica: *Mycena obducta*.

There is no other section of *Mycena* combining such characters as dry pileus, dry stipe arising from a whorl of radiating fibrils, smooth cheilocystidia with acute to rostrate apices, and a pileipellis made up of profusely branched and diverticulate hyphae. It seems best placed near section *Fragilipedes*.

Mycena obducta* Maas G. and de Meijer, *spec. nov.* – Figs. 22 and 23

Basidiomata solitaria vel dispersa. Pileus 5–12 mm latus, 2–5.5 mm altus, e conico convexus, siccus, levis, striatus, pruinosus, hygrophanus, obscure brunneus, centro obscurior. Caro tenuis, pileo concolor, odore fungoideo. Lamellae 14–17 stipitem attingentes, molles, ventricosae, usque ad c. 2.5 mm latae, late adnatae, dente decurrentes, interdum intervenosae, albae, margine concolores. Stipes 20–40 × 0.8–1.5 mm, cavus, fragilis, aequalis, cylindraceus, siccus, levis, totus subfloccoso-pruinosus, basin versus dense albo-tomentosus, e pallido griseo-brunneus, apice pallidior vel albus, basi fibrillis radiantibus albis substrato affixus.

Basidia immatura, 25–32 × 7–9 μm, clavata, 4-sporigera, fibulata. Sporae immaturae, 8.1–10 × 4.5–4.7 μm, inaequilateraliter ellipsoideae, leves, amyloideae. Cheilocystidia 20–55 × 6.5–11 × 1.8–2.5 μm, subfusiformia, fibulata, levia. Pleurocystidia similia, nonnulla guttulis oleaginosis repleta. Trama lamellarum iodi ope vinescens. Hyphae pileipellis 1.8–2.7 μm latae, fibulatae, valde ramosae, ramis diverticulatis. Hyphae stipitis corticales 2.5–3.5 μm latae, fibulatae, leves, cellulae terminales (caulocystidia) 22.5–110 × 3.5–9 μm, apicibus furcatis, levibus vel diverticulatis.

Foliicola.

Holotypus: A.A.R. de Meijer PAC-2978 (No. 990.200–081; L); isotypus: MBM 190326.

Basidiomata solitary to scattered. Pileus 5–12 mm across, 2–5.5 mm high, at

---

*Etymology: obductus, covered, in reference to the striking pileipellis covering the pileus.

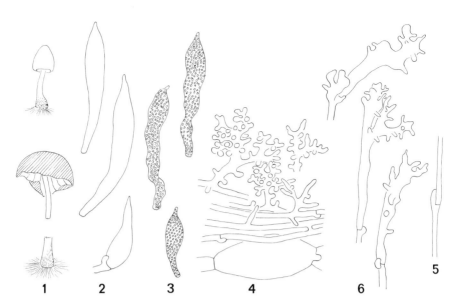

Fig. 22 (1–6) *Mycena obducta* (de Meijer ᴘᴀᴄ-2978). – 1. Habitus of young and old specimen, and basal part of the stipe. – 2. Cheilocystidia. – 3. Pleurocystidia. – 4. Hyphae of the pileipellis. – 5. Hypha of the cortical layer of the stipe. – 6. Terminal cells.
Fig. 1, × 2.5; all others, × 700.

first conical, becoming convex, dry, smooth, translucent-striate, pruinose, hygrophanous, fairly dark brown (5E4), between the striae grey-brown with a slight orange tint (5C3), with the centre very dark brown (5F4, 6F4). Context thin, concolorous with the pileus. Odour fungoid, taste mild. Lamellae 14–17 reaching the stipe, tender, ventricose, up to c. 2.5 mm broad, broadly adnate, decurrent with a tooth, some intervenose, white, with convex, concolorous edge. Stipe 20–40 × 0.8–1.5 mm, hollow, fragile, equal, terete, dry, smooth, subfloccose-pruinose all over, densely white-tomentose towards the base, at first entirely pale, then fairly dark brown (5E4), with only the apex pale to white, attached to the substratum by a whorl of fine, radiating, whitish fibrils.

Basidia (none seen mature) 25–32 × 7–9 μm, clavate, with four incipient sterigmata, clamped. Spores (few seen, very immature) 8.1–10 × 4.5–4.7 μm (Q = 2.0), pip-shaped, smooth, amyloid. Cheilocystidia 20–55 × 6.5–11 × 1.8–2.5 μm, forming a sterile band (lamellar edge homogeneous), subfusiform, subclavate, subcylindrical, clamped, smooth, with acute apex, or rostrate. Pleurocystidia similar, some densely filled with oily droplets. Lamellar trama vinescent in Melzer's reagent. Pileipellis a cutis of repent, radiately aligned hyphae which are 1.8–2.7 μm wide, clamped, in part smooth, the uppermost increasingly branched, the branches up to 5–6 μm wide, much branched and covered with globose warts and short excrescences 2–9 × 1.8–2.7 μm, the whole forming a densely tangled mass. Hypoderm made up of parallel hyphae with inflated cells up to 25 μm wide. Hyphae of the cortical layer of the stipe 2.5–3.5 μm wide, clamped, smooth, the terminal cells

66

(caulocystidia) 22.5–110 × 3.5–9 μm, more or less diverticulate, apically furcate and almost smooth to covered with cylindrical excrescences 1.8–9 × 1.8–4.5 μm.

On dead leaves of a dicotyledonous tree in dense ombrophilous forest, 10 m alt.

Holotype: '*Mycena obducta* Maas G. and de Meijer / 21 Dec. 1994 / Paraná: Paranaguá, Alexandra / A.A.R. de Meijer PAC-2978' (No. 990.200–081; L); isotype: MBM 190326.

Additional material: '28 Dec. 1994 / Paraná: Curitiba, Morretes, Parque Marumbi, Estação Marumbi / A.A.R. de Meijer MA-3004 / on dead leaves of a dicotyledonous tree in dense ombrophilous forest, 450 m alt.' (No. 990.200–138; L); duplicate: MBM 190327.

'27 June 1995 / Paraná: Morretes, Porto de Cima, Parque Marumbi, rio Nhundiaquara / A.A.R. de Meijer MA-3099 / on dead leaves and twigs of a dicotyledonous tree in dense ombrophilous forest, 20 m alt.' (No. 991.343–773; L); duplicate: MBM 190328.

Singer (1989: 8) described *Mycena micromelaena* from Brazil with characters which remind one of those of *M. obducta*. Singer's species appears to have a very dark pileus; white, adnate-subdecurrent lamellae; a white stipe which springs from a basal patch of radiating fibrils; spores of about the same size; cheilocystidia and pleurocystidia which are identical to each other; while the material was said to grow on fallen leaves of a dicotyledonous tree. The differences, however, between Singer's species and *M. obducta*, although few in number, cannot be ignored. The pileus of *Mycena micromelaena* is convex but has its centre applanate or somewhat depressed (at first conical, then convex in *M. obducta*); its stipe is stated to be macroscopically glabrous (subfloccose-pruinose all over in *obducta*); its basidia measure 16–22.5 × 6–7 μm (immature, 25–32 × 7–9 μm in *obducta*); its cheilocystidia are described as 'ex integro subtiliter diverticulatis' and obtuse (smooth and with acute apex in *obducta*).

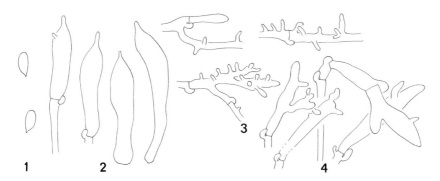

Fig. 23 (1–4) *Mycena obducta* (de Meijer MA-3099). – 1. Spores. – 2. Cheilocystidia. – 3. Hyphae of the pileipellis. – 4. Terminal cells of hyphae of the cortical layer of the stipe.
All figs., × 700.

12. MYCENA sect. **Indutae*** Maas G. and de Meijer, *sect. nov.*

Basidiomata statura media. Pileus udus lubricus, flavus. Caro odore fungoideo. Lamellae paucae, molles, arcuatae, albae, margine (ut videtur) viscidae, concolores. Stipes firmus, haud viscidus, totus puberulus, basi flocculosus, fibrillis crassis, radiantibus substrato affixus.

Basidia clavata, fibulata. Sporae inaequilateraliter ellipsoideae, leves, amyloideae. Cheilocystidia subcylindracea, fibulata, in materiam gelatinosam immersa, apice dilatata, ramosa diverticulataque. Pleurocystidia subfusiformia, fibulata. Trama lamellarum iodi ope vinescens. Hyphae pileipellis fibulatae, in materiam gelatinosam immersae, diverticulatae. Hyphae stipitis corticales fibulatae, haud in materiam gelatinosam immersae, diverticulatae.

Lignicola.

Species typica: *Mycena gelatinomarginata.*

Lodge (1988: 111) placed *Mycena gelatinomarginata* in section *Carolinenses* Maas G. and offered a number of arguments for this disposition, some of which need a closer look. The cheilocystidia, as illustrated in the author's figure 1G are very differently ornamented from those of the type of *M. carolinensis* Smith and Hesler (Maas Geesteranus, 1986: 96). An even more important difference lies in the fact that the cheilocystidia of *M. carolinensis* are not embedded in gelatinous matter, while also they do not, as is the case in *M. gelatinomarginata,* arise from a bundle of hyphae parallel to the lamellar edge. Finally the caulocystidia depicted by Lodge (fig. 1F) are totally different from their counterparts in *M. carolinensis.*

These differences warrant the erection of a new section which is certainly not close to section *Carolinensis.* It is equally not close to sections *Hygrocyboideae* (Fr.) Sing. (Maas Geesteranus, 1989: 89) and *Caespitosae* (A.H. Smith ex Sing.) Maas G. (1989: 360).

Perhaps, the best place for this section is between sections *Fragilipedes* (Fr.) Quél. and *Lactipedes* (Fr.) Quél. (Maas Geesteranus, 1988: 378).

MYCENA GELATINOMARGINATA Lodge – Fig. 24

Mycena gelatinomarginata Lodge in Trans. Br. mycol. Soc. 91: 109, fig. 1. 1988. – Holotype: Lodge PR 84 (F, 1068452, not seen); paratype: Lodge PR 404 (988.233-032; L).

Basidiomata scattered. Pileus 5–11 mm across, up to 4 mm high, convex, somewhat depressed at the centre with age, lubricous when moist, shallowly sulcate, translucent-striate, appearing glabrous, slightly hygrophanous, with the centre and striae fairly pale yellow (4A4), pale yellow between the striae (3A3), drying dingy whitish. Context thin, yellowish white to pale yellowish grey (4A2–4B2). Odour fungoid. Taste not recorded. Lamellae 11–14 reaching the stipe, tender, arcuate, up to 2.5 mm broad, decurrent, white, with concolorous edge (somewhat glassy in some specimens when dry, glistening in others). Stipe 4–7 × 0.3–0.7 mm, hollow, firm, curved, equal, terete for the greater part, with subbulbous base, dry, smooth, white-pruinose to white-puberulous all over, towards the base more flocculose, fairly pale yellow

*Etymology: indutus, clothed, referring to the densely clothed stipe.

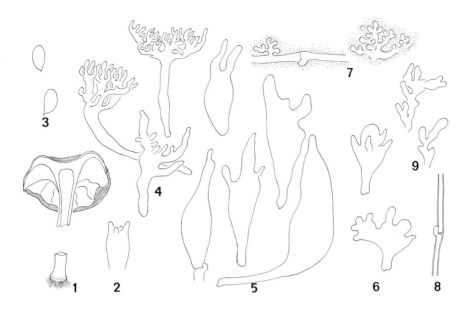

Fig. 24 (1–9) *Mycena gelatinomarginata* (de Meijer MA-2943). – 1. Section of the pileus and basal part of the stipe. – 2. Immature basidium. – 3. Spores. – 4. Cheilocystidia. – 5. Pleurocystidia. – 6. Intermediates between cheilo- and pleurocystidia. – 7. Hypha of the pileipellis. – 8. Hypha of the cortical layer of the stipe. – 9. Caulocystidia.

Fig. 1, × 4; all others, × 700.

(4A4), pale greyish (orange-)brown (5C4) below, attached to the substratum by a dense whorl of radiating, coarse, short, white fibrils.

Basidia (none seen mature) 25–30 × 6.5–8 μm, clavate, with four incipient sterigmata, clamped. Spores 8.1–9.0 × 4.9–5.8 μm (Q = 1.8), pip-shaped, smooth, amyloid. Cheilocystidia 27–50 × 5.5–9 μm, forming a sterile band (lamellar edge homogeneous), cylindrical to subclavate, apically more or less strongly branched and flaring, clamped, long- and short-stalked, at least up to the apical branches embedded in gelatinous matter, the branches more or less densely covered with cylindrical excrescences 5.5–12 × 2–3 μm. Pleurocystidia 50–67 × 12.5–20 × 2.5–10 μm, subfusiform to sublageniform, clamped, long- and short-stalked, with at least the stalks of the pleurocystidia near the lamellar edge embedded in gelatinous matter, generally simple or with two necks or with one or two lateral excrescences. Intermediates between cheilocystidia and pleurocystidia not rare. Lamellar trama vinescent in Melzer's reagent. Pileipellis a cutis of repent, radiately aligned hyphae which are 2.7–4.5 μm wide, clamped, embedded in gelatinous matter, covered with much branched excrescences (hardly discernible in the material available). Hypoderm made up of parallel, inflated hyphae up to 30 μm wide. Hyphae of the cortical layer of the stipe 2.7–3.5 μm wide, clamped, somewhat thick-walled, the outermost thin-walled, not embedded in gelatinous matter, (in the material available) covered with much torn and collapsed, thin-walled, branched excrescences (caulocystidia) – 27 × 2.7–4.5 μm.

Found on a decayed twig of a dicotyledonous tree in dense ombrophilous forest, 1000 m alt.

Material examined: '*Mycena gelatinomarginata* Lodge / 17 Nov. 1994 / Paraná: Morretes, Parque Marumbi, along road BR-277 / A.A.R. de Meijer MA-2943' (No. 990.200–136; L); duplicate: MBM 188520.

Investigation of the paratype of *Mycena gelatinomarginata* (at Leiden) and comparison with collection de Meijer MA-2943 necessitates a comment on the illustration of the cheilocystidia published by Lodge (1988: 110, fig. 1G). Two of the drawings (first and second rows on the right) actually represent true cheilocystidia; the others seem to be in part misshapen pleurocystidia and in part intermediates between cheilo- and pleurocystidia which appear to be not rare close to the lamellar edge.

It proved uncommonly difficult to give a satisfactory rendering of both the excrescences of the hyphae of the pileipellis in collection de Meijer MA-2943 and its caulocystidia. Possibly, Lodge experienced similar difficulties with her type material, and this may have resulted in her unusual drawings.

The original description of *M. gelatinomarginata* mentions various shades of orange colours not observed in collection de Meijer MA-2943. It is not uncommon, however, for the colour of the young basidiome to change or become paler with age.

13. MYCENA sect. **Saniosae** Maas G. and de Meijer, *sect. nov.*

Basidiomata statura media. Pileus velut glaber, rubrobrunneus. Caro tenuis, fracta fluidum rubrum exsudans. Lamellae molles, pallidae, margine rubrobrunneo. Stipes fragilis, velut glaber, pileo pallidior, basi fibrillis radiantibus substrato affixus.

Basidia clavata, 4-sporigera, (verisimiliter) fibulata. Sporae inaequilateraliter ellipsoideae, leves, amyloideae. Cheilocystidia clavata, fibulata, sucum rubrobrunneum continentia, apice diverticulata. Pleurocystidia nulla. Trama lamellarum iodi ope vinescens. Hyphae pileipellis et hyphae stipitis corticales fibulatae, sparse diverticulatae.

Foliicola.

Species typica: *Mycena saniosa*.

In the key to the sections of *Mycena* (Maas Geesteranus, 1992: 1) *Mycena saniosa* would readily key out as a member of section *Crocatae* Maas G., but the differences are shown in the following.

In *Mycena crocata* (Schrad.: Fr.) Kummer, the pileus is delicately pruinose, becoming somewhat glutinous when moist (appearing glabrous, dry in *M. saniosa*); 22 – 29 lamellae reach the stipe (11–14 in *saniosa*) and their edge is whitish (reddish brown in *saniosa*); when bruised, the fluid is yellowish orange to orange-red and remains unchanged in the herbarium (dark red in *saniosa* and disappearing in the herbarium); pleurocystidia are present (none in *saniosa*).

These differences warrant the erection of a section in its own right, which may be placed near section *Sanguinolentae* Maas G. (1988: 389).

Mycena saniosa* Maas G. and de Meijer, *spec. nov.* – Fig. 25 (1–5)

Basidiomata dispersa. Pileus 6.5–8 mm latus, convexus, centro paulo depressus, siccus, sulcatus, striatus, velut glaber, rubrobrunneus. Caro tenuis, fracta fluidum rubrum exsudans, odore nullo. Lamellae 11–14 stipitem attingentes, molles, horizontales, late adnatae, dente decurrentes, usque ad 1.5 mm latae, pallide incarnatae, margine rubrobrunneo. Stipes 40–45 × 0.5 mm, cavus, fragilis, aequalis, cylindraceus, siccus, levis, glaber, pallide incarnatus, totus minutissime rubro-brunneo-punctatus, basi fibrillis sparsis, radiantibus substrato affixus.

Basidia 9 μm lata, clavata, 4-sporigera. Sporae 7.6–8.1 × 5.4 μm, inaequilateraliter ellipsoi-deae, leves, amyloideae. Cheilocystidia 18–27 × 7–11 μm, clavata, fibulata, sucum rubro-brunneum continentia, apice surculis crassis 2.5–6.5 × 1.5–2.5 μm munita. Pleurocystidia nulla. Trama lamellarum iodi ope vinescens. Hyphae pileipellis 4.5–7 μm latae, fibulatae, sparse di-verticulatae. Hyphae stipitis corticales 1.8 μm latae, sparse diverticulatae.

Foliicola.

Holotypus: A.A.R. de Meijer ᴍᴀ-3006 (No. 990.200–152; L); notulae: ᴍʙᴍ 190347.

Basidiomata scattered. Pileus 6.5–8 mm across, convex, centrally slightly depressed, dry, sulcate, translucent-striate, appearing glabrous, the centre and striae reddish brown (8D4), between the striae fairly pale pinkish grey (7B3). Context thin, exuding a dark red juice when broken. Odour none, taste not recorded. Lamellae 11–14 reaching the stipe, tender, horizontal, broadly adnate, decurrent with a tooth, up to 1.5 mm broad, pale flesh-colour or somewhat more greyish, with reddish brown edge. Stipe 40–45 × 0.5 mm, hollow, fragile, equal, terete, dry, smooth, appearing glabrous, pale flesh-colour, entirely but very minutely punctate with dark red dots, the base attached to the substratum by a few, fine fibrils.

Basidia immature, 9 μm broad, clavate, with four incipient sterigmata, clamped (although clamps not observed). Spores (few seen, immature) 7.6–8.1 × 5.4 μm (Q = 1.8), pip-shaped, smooth, weakly amyloid. Cheilocystidia 18–27 × 7–11 μm, forming a dense sterile band (lamellar edge homo-geneous), clavate, clamped, with reddish contents, apically covered with coarse, unevenly spaced, straight to somewhat curved, more or less regularly shaped cylindrical excrescences 2.5–6.5 × 1.5–2.5 μm. Pleurocystidia absent. Lamellar trama vinescent in Melzer's reagent. Pileipellis a cutis of repent, radiately aligned hyphae which are 4.5–7 μm wide, clamped, sparsely covered with simple to somewhat branched, obtuse excrescences 4.5–12.5 × 2.7–3.5 μm. Hyphae of the hypoderm with inflated cells up to 25 μm. Hyphae of the cortical layer of the stipe 1.8 μm wide, sparsely covered with simple, obtuse excrescences 1.8–2.7 × 1.8 μm, terminal cells not observed.

On dead leaf of a dicotyledonous tree in dense ombrophilous forest, 450 m alt.

Holotype: '*Mycena saniosa* Maas G. and de Meijer / 28 Dec. 1994 / Paraná: Morretes, Parque Marumbi, Estação Marumbi / A.A.R. de Meijer ᴍᴀ-3006' (No. 990.200–152; L); notes and drawings: ᴍʙᴍ 190347.

Although the holotype consists of no more than two specimens, it was

---

*Etymology: saniosus, full of blood, referring to the context exuding a red drop when broken.

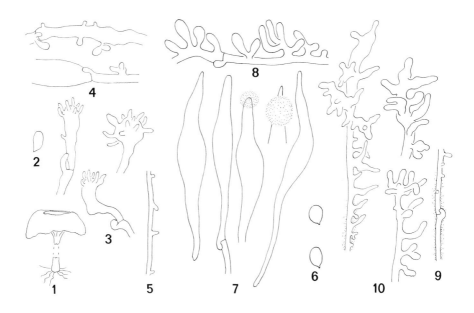

Fig. 25 (1–5) *Mycena saniosa* (de Meijer MA-3006). – 1. Habitus and basal part of the stipe. – 2. Spore. – 3. Cheilocystidia. – 4. Hyphae of the pileipellis. – 5. Hypha of the cortical layer of the stipe. (6–10) *Mycena rubrofarcta* (de Meijer CUI-2197). – 6. Spores. – 7. Cheilocystidia. – 8. Hypha of the pileipellis. – 9. Hypha of the cortical layer of the stipe. – 10. Terminal cells. Fig. 1, × 4; all others, × 700.

decided in this case to give a formal description and preserve the material. Many South American Mycenas occur solitary or in twos and it may take indefinitely before another conspecific collection will be found.

Macroscopically, *Mycena saniosa* could be confused with a species for which Raithelhuber (1984: 12) proposed the new name *Mycena anchietana* to replace *M. sanguinolenta* (Alb. and Schw.: Fr.) Kummer sensu Rick. Both have a reddish brown pileus, distant pale reddish lamellae with a dark edge ('mit schwarz-purpurner Schneide' according to Raithelhuber), and a pale flesh-colour stipe which exudes a reddish brown fluid [when broken]. The species was also said to have amyloid spores. No information is available on the surface hyphae of both pileus and stipe, but the cheilocystidia are described as being scanty and smooth. This alone proves *M. anchietana* to be a different species from *M. saniosa*.

14. MYCENA section GALACTOPODA (Earle) Maas G.

Mycena sect. *Galactopoda* (Earle) Maas G. in Proc. K. Ned. Akad. Wet. (Ser. C) **91**: 396. 1988. – Type species: *Mycena haematopus* (Pers.: Fr.) Kummer.

For further synonymy, see Maas Geesteranus, l.c.

Basidiomata medium-sized to large. Pileus densely powdered, glabrescent, brownish flesh-colour to dark brown with a purplish shade. Context thin. Odour weak to pleasant. Lamellae tender, ascending, adnate, whitish to pinkish, the edge concolorous or blood red. Stipe fragile, pruinose, glabrescent for the greater part, exuding a blood red fluid when cut, blackening in the herbarium, covered with coarse, whitish fibrils at the base.

Basidia clavate, 4-spored, clamped. Spores pip-shaped, smooth, amyloid. Cheilocystidia fusiform, with colourless or reddish brown contents, clamped, with slender neck. Pleurocystidia similar, if present. Lamellar trama vinescent in Melzer's reagent. Hyphae of the pileipellis clamped, covered with excrescences and diverticulate side-branches. Hyphae of the cortical layer of the stipe clamped, smooth, the terminal cells (caulocystidia) much branched and diverticulate, dissimilar to the cheilocystidia.

Growing on decaying wood of deciduous trees, less frequently of conifers.

Mycena rubrofarcta* Maas G. and de Meijer, *spec. nov.* – Fig. 25 (6–10)

Basidiomata gregaria. Pileus 4–19 mm latus, e conico planoconvexus, siccus, levis, striatus, e pruinoso glaber, hygrophanus, initio obscure purpureobrunneus, deinde pallide incarnatus, striis obscure brunneis munitus. Caro firma, pileo concolor, odore grato, sucum rubrum emittens. Lamellae 15–16 stipitem attingentes, molles, adscendentes, usque ad 3 mm latae, ventricosae, adnexae vel late adnatae denteque decurrentes, pallide incarnatae. Stipes 23–40 × 0.6–1.8 mm, cavus, fragilis, aequalis, levis, subpruinosus, glabrescens, initio obscure griseobrunneus, deinde pallidior, basi fibrillis crassis instructus.

Basidia 22.5–27 × 6.5–7 μm, clavata, 4-sporigera, fibulata, sterigmatibus c. 4.5 μm longis praedita. Sporae 6.5–7.2 × 4.8–5.4 μm, inaequilateraliter ellipsoideae, leves, amyloideae. Cheilocystidia 45–80 × 5.5–11.5 × 1.8–3.5 μm, fusiformia, fibulata, levia. Pleurocystidia similia. Trama lamellarum iodi ope vinescens. Hyphae pileipellis 2.5–4.5 μm latae, fibulatae, diverticulatae. Hyphae stipitis corticales 1.8–2.5 μm latae, fibulatae, magna ex parte leves, cellulae terminales 5–7 μm latae, varie diverticulatae.

Lignicola.

Holotypus: A.A.R. de Meijer cui-2197 (No. 988.233–024; L); isotypus: мвм 190345.

Basidiomata gregarious. Pileus 4–19 mm across, at first conical, finally planoconvex, dry, smooth, translucent-striate, pruinose, glabrescent, hygrophanous, very dark brown with some purplish shade (8EF5) when young, with paler margin, turning pale flesh-colour (5A3) with the centre and striae remaining very dark brown (8F5). Context firm, concolorous with the pileus, exuding a dark red juice when cut. Odour rather pleasant. Taste not recorded. Lamellae 15–16 reaching the stipe, tender, ascending, up to 3 mm broad, ventricose, adnexed to broadly adnate and decurrent with a tooth, smooth to ribbed, dorsally intervenose, pale flesh-colour (5A3). Stipe 23–40 × 0.6–1.8 mm, hollow, fragile, equal, terete, smooth, somewhat pruinose, especially near the apex, glabrescent, at first dark brown with some purplish shade (7E5), turning somewhat paler with age (7D4), exuding a dark red drop when cut, the base densely covered with coarse fibrils. The whole fungus blackening when dried.

Basidia (none seen mature) 22.5–27 × 6.5–7 μm, clavate, 4-spored, clamped, with sterigmata c. 4.5 μm long. Spores 6.5–7.2 × 4.8–5.4 μm (Q =

---

* Etymology: rubrofarctus, red-filled, referring to the red juice exuded by the context or the stipe when cut.

1.4), fairly broadly pip-shaped, smooth, amyloid. Cheilocystidia 45–80 × 5.5–11.5 × 1.8–3.5 μm, locally forming a sterile band, slender-fusiform, clamped, short-stalked (rather few) to extremely long-stalked (numerous), some having their tips surrounded by a globose mass of exudate. Pleuro-cystidia scattered, similar. Lamellar trama vinescent in Melzer's reagent. Pileipellis a cutis made up of radiately aligned repent hyphae which are 2.5–4.5 μm wide, clamped, not gelatinized, covered with cylindrical to somewhat clavate, simple to furcate or loosely branched excrescences 6.5–14.5 × 3.5–4.5 μm. Hyphae of the hypoderm up to 15 μm wide, parallel, thin-walled. Hyphae of the cortical layer of the stipe 1.8–2.5 μm wide, clamped, smooth for the greater part, towards the terminal cell showing a few, short, simple excrescences, somewhat gelatinizing, the terminal cells (caulocystidia) 5–7 μm wide, covered with cylindrical to very irregularly shaped, simple to much branched, thin-walled, easily collapsed excrescences 2–11 × 2–9 μm.

On a decayed stump of a dicotyledonous tree in mixed ombrophilous forest, 900 m alt.

Holotype: '*Mycena rubrofarcta* Maas G. and de Meijer / 18 March 1992 / Paraná: Curitiba, Centro Civico Distr., Bosque João Paulo II / A.A.R. de Meijer CUI-2197' (No. 988.233–024; L), isotype: MBM 190345.

Mycena rubrofarcta is remarkably close to *M. haematopus* (Pers.: Fr.) Kummer, for which it could easily have been mistaken in the field. They even resemble each other in that of both at least their stipes turn black on being dried. The two species are best distinguished by their microscopic characters. In *M. rubrofarcta*, the spores are 6.5–7.2 × 4.8–5.4 μm, the excrescences of the hyphae of the pileipellis as well as of the caulocystidia are loosely branched, the cheilocystidia are short-stalked to long-stalked and many even extremely long-stalked. In *M. haematopus* the spores are 9.0–9.5 × 5.3–5.8 μm (Maas Geesteranus, 1992: 335) ['10 × 7 μ' (Kühner, 1938: 221); '8–11 × 5–7 μ' (A.H. Smith, 1947: 141)], the excrescences of the hyphae of the pileipellis as well as of the caulocystidia are tightly branched, the cheilocystidia are short-stalked to sessile.

15. MYCENA sect. **Nigrescentes** Maas G. and de Meijer, *sect. nov.*

Basidiomata parva. Pileus siccus, rubrobrunneus vel atrobrunneus. Caro odore fungoideo. Lamellae paucae, arcuatae, margine rubrobrunneae vel atrobrunneae. Stipes fragilis, siccus, pileo concolor vel pallidior, deorsum fibrillis instructus. Siccatus totus fungus nigrescens.
Basidia clavata, 4-sporigera, fibulata. Sporae inaequilateraliter ellipsoideae, leves, amyloideae. Cheilocystidia clavata, fibulata, sucum brunneum continentia, surculis brevibus instructa. Pleurocystidia nulla. Trama lamellarum iodi ope vinescens. Hyphae pileipellis atque stipitis corticales fibulatae, pro parte surculis crassis dense munitae.
Lignicola.
Species typica: *Mycena nigrescens.*

In the key to the sections of *Mycena* (Maas Geesteranus, 1992: 1), *M. ni-grescens* could with some doubt be identified as a member of section *Ru-*

bromarginatae Sing. ex Maas G. (1980: 106). Some of the characters of this section, however, are clearly different from those of *M. nigrescens*. Members of section *Rubromarginatae* do not have arcuate, long decurrent lamellae; if some of their cheilocystidia are clavate, these are generally mixed with others which are fusiform, lageniform or utriform; in many cases, these cheilocystidia are smooth but, if covered with excrescences, the latter are either long and slender or very coarse; with the exception of *M. renati* Quél., the terminal cells of the hyphae of both the pileipellis and the cortical layer of the stipe are covered with excrescences which are completely differently shaped from their counterparts in *M. nigrescens*. Finally, the blackening of pileus and stipe of *Mycena nigrescens* when dried may well indicate that the cell sap in this species differs from that in the *Rubromarginatae*.

Section *Nigrescentes* may be placed near section *Galactopoda* (Earle) Maas G. (1988: 396), but is separated by the arcuate lamellae and clavate cheilocystidia.

KEY TO THE SPECIES

1. Pileus convex, finally with the centre somewhat depressed. Lamellae not triangular. Stipe with ozonium-like growth at the base. Cheilocystidia short-stalked: . . . . *M. nigrescens*
1. Pileus grossly umbonate. Lamellae triangular. Stipe without ozonium-like growth at the base. Cheilocystidia sessile: . . . . *M. furva*

Mycena nigrescens* Maas G. and de Meijer, *spec. nov.* – Fig. 26

Basidiomata gregaria vel caespitosa. Pileus 1.5–11 mm latus, 1–4 mm altus, convexus, initio margine involutus, centro depressus, siccus, subsulcatus striatusque, glaber, haud hygrophanus, rubrobrunneus, siccatus nigrescens. Caro tenuis, odore fungoideo. Lamellae 10–15 stipitem attingentes, haud molles, arcuatae, usque ad 2.5 mm latae, late adnatae, longe decurrentes, pallidae, margine rubrobrunneo. Stipes 6–20 × 0.6–1 mm, cavus, fragilis, subaequalis, cylindraceus, siccus, levis, glaber, e rubrobrunneo griseoflavus, siccatus nigrescens, basi spongiosus atque hirsutus.

Basidia 22.5–24 × 5.5–6.5 μm, clavata, 4-sporigera, fibulata. Sporae 7.0–7.4 × 3.1–3.6 μm, inaequilateraliter ellipsoideae, leves, amyloideae. Cheilocystidia 18–24 × (4.5–)6.5–14.5 μm, clavata, fibulata, sucum brunneum continentia, surculis cylindraceis 2–3 × 1.5–2 μm instructa. Pleurocystidia nulla. Trama lamellarum iodi ope vinescens. Hyphae pileipellis 2.7–5.5 μm latae, fibulatae, ramosae, leves, cellulae terminales 5.5–8 μm latae, surculis crassis munitae. Hyphae stipitis corticales 2.7–4.5 μm latae, fibulatae, pro parte leves, cellulae terminales 3.5–9 μm latae, surculis crassis instructae.

Lignicola.

Holotypus: A.A.R. de Meijer CUB-2931 (No. 990.200–095; L); isotype: MBM 190323.

Basidiomata gregarious to cespitose. Pileus 1.5–11 mm across, 1–4 mm high, convex, at first with involute margin, finally with the centre somewhat depressed, dry, shallowly sulcate, translucent-striate, appearing glabrous, not hygrophanous, dark red-brown (9E6–9F6 when young, 8E5 when mature), fairly pale greyish orange-brown (5C4) between the striae, the whole pileus turning almost black when dried. Context thin, concolorous with the pileus

*Etymology: nigrescens, blackening, referring to the basidiomata turning almost black when dried.

75

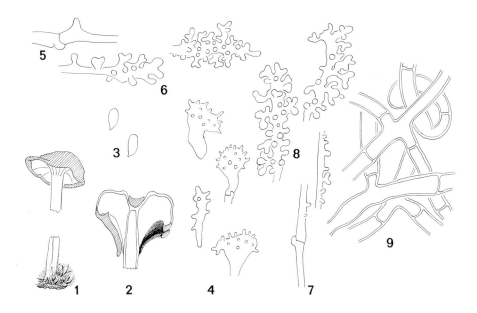

Fig. 26 (1–9) *Mycena nigrescens* (de Meijer cub-2931). – 1. Habitus and basal part of the stipe. – 2. Section of the pileus. – 3. Spores. – 4. Cheilocystidia. – 5. Fragment of a hypha of the pileipellis. – 6. Terminal cells of hyphae of the pileipellis. – 7. Hyphae of the cortical layer of the stipe. – 8. Terminal cells. – 9. Hyphae of the spongy tissue at the base of the stipe. Figs. 1–2, × 4; all others, × 700.

surface. Odour fungoid, taste slightly bitterish (?). Lamellae 10–15 reaching the stipe, firm, arcuate but not triangular, up to 2.5 mm broad, broadly adnate, far decurrent, very pale, not pure white, with dark red-brown edge. Stipe 6–20 × 0.6–1 mm, hollow, fragile, more or less equal, terete, dry, smooth, appearing glabrous for the greater part, at first dark red-brown (9E6–9F6), gradually turning greyish yellow (4B4), the base more or less copiously covered with a fine, pale, spongy tissue [comparable to the ozonium at the base of the stipe of *Coprinus radians* (Desmaz.) Fr.], from which emerge long, coarse fibrils. The whole fungus blackening when dried.

Basidia (none seen mature) 22.5–24 × 5.5–6.5 μm, slender-clavate, with four incipient sterigmata, clamped. Spores 7.0–7.4 × 3.1–3.6 μm (Q = 2.2), pip-shaped, smooth, amyloid. Cheilocystidia 18–24 × (4.5–)6.5–14.5 μm, hardly protruding and very difficult to extricate from the surrounding tissue, forming a sterile band (lamellar edge homogeneous), clavate, fairly short-stalked, clamped, filled with brownish sap, apically covered with fairly few, cylindrical excrescences 2–3 × 1.5–2 μm. Pleurocystidia absent. Lamellar trama vinescent in Melzer's reagent. Pileipellis a cutis of repent, radiately aligned hyphae which are 2.7–5.5 μm wide, clamped, much branched, partly smooth, towards their tips somewhat more diverticulate, with the terminal cells 5.5–8 μm wide, densely covered with coarse, simple to branched, cylindrical, round-tipped excrescences 3.5–8 × 2.5–6.5 μm which form intricate, coralloid masses. Hypoderm made up of parallel, much inflated hy-

76

phae. Hyphae of the cortical layer of the stipe 2.7–4.5 μm wide, clamped, partly smooth, towards their tips increasingly diverticulate, the terminal cells 3.5–9 μm wide, generally branched, densely covered with coarse, simple to branched, cylindrical, round-tipped excrescences 2.7–7 × 2–4.5 μm. Hyphae of the spongy tissue at the base of the stipe 5.5–7 μm wide, septate, without clamps, much branched, thick-walled (1 μm), smooth. Fibrils emerging from the spongy tissue made up of bundles of firmly agglutinated hyphae which are 2.7 μm wide, rather thick-walled, smooth, almost aseptate, clampless.

On decayed branch of a dicotyledonous tree in mixed ombrophilous forest, 900 m alt.

Holotype: '*Mycena nigrescens* Maas G. and de Meijer / 14 Nov. 1994 / Paraná: Curitiba, Santo Inacio Distr., Parque Barigui / A.A.R. de Meijer CUB-2931' (No. 990.200–095; L); isotype: MBM 190323.

Mycena fuscocystidiata is a species described by Singer (1989: 72) from Columbia and in many respects remarkably similar to *M. nigrescens*. The important difference between the two species is that *M. fuscocystidiata* has cheilocystidia which are apparently smooth, and possesses pleurocystidia, while its basal mycelium is stated to be 'sparso.'

In *Mycena furva*, a species of the same section, the stipe was found to exude a red juice when broken. Although this was not observed in *M. nigrescens* it seems reasonable to assume that the stipe in a young and fresh specimen would equally exude a red drop when cut.

Mycena furva* Maas G. and de Meijer, *spec. nov.* – Fig. 27

Basidiomata dispersa. Pileus 4.5–6.5 mm latus, usque ad 4 mm altus, convexus, valde umbonatus, siccus, haud striatus, glaber ut videtur, haud hygrophanus, aurantiacobrunneus, centro atrobrunneus, siccatus nigrescens. Caro pallida, odore fungoideo. Lamellae 14–16 stipitem attingentes, arcuatae, usque ad 2 mm latae, late adnatae, longe decurrentes, pallidae, margine atrobrunneo. Stipes 17–26 × 1–1.2 mm, cavus, fragilis, aequalis, cylindraceus, siccus, levis, glaber ut videtur, pallide griseobrunneus, siccatus nigrescens, basim versus fibrillis instructus, fractus sucum obscure rubrum stillans.

Basidia 22.5–25 × 7–9 μm, clavata, 4-sporigera, fibulata. Sporae c. 7 × 4.5 μm, inaequilateraliter ellipsoideae, leves, amyloideae. Cheilocystidia 16–22.5 × 8–20.5 μm, globosa vel ellipsoidea, fibulata, sessilia, sucum brunneum continentia, surculis cylindraceis 1–3.5 × 1–2.5 μm munita. Pleurocystidia nulla. Trama lamellarum iodi ope vinescens. Hyphae pileipellis 2.5–4.5 μm latae, fibulatae, ramosae-diverticulatae. Hyphae stipitis corticales 2.7 μm latae, fibulatae, diverticulatae.

Lignicola.

Holotypus: A.A.R. de Meijer RS-3023 (No. 990.200–041; L); notulae: MBM 188518.

Basidiomata scattered. Pileus 4.5–6.5 mm across, up to 4 mm high, convex, grossly umbonate, dry, not translucent-striate, appearing glabrous, not hygrophanous, orange-brown (7C5), at the centre very dark brown (9F5), turning almost black when dried. Context concolorous with the pileus above, pallid with some pinkish hue farther below. Odour fungoid, taste not re-

*Etymology: furvus, dark, black, in reference to the basidiomata turning almost black when dried.

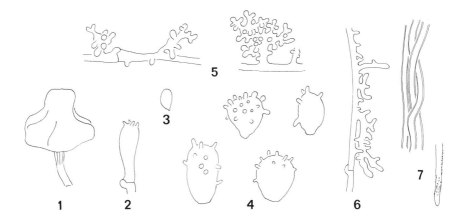

Fig. 27 (1–7) *Mycena furva* (de Meijer RS-3023). – 1. Habitus. – 2. Basidium. – 3. Spore. – 4. Chei-locystidia. – 5. Hyphae of the pileipellis. – 6. Hypha of the cortical layer of the stipe. – 7. Hyphae of a fibril taken near the base of the stipe.
Fig. 1, × 7; all others, × 700.

corded. Lamellae 14–16 reaching the stipe, arcuate, triangular, up to 2 mm broad, broadly adnate, far decurrent, very pale pinkish grey (between 7A2 and 7B2), with very dark brown edge. Stipe 17–26 × 1–1.2 mm, hollow, fragile, equal, terete, dry, smooth, appaearing glabrous, very pale orange-grey-brown (5B3), turning almost black when dried, towards the base covered with long, fairly coarse fibrils, exuding a dark red juice when cut.

Basidia (none seen mature) 22.5–25 × 7–9 µm, clavate, with four incipient sterigmata, clamped. Spores (immature) c. 7 × 4.5 µm (Q = 1.8), pip-shaped, smooth, amyloid. Cheilocystidia 16–22.5 × 8–20.5 µm, little protruding, crowded in some places, occurring mixed with basidia in others, globose, ellipsoid, sessile, clamped, filled with brownish sap, apically covered with fairly few, cylindrical or somewhat inflated excrescences 1–3.5 × 1–2.5 µm. Pleurocystidia absent. Lamellar trama vinescent in Melzer's reagent. Pileipellis a cutis of repent, radiately aligned hyphae which are 2.5–4.5 µm wide, clamped, in some parts almost smooth, in others very densely and intricately branched-diverticulate with the terminal excrescences 2.5–5.5 µm wide, the whole forming dense coralloid masses. Hypoderm made up of parallel, much inflated hyphae. Hyphae of the cortical layer of the stipe 2.7 µm wide, clamped, covered with simple to much branched excrescences 2–30 × 2–3 µm (which proved difficult to discern). Fibrils from the base of the stipe made up of bundles of firmly agglutinated hyphae which are 1.8–2.7 µm wide, rather thick-walled, smooth (except for the roughened tips), almost aseptate, clampless.

On decayed stump of a dicotyledonous tree in secondary mixed om-brophilous forest, 900 m alt.

Holotype: '*Mycena furva* Maas G. and de Meijer / 11 Feb. 1995 / Paraná:

Rio Branco do Sul, Areias Distr. / A.A.R. de Meijer RS–3023' (No. 990.200–041; L); notes and drawings: MBM 188518.

16. MYCENA section FULIGINELLAE (A.H. Smith ex Sing.) Maas G.

Mycena sect. Fuliginellae A.H. Smith, N. Am. Spec. Mycena: 42, 401, 429. 1917 (not val. publ.: no Latin descr.). – *Mycena* subsect. *Fuliginellae* (A.H. Smith) Sing. in Lilloa **22**: 362 ('1949') 1951 (not val. publ.: no Latin descr.). – *Mycena* subsect. *Fuliginellae* A.H. Smith ex Sing. in Sydowia **15**: 65. 1962. – *Mycena* sect. *Fuliginellae* (A.H. Smith ex Sing.) Maas G. in Proc. K. Ned. Akad. Wet. (Ser. C) **83**: 406. 1980. – Holotype: *Mycena vulgaris.*
   For further synonymy, see Maas Geesteranus, l.c.

Basidiomata medium-sized. Pileus covered with a gelatinous pellicle, viscid, grey or grey-brown in various shades to pallid or white. Flesh pliant, pallid. Odour rancid, farinaceous, indistinctive or unknown. Lamellae ascending or arcuate, broadly adnate, white to greyish, the edge gelatinized. Stipe hollow, glutinous to viscid, pruinose to puberulous above, glabrous farther below, grey or grey-brown to white, never yellow.
   Basidia clavate, 4-spored, clamped. Spores pip-shaped, smooth, amyloid. Cheilocystidia forming a sterile band, clavate to cylindrical, clamped, covered with unevenly spaced, coarse excrescences or apically much branched and terminated by very numerous excrescences. Pleurocystidia present or absent. Lamellar trama brownish vinescent in Melzer's reagent. Hyphae of the pileipellis clamped, embedded in gelatinous matter, smooth to diverticulate. Hyphae of the cortical layer of the stipe clamped, with gelatinizing cell-walls or embedded in gelatinous matter, smooth or sparsely diverticulate, terminal cells (caulocystidia) variously shaped, diverticulate.
   Growing on coniferous wood or on fallen needles, also on dead leaves of dicotyledonous trees.

As is shown by *Mycena dispar,* it is no longer true that members of section *Fuliginellae* are exclusively associated with coniferous trees. A further change in the original description of the section is that the pellicle covering the pileus and the gelatinous lamellar edge are no longer described as separable, since these characters have not been demonstrated in *M. dispar.*

KEY TO THE SPECIES

1. Pleurocystidia present. Terminal cells of the hyphae of the cortical layer of the stipe covered with numerous fine excrescences: . . . . *M. austini*
1. Pleurocystidia absent. Terminal cells of the hyphae of the cortical layer of the stipe much branched, branches very coarse: . . . . *M. dispar*

MYCENA AUSTINII (Peck) Kühn. – Fig. 28

Agaricus austinii Peck in Rep. N.Y. St. Mus. **28**: 48. 1876. – *Omphalia austinii* (Peck) Sacc., Syll. Fung. **5**: 336. 1887. – *Omphalopsis austinii* (Peck) Murrill in N. Am. Flora **9**: 312. 1916. – *Mycena austinii* (Peck) Kühn., Genre Mycena: 394. 1938. – Holotype: 'Agaricus Austinii Pk / Providence, Saratoga Co. / C.H. Peck / Omphalia' (NYS).

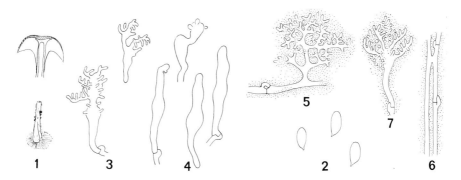

Fig. 28 (1–7) *Mycena austinii* (de Meijer CUB-2928). – 1. Section of pileus and basal part of the stipe. – 2. Spores. – 3. Cheilocystidia. – 4. Pleurocystidia. – 5. Hypha of the pileipellis. – 6. Hyphae of the cortical layer of the stipe. – 7. Terminal cell.

Fig. 1, × 3; all others, × 700.

Basidiomata scattered. Pileus (1.5–)4–8 mm across, up to 2.5 mm high, viscid, covered with a tenacious pellicle, convex with depressed or somewhat umbilicate centre, translucent-striate, appearing glabrous, strongly hygrophanous, centre and striae grey-brown (5D3–5D5), yellowish white between the striae, drying pale yellowish white (4A2). Context thin, whitish. Odour fungoid, taste not recorded. Lamellae 12–15 reaching the stipe, occasionally furcate near the pileus margin, tender, arcuate, broadly adnate, up to 1.5 mm broad, long decurrent down the stipe, white, edge concave, gelatinized, white. Stipe (3–)13–32 × 0.6–0.8 mm, hollow, tenacious, equal, terete, viscid, covered with a gelatinous pellicle, delicately pruinose at the apex, glabrous for the greater part, white above, grey-brown (5D3–6D4) farther below, arising from a grey-brown (6D4) basal patch made up of radiating, agglutinated fibrils.

Basidia (few seen mature) c. 27 × 6.5–7 μm, slender-clavate, 4-spored, clamped, with sterigmata up to 7 μm long. Spores 7.6–9.2 × 3.6–4.5 μm (Q = 2.1), pip-shaped, smooth, amyloid. Cheilocystidia 13.5–30 x3.5–5.5 μm, forming a sterile band (lamellar edge homogeneous), clavate, clamped, embedded in gelatinous matter, apically more or less branched, covered with unevenly spaced, simple to furcate excrescences –10 × 1–2 μm. Pleurocystidia 30–36 × 5.5–6.5 × 2.7–3.5 μm, subfusiform, with a more or less wavy outline, clamped, smooth or occasionally with a few, short, rounded excrescences. Lamellar trama weakly brownish vinescent in Melzer's reagent. Pileipellis a cutis of repent, radiately aligned hyphae which are embedded in gelatinous matter, 1.8–2.7 μm wide, clamped, much branched, the branches being covered with excrescences 1.8–3.5 x1–2 μm. Hypoderm made up of parallel, inflated hyphae. Hyphae of the cortical layer of the stipe embedded in gelatinous matter, 1.8–2.7 μm wide, clamped, smooth for the greater part, near the apex of the stipe frequently covered with simple, cylindrical excrescences, the terminal cells up to 6 μm broad, clavate, much branched, the branches being covered with excrescences 1.5–3.5 × 1–2 μm.

On dead twigs and fallen leaves of *Araucaria angustifolia,* in mixed ombrophilous forest, 900 m alt.

Material examined: '*Mycena austinii* (Peck) Kühn. / 14 Nov. 1994 / Paraná: Curitiba, Santo Inácio Distr., Parque Barigui / A.A.R. de Meijer cu b-2928' (No. 990.200–134; L); duplicate: мвм 188495.

Smith (1947: 408) stated that he had never seen the species when fresh and copied Peck's description which succinctly gave the colour as 'white.' Maas Geesteranus (1989: 334), studying the colour of the type material, judged the fresh pileus to have been at least pallid. It is only now that the true colour is fully known and it is clear that Peck must have based his description on dried specimens.

Mycena dispar* Maas G. and de Meijer, *spec. nov.* – Fig. 29

Basidiomata dispersa. Pileus 2.5–8 mm latus, usque ad 4 mm altus, hemisphaericus, centro papillis obtusis minutisque instructus, haud sulcatus, striatus, udus viscidus, hygrophanus, griseobrunneus, centro obscure fuscus. Caro tenuis, pallide grisea, odore indistincto. Lamellae 10– 12 stipitem attingentes, molles, arcuatae, usque ad 2 mm vel ulterior latae, late adnatae, decurrentes, albae, margine concolore, gelatinoso. Stipes 17–47 × 0.4–0.7 mm, cavus, fragilis, aequalis, cylindraceus, levis, viscidus, albus, e disco basali pallide griseoflavo natus.

Basidia c. 22 × 7 µm, clavata, 4-sporigera, fibulata. Sporae 7.2–9.0 × 3.8–4.5 µm, inaequilateraliter ellipsoideae, leves, amyloideae. Cheilocystidia –90? × 3.5–5.5 µm, cylindracea, in materiam gelatinosam immersa, apice ramosa. Pleurocystidia nulla. Trama lamellarum iodi ope vinescens. Hyphae pileipellis 1.8–2.7 µm latae, fibulatae, in materiam gelatinosam immersae, diverticulatae. Hyphae stipitis corticales 1.8–2.7 µm latae, fibulatae, leves vel sparse diverticulatae, cellulae terminales (caulocystidia) 35–40 × 5–6.5 µm, in materiam gelatinosam immersae, apice ramosae.

Foliicola.

Holotypus: A.A.R. de Meijer мл-2944 (No. 990.200–137; L); notulae: мвм 188510.

Basidiomata scattered. Pileus 2.5–8 mm across, up to 4 mm high, hemispherical, centrally with minute, obtuse papillae, not sulcate, translucent-striate, viscid when moist, hygrophanous, the striae grey-brown (5D3), between the striae pale grey with a slight yellow tint (5B2), the centre very dark brown (5F4). Context thin, pale greyish. Odour indistinct. Lamellae 10–12 reaching the stipe, tender, arcuate, up to 2.2 mm broad, broadly adnate, decurrent, pure white, with gelatinous, concolorous edge. Stipe 17–47 × 0.4– 0.7 mm, hollow, fragile, equal, terete, smooth, viscid, white, arising from a cushion-shaped basal disc which is greyish yellow (4B4), and covered with and surrounded by a thin gelatinous film which when dry tends to break up into tiny, glistening fibrils.

Basidia (none seen mature) c. 22 × 7 µm, clavate, some with four incipient sterigmata, clamped. Spores 7.2–9.0 × 3.8–4.5 µm (Q = 1.9), pip-shaped, smooth, amyloid. Cheilocystidia –90? × 3.5–5.5 µm, forming a sterile band (lamellar edge homogeneous), arising from a fusiform basal cell (c. 27–30 × 7 µm), cylindrical, embedded in gelatinous matter, apically much branched,

---

*Etymology: dispar, unlike, not like the type species of the section.

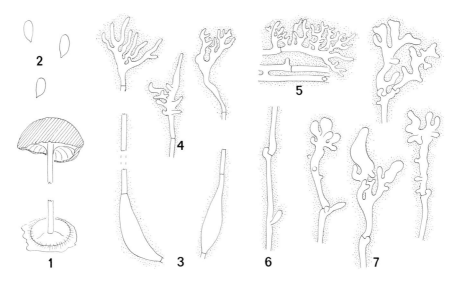

Fig. 29 (1–7) *Mycena dispar* (de Meijer MA-2944). – 1. Habitus and basal part of the stipe. – 2. Spores. – 3. Basal cells of the cheilocystidia. – 4. Cheilocystidia. – 5. Hyphae of the pileipellis. – 6. Hypha of the cortical layer of the stipe. – 7. Terminal cells.
Fig. 1, × 6; all others, × 700.

with the branches $10-13.5 \times 1.8-2.5\ \mu$m. Pleurocystidia absent. Lamellar trama vinescent in Melzer's reagent. Pileipellis an ixocutis of repent, radiately aligned hyphae $1.8-2.7\ \mu$m wide, clamped, embedded in gelatinous matter, the uppermost covered with branched excrescences $2.5-20 \times 2\ \mu$m. Hypoderm made up of parallel, inflated hyphae up to $25\ \mu$m wide. Hyphae of the cortical layer of the stipe $1.8-2.7\ \mu$m wide, clamped, embedded in gelatinous matter, smooth or with few excrescences, the terminal cells (caulocystidia) $35-40 \times 5-6.5\ \mu$m, clamped, variously branched, with very coarse branches $7-25 \times 2.5-6.5\ \mu$m.

On dead, non-leathery leaves of a dicotyledonous tree, 1000 m alt.

Holotype: '*Mycena dispar* Maas G. and de Meijer / 19 Nov. 1994 / Paraná: Morretes, Parque Marumbi, along road BR-277 / A.A.R. de Meijer MA-2944' (No. 990.200–137; L); notes and drawings: MBM 188510.

Mycena dispar differs from *Mycena vulgaris,* the type species of the section, in having fewer lamellae ($14-25$ reaching the stipe in *vulgaris*), in the stipe springing from a basal disc (instead of being covered with coarse fibrils as in *vulgaris*), in the fusiform basal cells of the cheilocystidia, and the very coarse, $2.5-6.5\ \mu$m wide apical branches of the caulocystidia (only $1\ \mu$m wide in *vulgaris*).

Going by the original description, *Mycena idroboi* Sing. (1973: 41) could be mistaken for *M. dispar* on account of its following features: its pileus is fuscous, the lamellae are decurrent and white, the stipe is viscid, the cheilocystidia are embedded in gelatinous matter, pleurocystidia are absent, and the hyphae of the pileipellis are described as diverticulate and subgelatinous. Although a drawing of the microscopic elements would have more readily shown the difference between the two species, Singer's description contains sufficient information to be able to conclude that *M. dispar* and *M. idroboi* are two different species and that the latter may not even be a member of section *Fuliginellae*. 1) The pileipellis of *Mycena idroboi* is said to possess some scattered 'dermatocystidia' resembling the cheilocystidia; 2) these cheilocystidia are 'clavate-ventricose' and both apically and subapically covered with finger-like excrescences, reliably illustrated by Raithelhuber (1984: figs. 93 and 94); 3) no mention was made by Singer of the presence of caulocystidia.

An uncertainty in the description of the present species is that part of the cheilocystidia which has been called 'basal cell', but dense gelatinous matter prevented further investigation, while clamp connections were not observed.

17. MYCENA section INSIGNES Maas G.

Mycena section *Insignes* Maas G. in Proc. K. Ned. Akad. Wet. (Ser. C) **92**: 343. 1989. – Type species *Mycena insignis* A.H. Smith.

Basidiomata medium-sized to large. Pileus viscid, pruinose or glabrous, black-brown, grey-brown, whitish. Context thin. Odour strong in one species, indistinctive or unknown in others. Lamellae tender, arcuate or ascending, broadly adnate, whitish, the edge not gelatinized, concolorous. Stipe hollow, pruinose or puberulous above, glabrescent farther below, viscid, more or less concolorous with the pileus or whitish, generally covered with fibrils at the base.

Basidia clavate, 4-spored, clamped. Spores pip-shaped, smooth, amyloid. Cheilocystidia not embedded in gelatinous matter, fusiform, lageniform, subclavate, clamped, smooth or covered with a few, coarse excrescences. Pleurocystidia similar or absent. Lamellar trama generally but often faintly brownish vinescent in Melzer's reagent. Hyphae of the pileipellis clamped, embedded in gelatinous matter, smooth or diverticulate. Hyphae of the cortical layer of the stipe clamped, embedded in gelatinous matter, smooth or somewhat diverticulate, the terminal cells (caulocystidia) smooth or some-what branched.

Growing on vegetable debris, mostly on fallen conifer needles.

KEY TO THE SPECIES

1. Hyphae of the pileipellis diverticulate.
    2. Spores 3–3.7 μm long. Cheilocystidia smooth: . . . . *M. demissa*
    2. Spores 5.5–7.5 μm long. Cheilocystidia covered with coarse excrescences: . . . *M. surculosa*
1. Hyphae of the pileipellis smooth, covered with a massive gelatinous layer. Cheilocystidia covered with excrescences: . . . . *M. conspersa*

Mycena conspersa* Maas G. and de Meijer, *spec. nov. –* Fig. 30

Basidiomata dispersa. Pileus 2–6 mm latus, 3–4 mm altus, e conico-convexo campanulatus, siccus ut videtur, levis, striatus, glaber, atrobrunneus. Caro tenuis, odore nitroso. Lamellae c. 13 stipitem attingentes, molles, adscendentes, ventricosae, usque ad 1.3 mm latae, adnexae, haud intervenosae, pallide griseae, margine convexae, concolores. Stipes 9–25 × 0.5 mm, cavus, fragilis, aequalis, cylindraceus, levis, siccus ut videtur, totus pruinosus, pallide flavidogriseus, basi subpubescens, e disco albo-fibrilloso natus.

Basidia 18–20 × 7–9 µm, clavata. Sporae 7.0–8.1 × 4.6–5.8 µm, inaequilateraliter ellipsoideae, leves, amyloideae. Cheilocystidia 12.5–19 × 8–11.5 µm, clavata, fibulata, surculis crassis 3.5–13.5 × 1–2 µm munita. Pleurocystidia nulla. Trama lamellarum iodi ope brunneovinescens. Hyphae pileipellis 2.5–8 µm latae, fibulatae, leves, strato crasso gelatinoso obtectae. Hyphae stipitis corticales 2.7–3.5 µm latae, fibulatae, parum gelatinosae, surculis et caulocystidiis plerumque ramosis instructae.

Ramicola.

Holotypus: A.A.R. de Meijer CUB-3199 (No. 991.343–733; L); isotypus: MBM 188502.

Basidiomata scattered. Pileus 2–6 mm across, 3–4 mm high, conical-convex, then campanulate, smooth, translucent-striate, glabrous, appearing dry but actually covered with a gelatinous layer, strongly hygrophanous, the striae black-brown (5F2), between the striae grey (5C1), drying evenly pale grey (4B1). Context thin. Odour distinctly nitrous when broken. Lamellae c. 13 reaching the stipe, tender, ascending, ventricose, up to 1.3 mm broad, adnexed, not intervenose, pale grey (4B1), with convex, concolorous edge. Stipe 9–25 × 0.5 mm, hollow, fragile, equal, terete, smooth, appearing dry, pruinose to subpubescent, especially below, pale yellowish grey (4B3), white above, springing from a small patch of fine, radiating, white fibrils which are not always equally well visible.

Basidia (immature) 18–20 × 7–9 µm, clavate, sterigmata not observed. Spores (possibly immature) 7.0–8.1 × 4.6–5.8 µm (Q = 1.5), broadly pip-shaped, smooth, amyloid. Cheilocystidia 12.5–19 × 8–11.5 µm, forming a sterile band (lamellar edge homogeneous), clavate, clamped, short-stalked, not embedded in gelatinous matter, covered with not very numerous, unevenly spaced, straight to somewhat curved, generally simple, cylindrical or tapering excrescences 3.5–13.5 × 1–2 µm. Pleurocystidia absent. Lamellar trama brownish vinescent in Melzer's reagent. Pileipellis a cutis of a few repent, radiately aligned hyphae which are 2.5–8 µm wide, clamped, smooth, covered with a massive gelatinous layer which in diluted KOH swells to a thickness of c. 60 µm. Hypoderm made up of parallel hyphae with inflated cells up to 35 µm wide. Hyphae of the cortical layer of stipe 2.7–3.5 µm wide, clamped, thinly covered with a gelatinous layer (or possibly most of the gelatinous matter dissolved in warm, diluted KOH), covered with simple to branched, variously shaped excrescences 1.5–18 × 1.5–4.5 µm which, farther down the stipe, pass into much branched caulocystidia – 40 × 2–4.5 µm, with some of the branches drawn out into whip-like points.

---

*Etymology: conspersus, dusted, speckled, referring to the covering of the stipe which shows up clearly especially when dry.

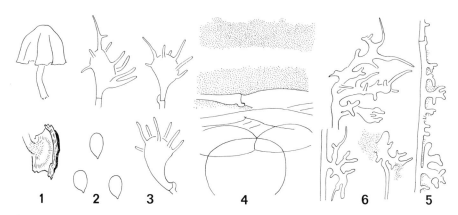

Fig. 30 (1–6) *Mycena conspersa* (de Meijer CUB-3199). – 1. Habitus and basal part of the stipe. – 2. Spores. – 3. Cheilocystidia. – 4. Pileipellis, covered with a thick gelatinous layer. – 5. Hypha of the cortical layer of the stipe. – 6. Caulocystidia.
Fig. 1, × 4; all others, × 700.

Growing on a decayed branch of a dicotyledonous tree, in mixed ombrophilous forest, 250 m alt.

Holotype: '*Mycena conspersa* Maas G. and de Meijer / 17 Jan. 1996 / Paraná: Altonia, forest at Estrada do Amendoim, 2 km N of Jardim Paredão / A.A.R. de Meijer CUB-3199' (No. 991.343–733; L); isotype: MBM 188502.

According to the collector's notes, the pileus and the stipe were taken to be dry, but microscopic investigation incontestably showed the presence of a thick gelatinous layer covering the pileipellis and remnants of gelatinous matter covering some of the caulocystidia. Also, the silvery and somewhat scaly aspect of the surface of both the pileus and stipe in the dried material caused by the contraction of the gelatinous covering is a sure sign of its presence.

The attachment of the stipe to the substratum by a patch of radiating fibrils seems to be uncommon in species of section *Insignes*, and was thus far known only in *Mycena roriduliformis* (Murrill) Dennis, *M. mitis* Maas G. (1992: 469) and in *Mycena calceata* Robich (1996: 245), recently described from Spain. It may not be a feature of great importance and, anyway, it is not equally well developed in some specimens of the holotype.

Equally uncommon in species of the *Insignes* is a strong odour. *Mycena odorifera* (Peck) Sacc. is an exception, having an odour which Peck called subalcaline. *Mycena conspersa* is another example, but with a strong nitrous smell.

Yet another special feature of *M. conspersa* is the strikingly different ornamentation of the cheilocystidia, but compare also those of *M. surculosa*.

Mycena demissa* Maas G. and de Meijer, *spec. nov.* – Fig. 31

Basidiomata dense gregaria vel subfasciculata. Pileus 5–20 mm latus, convexus vel plano-

*Etymology: demissus, sunken, referring to the depressed centre of the pileus.

85

convexus, plerumque centro depressus, sublubricus, levis, substriatus, hygrophanus, griseo-brunneus, centro obscurior. Caro tenuis, odore ignoto. Lamellae 23–26 stipitem attingentes, intervenosae, molles, aequales vel subarcuatae, 1 mm latae, late adnatae, decurrentes, albidae, margine recto vel concavo, concolore. Stipes 20–23 × 1–2 mm, cavus, fragilis, aequalis, cylindraceus, udus lubricus, levis, apice sparse puberulus, deorsum glaber, obscure brunneus.

Basidia 13.5–15 × 4.5–6.5 μm, clavata, 4-sporigera, fibulata. Sporae 3.7–4.5 × 2.3–2.7 μm, inaequilateraliter ellipsoideae, leves, amyloideae. Cheilocystidia 23–38 × 7–15 μm, clavata vel fusiformia, fibulata, levia vel surculis crassis instructa. Pleurocystidia nulla. Trama lamellarum iodi ope vinescens. Hyphae pileipellis 1–1.8 μm latae, fibulatae, in materiam gelatinosam immersae, dense diverticulatae. Hyphae stipitis corticales 1.8–3.5 μm latae, fibulatae, leves, in materiam gelatinosam immersae, caulocystidia 14–60 × 3.5–13.5 μm, versiformia.

Lignicola.

Holotypus: A.A.R. de Meijer PAC-2763 (No. 988.233–070; L); isotypus: MBM 188505.

Basidiomata densely gregarious to subfasciculate. Pileus 5–20 mm across, convex to planoconvex, centrally often more or less depressed, with involute margin, clammy to the touch, lubricous when moist, smooth, vaguely striate, appearing glabrous, hygrophanous, grey-brown (5D4), darker and somewhat more brown at the centre (6E4). Context thin. Odour not recorded. Lamellae 23–26 reaching the stipe, dorsally intervenose, tender, straight to more or less arcuate, 1 mm broad, broadly adnate and decurrent, whitish, with concave, concolorous edge. Stipe 20–23 × 1–2 mm, hollow, fragile, equal, terete, lubricous when moist, smooth, sparsely puberulous near the apex, glabrous farther below, dark brown (7E5), the base attached to the sub-

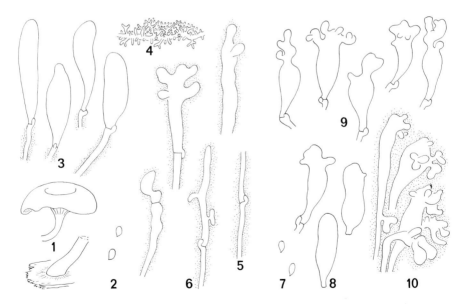

Fig. 31 (1–6) *Mycena demissa* (de Meijer PAC-2763). – 1. Habitus and basal part of the stipe. – 2. Spores. – 3. Cheilocystidia. – 4. Hypha of the pileipellis. – 5. Hypha of the cortical layer of the stipe. – 6. Caulocystidia.

(7–10) *Mycena demissa* (de Meijer MA-3003). – 7. Spores. – 8. Cheilocystidia. – 9. Cheilocystidia near the pileus margin. – 10. Caulocystidia.

Fig. 1, × 3; all others, × 700.

stratum by a small patch of radiating, white fibrils which are not always readily visible.

Basidia (none seen mature) $13.5-15 \times 4.5-6.5 \mu$m, clavate, with four incipient sterigmata, clamped. Spores $3.7-4.5 \times 2.3-2.7 \mu$m (Q = 1.6), pip-shaped, smooth, amyloid. Cheilocystidia $23-38 \times 7-15 \mu$m, forming a sterile band (lamellar edge homogeneous), clavate or somewhat fusiform, clamped, smooth or, particularly towards the pileus margin, more or less branched or covered with coarse, blunt excrescences $2.5-8 \times 2.5-4.5 \mu$m, not embedded in gelatinous matter (although the hyphae from which they arise are). Pleurocystidia absent. Lamellar trama vinescent in Melzer's reagent. Pileipellis an ixocutis of repent, radiately aligned hyphae which are $1-1.8 \mu$m wide, clamped, densely covered with cylindrical, simple to much branched excrescences $1.5-7 \times 0.9-1.5 \mu$m, forming dense masses. Hypoderm made up of parallel, thin-walled hyphae, whose cells are inflated. Hyphae of the cortical layer of the stipe $1.8-3.5 \mu$m wide, clamped, smooth, embedded in gelatinous matter, the caulocystidia $14-60 \times 3.5-13.5 \mu$m, clustered, simple, apically broadened and covered with coarse, blunt excrescences $3.5-9 \times 2.5-4.5 \mu$m, or very much branched, variously shaped, clamped.

On decayed stub of a dicotyledonous tree in dense ombrophilous forest, 10 m alt.

Holotype: '*Mycena demissa* Maas G. and de Meijer / 1 June 1993 / Paraná: Paranaguá, Alexandra, at the crossing of the roads BR-277 and PR 407 / A.A.R. de Meijer PAC-2763' (No. 988.233–070; L); isotype: MBM 188505.

Additional material: '28 Dec. 1994 / Paraná: Morretes, Parque Marumbi, Estação Marumbi / A.A.R. de Meijer MA-3003 / on decayed branch of a dicotyledonous tree in dense ombrophilous forest, 450 m alt.' (No. 990.200–142; L); duplicate: MBM 188506.

'23 April 1995 / Paraná: Curitiba, Parque Municipal do Iguaçu, Zoológico / A.A.R. de Meijer CUf-3058 / among liverworts on decayed dicotyledonous tree in mixed ombrophilous forest, 900 m alt. (No. 990.200–166; L).

The nearest relative of *M. demissa* among the members of section *Insignes* in the South American area is *Mycena roriduliformis* (Murrill) Dennis, and it may even be asked whether the two are different. Both species are lignicolous, their lamellae are arcuate, the stipes spring from a basal patch of radiating fibrils, their spores are practically the same and smaller than those of any other species of the section, and their caulocystidia show certain similarities. But the pileus in *M. roriduliformis* is isabelline (*demissa*: grey-brown to dark brown); 14–17 of its lamellae reach the stipe (*demissa*: 23–26); its stipe is paler concolorous with the pileus (*demissa*: very dark brown). For the time being but not without some doubt *M. roriduliformis* and *M. demissa* are kept separated.

Another species that requires a close look is *Mycena intervenosa* Sing. (1989: 77) which Singer considered related to *M. roriduliformis,* although the pileus of his species was said to be 'haud viscoso' and the stipe 'sicco.' To judge from these features, *M. intervenosa* may not be a member of section *Insignes,* but it cannot be denied that certain elements in its description are not unlike those of *M. demissa.* The difference between the two species is that in *M. demissa* the stipe is dark brown (*intervenosa*: white with fuscidulous base); the hyphae of the pileipellis densely diverticulate (*intervenosa*: smooth); the caulocystidia either coarsely diverticulate or apically branched (*intervenosa*: smooth).

Since several of the South American members of section *Insignes* had been reported to grow on fallen conifer needles, this association was thought to be a special feature of these species. This now turns out not to be the case; compare also *Mycena mitis* Maas G. (1992: 469), *M. corrugans* Maas G. (1992: 471) and *M. calceata* Robich (1996: 245), recently described from Spain.

Mycena surculosa* Maas G. and de Meijer, *spec. nov.* – Fig. 32

Basidiomata dispersa. Pileus 3–5 mm latus, convexus vel campanulatus, siccus, levis, striatus, albus, striis tamen griseis atque centro obscure brunneo. Caro tenuis, odore indistincto. Lamellae 10–12 stipitem attingentes, molles, arcuatae, 0.5–1 mm latae, decurrentes, albae, margine concavae, concolores. Stipes 20–40 × 0.2–0.4 mm, cavus, fragilis, aequalis, cylindraceus, e viscido siccus, levis, sparse puberulus, albus, e disco basali 1 mm lato citrino natus.

Basidia 20–23 × 5.5–7 μm, clavata, 4-sporigera, fibulata. Sporae (5.5–)7.2–8.1 × 3.5–4.5 μm, inaequilateraliter ellipsoideae, leves, amyloideae. Cheilocystidia 15–28 × 3.5–7 μm, clavata vel interdum subcylindracea, fibulata, surculis lateralibus vel apicalibus 3.5–11.5 × 1.5–2.5 μm instructa, haud in materiam gelatinosam immersa. Pleurocystidia nulla. Trama lamellarum iodi ope brunneovinescens. Hyphae pileipellis 0.9–2.5 μm latae, fibulatae, leves, ramis lateralibus brevibusque dense diverticulatis atque materia gelatinosa circumdatis instructa. Hyphae stipitis corticales 1.8–2.5 μm latae, fibulatae, leves, subgelatinosae, cellulae terminales 40–90 × 2.5–9 μm, varie diverticulatae.

Foliicola.

Holotypus: A.A.R. de Meijer MA-2098 (No. 988.233–005; L); isotypus: MBM 190352.

Basidiomata scattered. Pileus 3–5 mm across, convex to campanulate, centrally plane to depressed, dry, smooth, striate, white with dark grey-brown (7E2) to pale grey (7B2) striae and black-brown (7F3) centre. Context thin. Odour indistinct. Lamellae 10–12 reaching the stipe, tender, arcuate, 0.5–1 mm broad, decurrent, white, with concave, concolorous edge. Stipe 20–40 × 0.2–0.4 mm, hollow, fragile, equal, terete, viscid but drying soon, smooth, sparsely puberulous all over, springing from a cushion-like, somewhat cottony, pale citrine basal patch up to 1 mm across which, when dried, at its circumference shows minute, silky fibrils embedded in a transparent gelatinous film.

Basidia (none seen mature) 20–23 × 5.5–7 μm, clavate, with four incipient sterigmata, clamped. Spores (5.5–)7.2–8.1 × 3.5–4.5 μm (Q = 2.0), pip-shaped, smooth, amyloid. Cheilocystidia 15–28 × 3.5–7 μm, forming a sterile band (lamellar edge homogeneous), clavate or less frequently sub-

*Etymology: surculosus, full of sprouts, in reference to the densely diverticulate side-branches of the hyphae of the pileipellis.

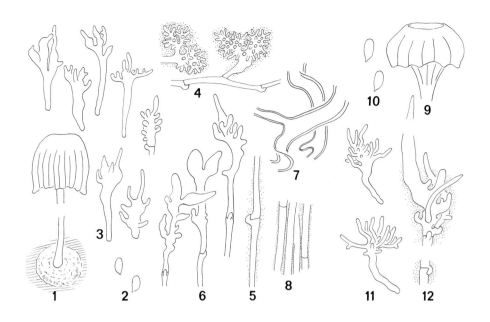

Fig. 32 (1–8) *Mycena surculosa* (de Meijer MA-2098). – 1. Habitus and basal part of the stipe. – 2. Spores. – 3. Cheilocystidia. – 4. Hypha of the pileipellis and terminal cells. – 5. Hypha of the cortical layer of the stipe. – 6. Terminal cells. – 7. Hyphae near the centre of the basal disc. – 8. Hyphae of the edge of the basal disc.
(9–12) *Mycena surculosa* (de Meijer MA-3097). – 9. Habitus. – 10. Spores. – 11. Cheilocystidia. – 12. Terminal cell.
Figs. 1 and 9, × 7.5; all others, × 700.

cylindrical, clamped, apically and sometimes also laterally covered with comparatively few, rather coarse, variously shaped excrescences 3.5–11.5 × 1.5–2.5 μm, not embedded in gelatinous matter. Pleurocystidia absent. Lamellar trama brownish vinescent in Melzer's reagent. Pileipellis a cutis of repent, radiately aligned hyphae which are 0.9–2.5 μm wide, clamped, smooth, much branched and with short, apically 4.5–7 μm broad sidebranches which are densely covered with simple to furcate, cylindrical, somewhat gelatinized excrescences 4.5–6.5 × 1–2 μm. Hypoderm made up of parallel, thin-walled, more or less inflated hyphae. Hyphae of the cortical layer of the stipe 1.8–2.5 μm wide, clamped, smooth, somewhat gelatinized, the terminal cells 40–90 × 2.5–9 μm, covered with coarse excrescences, some of which may reach 50 μm in length. Hyphae of the basal patch around the point of insertion of the stipe up to 8 μm wide, tightly interwoven, much branched and contorted, thick-walled, clampless; those at the circumference of the patch 2.5–4.5 μm wide, parallel, unbranched, embedded in gelatinous matter.

On dead, coriaceous leaves of a dicotyledonous tree in dense ombrophilous forest, 1000 m alt.

Holotype: '*Mycena surculosa* Maas G. and de Meijer / 19 Jan. 1992 /

Paraná: Quatro Barras, Parque Marumbi, Itupava track / A.A.R. de Meijer MA-2098' (No. 988.233–005; L); isotype: MBM 190352.

Additional material: '27 June 1995 / Paraná: Morretes, Porto de Cima, Parque Marumbi, near Nhundiaquara River / A.A.R. de Meijer MA-3097 / on dead leaves of a dicotyledonous tree in dense ombrophilous forest, 20 m alt.' (No. 991.343–788; L); duplicate: MBM 190353.

In the members of section *Insignes*, the amount of gelatinous matter covering the cortical hyphae of the stipe may vary considerably. The hyphae may be completely covered by a gelatinous layer, as in *M. insignis* A.H. Smith, but in *M. pseudoclavicularis* A.H. Smith (Maas Geesteranus, 1992: 376, 380) the hyphae may be locally devoid of any covering. In the present species, the cortical hyphae in the upper part of the stipe appear to be perfectly dry, whereas those near the base of the stipe show some scattered gelatinous accumulations.

Mycena surculosa seems most closely related with *M. insignis*, with which it has arcuate lamellae and strangely shaped and ornamented cheilocystidia and terminal cells of the cortical hyphae of the stipe in common. It shares the possession of a basal patch to the stipe with *M. roriduliformis* (Murrill) Dennis.

18. MYCENA section EUSPEIREAE Maas G.

Mycena sect. *Euspeireae* Maas G. in Proc. K. Ned. Akad. Wet. (Ser. C) **92**: 355. 1989. – Type species: *Mycena euspeirea* (Berk. and Curt.) Sacc.

Basidiomata medium-sized. Pileus viscid to lubricous, covered with a gelatinous, separable pellicle, white or isabelline to grey-brown. Context thin. Odour not recorded or absent. Lamellae tender, ascending or arcuate, adnate or decurrent, white or darkening, the edge not gelatinized (not separable as a tough thread). Stipe viscid, puberulous or appearing glabrous, white or turning grey-brown, the base covered with fibrils.

Basidia 4-spored, clamped. Spores pip-shaped, smooth, amyloid. Cheilocystidia not embedded in gelatinous matter, generally fusiform, clamped, smooth or with few excrescences. Pleurocystidia similar. Lamellar trama vinescent in Melzer's reagent. Hyphae of the pileipellis clamped, embedded in gelatinous matter, smooth or diverticulate. Hyphae of the cortical layer of the stipe clamped, embedded in gelatinous matter, smooth, the terminal cells smooth or branched and/or diverticulate.

Lignicolous.

Mycena tapeina* Maas G. and de Meijer, *spec. nov.* – Fig. 33

Basidiomata caespitosa. Pileus 8–18 mm latus, planoconvexus, centro plerumque depressus, umidus lubricus, levis, striatus, pallide griseoflavus. Caro tenuis, odore nullo. Lamellae c. 18

*Etymology: ταπεινός, low lying, referring to the hollowed centre of the pileus.

stipitem attingentes, sublentae, arcuatae, usque ad 2 mm latae, decurrentes, albae, margine concavo, albo. Stipes 30–70 × 1.2–2.2 mm, cavus, fragilis, aequalis, cylindraceus, umidus viscidus, levis, quasi glaber, albus, deorsum pallide griseobrunneus flavidotinctus, basi albotomentosus.

Basidia c. 18 × 4.5 μm, clavata, 4-sporigera, fibulata. Sporae 3.5–5.3 × 2.4–2.7 μm, inaequilateraliter ellipsoideae, leves, amyloideae. Cheilocystidia 30–95 × 4.5–8 × 2.5–4.5 μm, fusiformia vel subcylindracea, fibulata, levia, apice raro surculis praedita. Pleurocystidia similia. Trama lamellarum iodi ope brunneovinescens. Hyphae pileipellis 1.8–2.7 μm latae, fibulatae, in materiam gelatinosam immersae, diverticulatae. Hyphae stipitis corticales 1.8–2.2 μm latae, fibulatae, in materiam gelatinosam immersae, leves, cellulae terminales 16–35 × 4.5–5.5 μm, clavatae.

Lignicola.

Holotypus: A.A.R. de Meijer PAC-2774 (No. 988.233–051; L); isotypus: MBM 190354.

Basidiomata cespitose. Pileus 8–18 mm across, planoconvex, frequently with depressed centre, flattening with age, lubricous when wet, smooth, striate, the centre and striae pale greyish yellowish (4B3), between the striae white, drying white, the margin finally often revolute. Context thin. Odour absent. Lamellae c. 18 reaching the stipe, rather toughish when dried, arcuate, up to 2 mm broad, decurrent, pure white when fresh, somewhat waxy when dried, with concave, white edge. Stipe 30–70 × 1.2–2.2 mm, hollow, fragile, equal, terete, somewhat viscid when wet, smooth, appearing glabrous, white, pale grey-brown (5B2) in the lower part, the base covered with a fine, white tomentum.

Basidia (none seen mature) c. 18 x4.5 μm, clavate, with four incipient sterigmata, clamped. Spores 3.5–5.3 × 2.4–2.7 μm (Q = 2.2), pip-shaped, smooth, amyloid. Cheilocystidia sparse, 30–95 × 4.5–8 × 2.5–4.5 μm, fusiform or, less frequently, subcylindrical, clamped, generally long-stalked to very long-stalked, smooth, occasionally apically with one or two excrescences, the projecting part not embedded in gelatinous matter. Pleurocystidia similar. Lamellar trama brownish vinescent in Melzer's reagent. Pileipellis an ixocutis of repent, radiately aligned hyphae which are 1.8–2.7 μm wide, clamped, covered with hardly distinguishable, simple to bran-

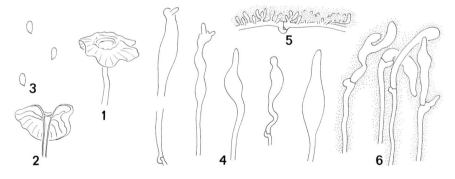

Fig. 33 (1–6) *Mycena tapeina* (de Meijer PAC-2774). – 1. Habitus. – 2. Section of pileus. – 3. Spores. – 4. Cheilocystidia. – 5. Hypha of the pileipellis. – 6. Hyphae of the cortical layer of the stipe and terminal cells.

Fig. 1, × 1.5; all others, × 700.

ched, cylindrical, thin-walled excrescences $3.5-6.5 \times 2.2-2.7$ μm. Hypoderm consisting of parallel hyphae with inflated cells up to 30 μm broad. Hyphae of the cortical layer of the stipe $1.8-2.2$ μm wide, clamped, embedded in gelatinous matter, smooth, the terminal cells $16-35 \times 4.5-5.5$ μm, clavate, more or less curved.

On the decayed trunk of a dicotyledonous tree in dense ombrophilous forest, 10 m alt.

Holotype: '*Mycena tapeina* Maas G. and de Meijer / 1 June 1993 / Paraná: Paranaguá, Alexandra / A.A.R. de Meijer PAC-2774' (No. 988.233–051; L); isotype: MBM 190354.

Of the two members of section *Euspeireae* thus far known – *M. euspeirea* (Berk. and Curt.) Sacc. and *M. glutinosa* Beardslee –, the pileus was described (Maas Geesteranus, 1993: 388, 390) as being covered by a gelatinous separable pellicle. This was not noticed in the present species when fresh, although microscopically the hyphae of the pileipellis are clearly seen to be embedded in gelatinous matter.

The three species have several characters in common, and one of these is the slight width of the spores.

19. MYCENA sect. CAESPITOSAE (A.H. Smith ex Sing.) Maas G.

Mycena sect. *Caespitosae* A.H. Smith, N. Am. Spec. *Mycena*: 41, 401, 406. 1947 (not val. publ.: no Latin descr.). – *Mycena* subsect. *Caespitosae* (A.H. Smith) Sing. in Lilloa **22**: 362. ('1949') 1951 (not val. publ.: no Latin descr.). – *Mycena* subsect. *Caespitosae* A.H. Smith ex Sing. in Sydowia **15**: 65. 1962. – *Mycena* sect. *Caespitosae* (A.H. Smith ex Sing.) Maas G. in Proc. K. Ned. Akad. Wet. (Ser. C) **83**: 407. 1980. – Holotype: *Mycena texensis* A.H. Smith.
For further synonymy, see Maas Geesteranus, l.c.

Basidiomata medium-sized to large, densely cespitose. Pileus covered with a gelatinous, separable pellicle, viscid, pruinose or glabrous, white to orange or more brownish orange, with concolorous or dark centre. Context pliant. Odour pleasant, subfarinaceous or unknown. Taste indistinctive or unknown. Lamellae arcuate or ascending, adnate, whitish, yellow or pale orange, the edge gelatinized (or not?), concolorous or deep orange. Stipe hollow, pruinose to pulverulent above, viscid, yellow or, at least partly, orange, covered with fibrils at the base.

Basidia clavate, 4-spored, clamped. Spores pip-shaped, smooth, amyloid. Cheilocystidia embedded in gelatinous matter (or not?), fusiform to clavate or subcylindrical, smooth or apically lobed or with a few coarse excrescences. Pleurocystidia scattered or absent. Lamellar trama vinescent in Melzer's reagent. Hyphae of the pileipellis clamped, embedded in gelatinous matter, diverticulate. Hyphae of the cortical layer of the stipe clamped, embedded in gelatinous matter, smooth, the terminal cells (caulocystidia) coarsely diverticulate to smooth.

Lignicolous.

Mycena paranaensis* Maas G. and de Meijer, *spec. nov.* – Figs. 34 and 35

Basidiomata fasciculata. Pileus 7–26 mm latus, primo convexus, interdum subumbonatus, deinde subapplanatus, centro depressus, viscosus, levis, striatus, glaber, hygrophanus, e obscure brunneo-aurantiaco vel brunneo pallidior, exsiccatus albus. Caro albidus, odore fungoideo. Lamellae 24–26 stipitem attingentes, flexibiles, arcuatae, usque ad 3 mm latae, late adnatae, decurrentes, flavae, margine viscoso, concavo, aurantiaco. Stipes 15–90 × 1.2–3 mm, cavus, firmus, aequalis, cylindraceus, viscosus, levis, superne pallide flavus, inferne brunneus, basi dense hirsutus.

Basidia 27–30 × 7–9 μm clavata, 4-sporigera, fibulata. Sporae 8.1–9.8 × 4.7–5.8 μm, inaequilateraliter ellipsoideae, leves, amyloideae. Cheilocystidia 22.5–48 × 6.5–15 × 1.5–4.5 μm, in materiam gelatinosam immersa, fusiformia, fibulata, sucum flavobrunneolum continentia, levia vel sursum furcata. Pleurocystidia similia, 35–50 × 11–12.5 μm. Trama lamellarum iodi ope tenuiter brunneo-vinescens. Hyphae pileipellis 1.8–4.5 μm latae, fibulatae, in materiam gelatinosam immersae, leves, cellulae terminales 75–120 × 4.5–7 μm, leves. Hyphae stipitis corticales 1.8–2.5 μm latae, fibulatae, in materiam gelatinosam immersae, leves, caulocystidia usque ad 13.5 μm lata, valde ramosa.

Lignicola.

Holotypus: A.A.R. de Meijer CUA-315 (No. 990.200–117; L); isotypus: MBM 190330.

Basidiomata fasciculate. Pileus 7–26 mm across, at first convex with strongly involute margin, occasionally somewhat umbonate, flattening with age, becoming plano-convex, sometimes centrally depressed, viscid, with a gelatinous, separable pellicle, smooth, translucent-striate, glabrous, hygrophanous, when very young brownish orange to brown (6C8–6D8), later with centre and striae fairly pale brownish orange (5B6–5B8) to more yellowish brown (5D6–5D8), between the striae maize-yellow (4A6), drying white. Context pale greyish, drying whitish. Odour fungoid, taste mild. Lamellae 24–26 reaching the stipe, pliant-tough, arcuate, up to 3 mm broad, broadly adnate, far decurrent, pale yellow to maize-yellow (4A6), becoming somewhat paler with age, with concave, viscid, orange-yellow edge. Stipe 15–90 x1.2–3 mm, hollow, firm, equal, terete, viscid, smooth, appearing tomentose after having been dried, pale yellow above (near 3A4 – 4A5), brown below (5D6–6D6), paler brownish-punctate (5C5), the base densely white-hirsute.

Basidia 27–30 × 7–9 μm, clavate, 4-spored, clamped, with sterigmata up to 7 μm long. Spores 8.1–9.8 × 4.7–5.8 μm (Q = 1.7), pip-shaped, smooth, amyloid. Cheilocystidia 22.5–48 × 6.5–15 × 1.5–4.5 μm, forming a sterile band (lamellar edge homogeneous), embedded in gelatinous matter, fusiform, subclavate, clamped, with yellowish brownish contents, smooth, apically with one or two necks, occasionally with the neck more or less torulose. Pleurocystidia similar, 35–50 × 11–12.5 μm. Lamellar trama brownish vinescent in Melzer's reagent. Pileipellis an ixocutis of repent, radiately aligned hyphae which are 1.8–4.5 μm wide, clamped, smooth, terminal cells 75–120 × 4.5–7 μm, smooth or with rare excrescences. Hyphae of the cortical layer of the stipe 1.8–2.5 μm wide, clamped, embedded in gelatinous matter, mostly smooth, in part giving rise to equally narrow, branched terminal cells, in part to very dense clusters of up to 13.5 μm broad, thick-walled (2 μm), profusely

*Etymology: specific epithet formed after the State of Paraná.

branched caulocystidia with simple to furcate excrescences 2.5–13.5 × 2.5–4.5 μm, all with yellowish brownish contents.

On dead, horizontal trunk of a dicotyledonous tree in seasonal semi-deciduous alluvial forest, 870 m alt.

Holotype: '*Mycena paranaensis* Maas G. and de Meijer / 24 Dec. 1979 / Paraná: Curitiba, Uberaba Distr., Reserva Biológica Cambuí / A.A.R. de Meijer cua-315' (No. 990.200–117; L); isotype: мвм 190330.

Additional material: '23 April 1995 / Paraná: Curitiba, Parque Municipal do Iguaçu, Zoologico / A.A.R. de Meijer cuf-3057 / among moss on decayed trunk of a dicotyledonous tree in mixed ombrophilous forest, 900 m alt.' (No. 990.200–180; L); duplicate: мвм 190331.

The basidiomes of the second collection were collected in a more advanced state of maturity than those of the type. The colour of the pilei appeared to have lost its orange component and matched the colour codes 5C4–5D4. The lamellae proved to be much farther decurrent down the stipe with decidedly orange edges, whereas the lamellar edges in the type collection were found to be for the greater part concolorous with the sides.

Of the two North American relatives, *Mycena texensis* A.H. Smith and *M. leaiana* (Berk.) Sacc., the former shares the arcuate lamellae with *M. paranaensis,* but is otherwise different in its much smaller spores, the different shape of the cheilocystidia, and the hyphae of the pileipellis. *Mycena leaiana* can be separated from *M. paranaensis* by its bright orange pileus,

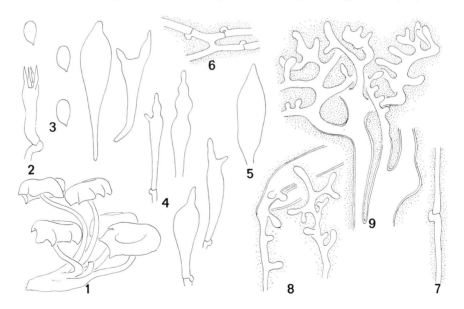

Fig. 34 (1–9) *Mycena paranaensis* (de Meijer cua-315). – 1. Habitus. – 2. Basidium. – 3. Spores. – 4. Cheilocystidia. – 5. Pleurocystidium. – 6. Hypha of the pileipellis. – 7. Hypha of the cortical layer of the stipe. – 8. Terminal cells (caulocystidia). – 9. Part of a cluster of caulocystidia.
Fig. 1, × 2; all others, × 700.

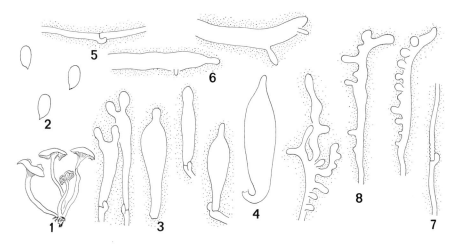

Fig. 35 (1–8) *Mycena paranaensis* (de Meijer cuf-3057). – 1. Habitus. – 2. Spores. – 3. Cheilocystidia. – 4. Pleurocystidium. – 5. Hypha of the pileipellis. – 6. Terminal cells of hyphae of the pileipellis. – 7. Hypha of the cortical layer of the stipe. – 8. Terminal cells of hyphae of the cortical layer of the stipe. Fig. 1, × 0.5; all others, × 700.

non-arcuate lamellae, and ornamented hyphae of the pileipellis and terminal cells.

Neither in *Mycena paranaensis* nor in the two North American species attention seems to have been given to the question whether the lamellar edge of fresh material can be detached as an elastic thread.

20. MYCENA section RORIDAE Kühn.

Mycena section *Roridae* Kühn. in Bull. bimens. Soc. linn. Lyon **10**: 125. 1931. – *Mycena* subsect. *Roridae* (Kühn.) Sing. in Lilloa **22**: 362. ('1949') 1951; Agar. mod. taxon., 3rd ed.: 394. 1975. – Type species: *Mycena rorida* (Fr.: Fr.) Quél.

  Mycena stirps *Rorida* A.H. Smith, N. Am. spec. *Mycena*: 41. 1947 (nomen nudum). – Type species: *Mycena rorida*.

Basidiomata medium-sized. Pileus dry, pruinose, variously coloured in shades of grey-brown. Context thin, pallid to pale brownish. Odour not distinctive. Lamellae tender, arcuate, decurrent, white to pallid, with concolorous edge. Stipe hollow, fragile, terete, thickly covered with a transparent slimy layer, whitish above, brownish below.

Basidia clavate, mostly 4-spored, clamped. Spores pip-shaped, smooth, amyloid. Cheilocystidia generally slender-clavate, clamped, not embedded in gelatinous matter, apically usually broadly rounded. Pleurocystidia absent. Lamellar trama vinescent in Melzer's reagent. Pileipellis hymeniform, generally made up of erect, inflated, smooth cells, not embedded in gelatinous matter. Hyphae of the cortical layer of the stipe clamped, smooth, embedded in gelatinous matter. Caulocystidia slender-clavate, usually smooth.

Growing on vegetable debris.

Singer (1975: 394), regarding section *Roridae* as a subsection, stated that it 'is very isolated among the viscid Mycenae, and it appears to be close to *Hydropus*.' He did not repeat this statement in a later edition (1986: 412).

As it seems, in a doctoral study at one of the German universities, the present section has been raised to generic level, and rightly so. Unfortunately, it is not known whether this study has been published.

KEY TO THE SPECIES

1. Cheilocystidia slender-clavate. Pleurocystidia absent.
   2. Pileus dark brown. Stipe grey-brown. Caulocystidia apically much swollen, broadly rounded: . . . . *M. fuscororida*
   2. Pileus white. Stipe white. Caulocystidia apically moderately swollen, not broadly rounded:
   . . . . *M. albororida*
1. Cheilocystidia broadly utriform. Pleurocystidia present. Caulocystidia apically much swollen, broadly rounded:

   . . . . *M. ornatororida*

Mycena albororida Maas G. and de Meijer, *spec. nov.* – Fig. 36

Basidiomata dispersa. Pileus 1–6 mm latus, hemisphaericus vel convexus, siccus, levis, striatus, glaber, albus, centro pallide griseoflavus. Caro tenuis, odore nullo. Lamellae c. 15 stipitem attingentes, molles, subarcuatae, usque ad 1.2 mm latae, paulo decurrentes, albae, margine concolores. Stipes 8–17 × 0.2–0.8 mm, cavus, fragilis, aequalis, cylindraceus, forte glutinosus, levis, albus, e disco basali vitreo 1 mm lato natus.

Basidia 16–18 × 6.5 μm, clavata, 4-sporigera, fibulata, sterigmatibus 3.5 μm longis munita. Sporae 8.1–9.6 × 4.2–5.4 μm, inaequilateraliter ellipsoideae, leves, amyloideae. Cheilocystidia 23–36 × 5.5–10 μm, clavata vel subcylindracea, apice interdum capitata, fibulata, haud in materiam gelatinosam immersa, interne oleosa. Pleurocystidia nulla. Trama lamellarum iodi ope brunneovinescens. Pileipellis e cellulis 22.5–30 × 13.5–16 μm, rectis, clavatis, levibus, haud in materiam gelatinosam immersis formata. Hyphae stipitis corticales 1.8–2.5 μm latae, fibulatae, leves, in materiam gelatinosam immersae, cellulae terminales 30–45 × 2.5–7 μm, simplices vel ramosae, subclavatae vel cylindraceae.

Foliicola.

Holotypus: A.A.R. de Meijer MA-1675 (No. 988.233–007; L); isotypus: MBM 188487.

Basidiomata scattered. Pileus 1–6 mm across, hemispherical to convex, depressed when dried, dry, smooth, striate, glabrous, white with pale greyish yellow centre. Context thin. Odour none. Lamellae c. 15 reaching the stipe, tender, somewhat arcuate, up to 1.2 mm broad, slightly decurrent, white, with concolorous edge. Stipe 8–17 × 0.2–0.8 mm, hollow, fragile, equal, terete, thickly covered with a transparent slimy layer, smooth, pure white, springing from a basal disc which in dried specimens is 1 mm across, transparent and very thin.

Basidia (none seen mature) 16–18 × 6.5 μm, clavate, 4-spored, clamped, with sterigmata 3.5 μm long. Spores 8.1–9.6 × 4.2–5.4 μm (Q = 1.8), pip-shaped, smooth, amyloid. Cheilocystidia 23–36 × 5.5–10 μm, forming a dense, sterile band (lamellar edge homogeneous), slender-clavate to subcylindrical, clamped, not immersed in gelatinous matter, rarely furcate or apically lobed, apically broadly rounded to more or less capitate, with oily

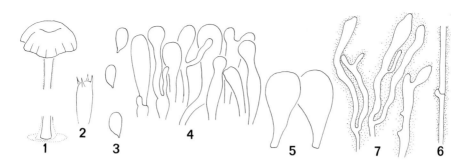

Fig. 36 (1–7) *Mycena albororida* (de Meijer MA-1675). – 1. Habitus and basal part of the stipe. – 2. Basidium. – 3. Spores. – 4. Cheilocystidia. – 5. Erect cells of the pileipellis. – 6. Hypha of the cortical layer of the stipe. – 7. Terminal cells (caulocystidia).
Fig. 1, × 10; all others, × 700.

contents. Pleurocystidia absent. Lamellar trama brownish vinescent in Melzer's reagent. Pileipellis hymeniform, made up of erect, broadly clavate, smooth cells 22.5–30 × 13.5–16 μm, not immersed in gelatinous matter. Hyphae of the cortical layer of the stipe 1.8–2.5 μm wide, clamped, smooth, embedded in gelatinous matter, the terminal cells 30–45 × 2.5–7 μm, simple to more or less branched, subclavate to cylindrical.

On dead leaves and decayed twig of a dicotyledonous tree in dense ombrophilous forest, 950 m alt.

Holotype: '*Mycena albororida* Maas G. and de Meijer / 2 May 1990 / Paraná: Piraquara, Parque Marumbi, Mananciais da Serra, / A.A.R. de Meijer MA-1675' (No. 988.233–007; L); isotype: MBM 188487.

This relative of *Mycena rorida* (Fr.: Fr.) Quél. earns the prefix *albo* on account of its pure white stipe, but a more dependable way to distinguish the two species is by comparing their cheilocystidia.

Horak (1978: 20–29) published a paper enumerating the species of *Mycena* sect. *Roridae* Kühn. then known from the Southern Hemisphere. Two of these, *M. lamprospora* (Corner) Horak and *M. irritans* Horak, have cheilocystidia which (in their author's drawing) look rather similar to those of *M. albororida*. To judge from the original description by Corner (1950: 427, as *M. rorida* var. *lamprospora*), *M. lamprospora* differs from *M. albororida* in the colour of the pileus ('pruinose with minute fuscous brown particles scattered toward the white margin, crowded over the deeply colored disc') and the irregularly lobed outline of several of the cheilocystidia (Corner's figure 3, on the left). *Mycena irritans* has a stipe which is white above, brown below; smaller spores (6–8 × 3–4 μm); spheropedunculate rather than clavate cells of the pileipellis.

A feature not mentioned in the description of any of the species of section *Roridae* is the film-like, transparent disc at the base of the stipe, so obvious in dried material of the present species.

Mycena fuscororida Maas G. and de Meijer, *spec. nov.* – Fig. 37

Basidiomata dispersa. Pileus 2–5 mm latus, e hemisphaerico convexus, centro interdum depressus, siccus, subsulcatus, striatus, glaber, hygrophanus, e fusco griseobrunneus. Caro tenuis, odore indistincto. Lamellae 10–18 stipitem attingentes, molles, arcuatae, c. 1 mm latae, decurrentes, albae, margine concolores. Stipes 4–10 × 0.5 mm, cavus, fragilis, aequalis, cylindraceus, basi latior (0.9 mm), dense pituitosus, levis, griseobrunneus, superne griseo-albus, e disco basali parvo vitreoque natus.

Basidia c. 25 × 7–9 μm, clavata, 4-sporigera, fibulata. Sporae 9.0–9.8 × 4.6–5.4 μm, inaequilateraliter ellipsoideae, leves, amyloideae. Cheilocystidia 40–58 × 4.5–5.5 × 7–11 μm, graciliter clavata, fibulata, haud in materiam gelatinosam immersa. Pleurocystidia nulla. Trama lamellarum iodi ope brunneovinescens. Pileipellis e cellulis levibus diversi generis formata: a) 40–65 × 8–18 μm, versiformibus, fibulatis; b) 22–35 × 11.5–14.5 μm, clavatis, fibulatis. Hyphae stipitis corticales 1.8–3.5 μm latae, fibulatae, leves, in materiam gelatinosam immersae, caulocystidia 24–33 × 4.5–10 μm, graciliter clavata.

Ramicola.

Holotypus: A.A.R. de Meijer MA-3048 (No. 990.200–054;L); notulae: MBM 188519.

Basidiomata scattered. Pileus 2–5 mm across, at first hemispherical, later convex, centrally sometimes slightly depressed, dry, smooth to sulcate, translucent-striate, glabrous, hygrophanous, at first very dark brown (fuscous; 5–6E3 to 5–6F3), gradually the centre and striae turning grey-brown (5D3–5E3), between the striae pale yellowish brown. Context thin. Odour indistinct. Lamellae 10–18 reaching the stipe, tender, arcuate, c. 1 mm broad, decurrent, white, with concave, concolorous edge. Stipe 4–10 × 0.5 mm, hollow, fragile, equal, terete, at the base broadened up to 0.9 mm, thickly covered with a transparent slimy layer, smooth, grey-brown (5D3), towards

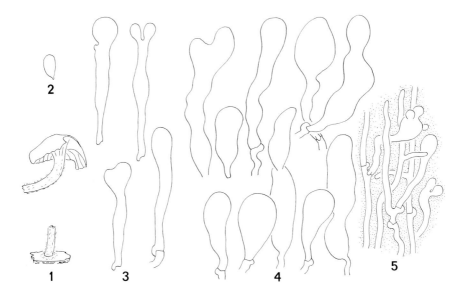

Fig. 37 (1–5) *Mycena fuscororida* (de Meijer MA-3048). – 1. Habitus and basal part of the stipe. – 2. Spore. – 3. Cheilocystidia. – 4. Erect cells of the pileipellis. – 5. Hyphae of the cortical layer of the stipe and caulocystidia.
Fig. 1, × 4; all others, × 700.

the apex greyish white, springing from an unobtrusive basal disc which in dried specimens is less than 1 mm across, transparent and very thin.

Basidia (none seen mature) c. 25 × 7–9 μm, clavate, 4-spored, clamped. Spores (very few seen) 9.0–9.8 × 4.6–5.4 μm (Q = 1.9), pip-shaped, smooth, amyloid. Cheilocystidia 40–58 × 4.5–5.5 × 7–11 μm, forming a dense, sterile band (lamellar edge homogeneous), slender-clavate, clamped, not embedded in gelatinous matter, apically more or less pronouncedly capitate, broadly rounded, rarely furcate. Pleurocystidia absent. Lamellar trama brownish vinescent in Melzer's reagent. Pileipellis hymeniform, made up of two kinds of erect, smooth cells, not embedded in gelatinous matter: a) 40–65 × 8–18 μm, subcylindrical, subclavate, sublageniform, clamped, straight to more or less curved, usually wavy in outline; b) 22–35 × 11.5–14.5 μm, clavate, clamped. Hyphae of the cortical layer of the stipe 1.8–3.5 μm wide, clamped, smooth, embedded in gelatinous matter (which readily dissolves in warm, diluted KOH), the caulocystidia 24–33 × 4.5–10 μm, slender-clavate, clamped, apically more or less pronouncedly capitate, sometimes with a few globose excrescences, more rarely furcate.

On dead twigs of a dicotyledonous tree in dense ombrophilous forest, 1200 m alt.

Holotype: 'Mycena fuscororida Maas G. and de Meijer / 16 March 1995 / Paraná: Quatro Barras, Parque Marumbi, Morro Sete / A.A.R. de Meijer MA-3048' (No. 990.200–054; L); notes and drawings: MBM 188519.

Mycena fuscororida shares the strikingly slender-clavate shape of its cheilocystidia with two other species of the rorida-group, M. austrororida Sing. and M. irritans Horak. The former, however, has yet another kind of cheilocystidia (Singer, 1959: 393, fig. 4) which are more broadly clavate, while its caulocystidia are utterly different from those of M. fuscororida. The second species, M. irritans, differs from M. fuscororida in its narrower spores (3–4 μm) and the different construction of the pileipellis.

The two kinds of cells of the pileipellis depicted in Fig. 2F might imply that Mycena lamprospora (Corner) Horak (1978: 23), described from material collected in Papua New Guinea, and M. fuscororida are closely related if not the same species. Reexamination of the Papuan material would no doubt give an answer to this question, but does not seem pertinent to the matter in hand. According to the original description and drawings given, the cheilocystidia and caulocystidia of Mycena rorida var. lamprospora Corner (1950: 427, fig. 3) are differently shaped from those in Horak's publication and, in any case, it is also beyond any doubt that the true M. rorida var. lamprospora and M. fuscororida are two separate taxa.

Mycena ornatororida* Maas G. and de Meijer, spec. nov. – Fig. 38

Basidiomata dispersa. Pileus 5–12 mm latus, e convexo applanatus, siccus, subsulcatus, striatus,

---

*Etymology: ornatus, adorned, in reference to the white lamellae having a dark brown edge.

glaber, haud hygrophanus, obscure brunneus, margine recurvatus. Caro tenuis, odore tenui. Lamellae 10–12 stipitem attingentes, molles, arcuatae, usque ad 3 mm latae, decurrentes, nonnullae furcatae, albae, margine obscure brunneae. Stipes 15–27 × 0.7–1.3 mm, cavus, fragilis, aequalis, cylindraceus, pituitosus, levis, albus, basi defractus.

Basidia 20–23 × 7–9 μm, clavata, 4-sporigera, fibulata, sterigmatibus 4.5 μm longis instructa. Sporae 8.1–11.5 × 3.8–4.5 μm, subcylindraceae, leves, amyloideae. Cheilocystidia 27–30 × 11–14.5 × 4.5–6.5 μm, late utriformia vel clavata, fibulata, haud in materiam gelatinosam immersa, interne brunneola. Pleurocystidia similia. Trama lamellarum iodi ope haud vinescens. Pileipellis e cellulis 22.5–40 × 12.5–20 μm, fibulatis, rectis, ellipsoideis vel spheropedunculatis, levibus, haud in materiam gelatinosam immersis formata. Hyphae stipitis corticales 1.8–2.5 μm latae, fibulatae, leves, in materiam gelatinosam immersae, caulocystidia 10–27 × 6.5–11 μm, sparsa, clavata vel ellipsoidea.

Lignicola.

Holotypus: A.A.R. de Meijer cua-389 (No. 990.200–147; L); notulae: мвм 190329.

Basidiomata scattered. Pileus 5–12 mm across, at first convex, then flattened, dry, shallowly sulcate, translucent-striate, glabrous, not hygrophanous, dark brown (Munsell 10YR3/3), somewhat darker than 6E4), with slightly recurved margin. Context thin, white when dry. Odour rather faint. Lamellae 10–12 reaching the stipe, tender, arcuate, up to 3 mm broad, far decurrent on the stipe, some furcate, white but with dark brown edge. Stipe 15–27 × 0.7–1.3 mm, hollow, fragile, equal, terete, thickly covered with a transparent slimy layer, smooth, white, broken off at the base.

Basidia 20–23 × 7–9 μm, clavate, 4-spored, clamped, with sterigmata 4.5 μm long. Spores 8.1–11.5 × 3.8–4.5 μm (Q = 2.3), almost cylindrical, smooth, weakly amyloid. Cheilocystidia 27–30 × 11–14.5 × 4.5–6.5 μm, broadly utriform, more rarely clavate, clamped, long- or short-stalked, not immersed in gelatinous matter, filled with brownish sap. Pleurocystidia similar, presumably colourless. Lamellar trama not vinescent in Melzer's reagent.

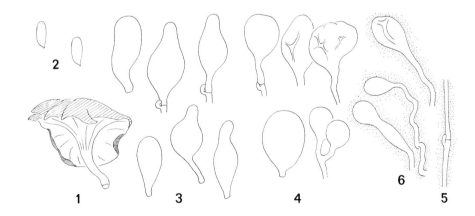

Fig. 38 (1–6) *Mycena ornatororida* (de Meijer cua-389). – 1. Habitus. – 2. Spores. – 3. Cheilocystidia. – 4. Erect cells of the pileipellis. – 5. Hypha of the cortical layer of the stipe. – 6. Caulocystidia. Fig. 1, × 5; all others, × 700.

Pileipellis hymeniform, made up of erect, ellipsoid to spheropedunculate, long- or short-stalked, thin-walled, smooth cells 22.5–40 × 12.5–20 µm, not immersed in gelatinous matter, filled with brownish sap. Hyphae of the cortical layer of the stipe 1.8–2.5 µm wide, clamped, smooth, embedded in gelatinous matter, caulocystidia very scarce, 10–27 × 6.5–11 µm, clavate or ellipsoid, thin-walled.

Found on very much decayed wood of a dicotyledonous tree in seasonal semi-deciduous alluvial forest, 870 m alt.

Holotype: '*Mycena ornatororida* Maas G. and de Meijer / 14 March 1980 / Paraná: Curitiba, Uberaba Distr., Reserva Biológica Cambuí / A.A.R. de Meijer CUa-389' (No. 990.200–147; L); notes and drawings: MBM 190329.

Of the species of section *Roridae* described by Horak from the Southern Hemisphere (1978) there is none which has white lamellae with a dark brown edge. There is also no other species of the section which combines broadly utriform cheilocystidia and clavate caulocystidia. Finally, the presence of pleurocystidia is unknown in the other species. A character which the present species shares with *M. rorida* (Fr.: Fr.) Quél. and *M. austrororida* Sing. is the length of the spores (up to 12 µm), but the spores of *austrororida* are almost twice as broad as those of *M. ornatororida*, while the cheilocystidia of both *rorida* and *austrororida* are widely different from those of *ornatororida*. The disposition of the present species in section *Roridae*, therefore, is not free from doubt.

21. MYCENA sect. **Cerasinae** Maas G. and de Meijer, *sect. nov.*

Basidiomata statura magna. Pileus purpureus. Caro odore grato. Lamellae molles, obscure purpureae. Stipes fragilis, glaber, purpureus.
    Basidia clavata, fibulata. Sporae inaequilateraliter ellipsoideae, leves, amyloideae. Cheilocystidia subutriformia vel clavata, fibulata, levia. Pleurocystidia nulla. Trama lamellarum iodi ope brunneovinescens. Hyphae pileipellis fibulatae, diverticulatae. Hyphae stipitis corticales fibulatae, maxima ex parte leves, cellulae terminales perrarae.
    Ad sarmenta.
    Species typica: *Mycena cerasina*.

Section *Cerasinae* may be placed near section *Calodontes* (Fr. ex Berk.) Quél. (Maas Geesteranus, 1989: 480).

Mycena cerasina* Maas G. and de Meijer, *spec. nov.* – Fig. 39 (1–6)

Basidiomata gregaria. Pileus 26–30 mm latus, 20–27 mm altus, conicus vel campanulatus, siccus, sulcatus, striatus, centro perforatus, hygrophanus, e purpureo pallide griseoroseus. Caro usque ad 1.8 mm crassa, odore grato. Lamellae c. 30 stipitem attingentes, molles, adscendentes, ventricosae, 6 mm latae, adnatae, obscure purpureae, margine convexae, concolores vel pallidiores. Stipes 90 × 3.5–5 mm, cavus, fragilis, aequalis, cylindraceus, plerumque contortus, siccus, levis, glaber, totus purpureus vel sursum purpureus, deorsum pallide flavus.
    Basidia 21.5–24 × 5.5–7 µm, clavata, 4-sporigera, fibulata. Sporae 6.7–7.5 × 2.8–3.6 µm,

*Etymology: cerasinus, an indefinite colour related to purple.

inaequilateraliter ellipsoideae, leves, amyloideae. Cheilocystidia 27–44 × 7–10 × 2.5–4.5 μm, subutriformia vel clavata, fibulata, levia. Pleurocystidia nulla. Trama lamellarum iode ope brunneovinescens. Hyphae pileipellis 1.8–4.5 μm latae, fibulatae, diverticulatae. Hyphae stipitis corticales 1.8–2.5 μm latae, fibulatae, maxima ex parte leves, cellulae terminales perrarae.

Ad sarmenta coniferarum.

Holotypus: A.A.R. de Meijer coa-1144 (No. 990.200–163; L); isotypus: MBM 188496.

Basidiomata gregarious. Pileus 26–30 mm across, 20–27 mm high, conical to campanulate, dry, sulcate, translucent-striate, with the centre perforated, hygrophanous, at first fairly dark greyish purple (13D4), drying much paler, greyish pink (12AB3). Context up to 1.8 mm thick. Odour sweet. Lamellae c. 30 reaching the stipe, tender, ascending, ventricose, 6 mm broad, adnate, dark purple (darker than the pileus, 13E4), with convex and concolorous or paler edge. Stipe 90 × 3.5–5 mm, hollow, fragile, equal, terete, often contorted, dry, smooth, glabrous, fairly dark greyish purple (13D4) throughout or purple above and pale yellow (4A4) below, the base covered with few coarse fibrils.

Basidia 21.5–24 × 5.5–7 μm, slender-clavate, 4-spored, clamped, with sterigmata 4.5 μm long. Spores 6.7–7.5 × 2.8–3.6 μm (Q = 2.0), pip-shaped, smooth, amyloid. Cheilocystidia 27–44 × 7–10 × 2.5–4.5 μm, in places forming a sterile band, subutriform to sublageniform, less frequently clavate, clamped, smooth. Pleurocystidia absent. Lamellar trama brownish vinescent in Melzer's reagent. Hyphae of the pileipellis 1.8–4.5 μm wide, clamped, covered with scattered, simple to somewhat branched, cylindrical, more or less curved excrescences 1–7 × 1–1.8 μm. Hypoderm made up of parallel,

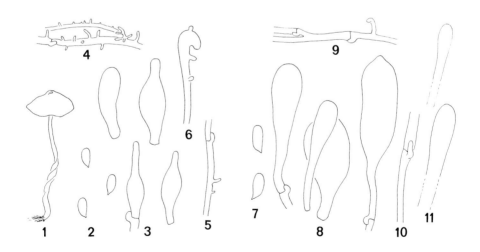

Fig. 39 (1–6) *Mycena cerasina* (de Meijer coa-1144). – 1. Habitus. – 2. Spores. – 3. Cheilocystidia. –
4. Hyphae of the pileipellis. – 5. Hypha of the cortical layer of the stipe. – 6. Terminal cell.
(7–10) *Mycena pura* (de Meijer coa-2827). – 7. Spores. – 8. Cheilocystidia. – 9. Hypha of the pileipellis. – 10. Hypha of the cortical layer of the stipe. – 11. Terminal cells.
Fig. 1, × 0.5; all others, × 700.

thin-walled, inflated hyphae up to 20 μm wide. Hyphae of the cortical layer of the stipe 1.8–2.5 μm wide, clamped, smooth, with rare short excrescences, terminal cells very rare (one seen), 6 μm wide.

On leaf litter in 8 years old stand of *Pinus taeda* (not an indigenous tree), 900 m alt.

Holotype: '*Mycena cerasina* Maas G. and de Meijer / 12 May 1988 / Paraná: Colombo, Estrada da Ribeira, EMBRAPA-Florestal / A.A.R. de Meijer COa-1144' (No. 990.200–163; L); isotype: MBM 188496.

Going by the shape of the cheilocystidia, the present species could well be taken for a member of section *Fragilipedes*. Also, purplish colours are not unknown in this section, but these tints disappear with age or when the material is dried, and no member of the *Fragilipedes* is deep purple in all parts. *Mycena cerasina* differs from section *Fragilipedes* in being purple throughout and, apparently, in the chemical composition of its colouring substance which remains dark even after drying. Some species of section *Calodontes* are also known to have dark purple colours; in fact, at first sight *M. cerasina* was mistaken for *Mycena diosma* Krieglsteiner and Schwöbel, but all members of the *Calodontes* have smooth hyphae of the pileipellis and numerous and, above all, voluminous caulocystidia.

22. MYCENA section CALODONTES (Fr. ex Berk.) Quél.

Agaricus subtrib. *Calodontes* Fr., Syst. mycol. **1**: 111. 1821 (inadmissible term denoting rank). – *Agaricus* [sect.] *Calodontes* Fr. ex Berk. in J.E. Smith, Engl. Flora **5** (2): 43. 1836; Fr., Epicr. Syst. mycol.: 99. 1838; Cooke, Handb. Br. Fungi **1**: 63. 1871 (formally accepted as section). – *Mycena* [sect.] *Calodontes* (Fr. ex Berk.) Quél. in Mém. Soc. Emul. Montbél. II **5**: 102. 1872. – *Mycena* subsect. *Calodontes* (Fr. ex Berk.) Métrod, Prodr. flore mycol. Madagasc. **3**: 20, 32. 1949. – Lectotype: *Agaricus pelianthinus* Fr.

Basidiomata medium-sized to large. Pileus glabrous, usually somewhat lubricous when moist, variously coloured, not infrequently with purplish or violaceous tints. Context thin. Odour and taste raphanoid. Lamellae tender, ascending to almost horizontal, adnate to more or less distinctly decurrent, white or flushed with colours of the pileus, the edge more intensely coloured than the sides or pale to white. Stipe fragile to firm or tough, variously coloured, not infrequently with purplish or violaceous tints, the base covered with coarse fibrils.

Basidia clavate, 4-spored, clamped. Spores pip-shaped to somewhat elongated, smooth, amyloid or inamyloid. Cheilocystidia often fusiform and in most cases apically broadly rounded, clamped, with purplish brown or colourless contents, generally smooth. Pleurocystidia similar or absent. Lamellar trama vinescent in Melzer's reagent. Hyphae of the pileipellis smooth, clamped. Hyphae of the cortical layer of the stipe smooth, clamped, terminal cells (caulocystidia) smooth.

Growing on vegetable debris, not on wood.

1. Spores amyloid.
   2. Cheilocystidia with broadly rounded apices; pleurocystidia usually present:
   . . . . 22.1. subsect. *Purae*
   2. Cheilocystidia with much narrowed necks, apically not broadly rounded; pleurocystidia
   absent: . . . . 22.2. subsect. *Generosae*
1. Spores inamyloid; pleurocystidia absent: . . . . 22.3. subsect. *Violacellae*

22.1. Subsection PURAE (Konr. and Maubl.) Maas G.

Mycena sect. *Purae* Konr. and Maubl., Ic. sel. Fung. **6**: 269. 1934. – *Mycena* sect. *Calodontes*
subsect. *Purae* (Konr. and Maubl.) Maas G. in Persoonia **11**: 112. 1980. – Lectotype: *Mycena*
pura (Pers.: Fr.) Kummer.
   For further synonymy, see Maas Geesteranus, l.c.

Basidiomata with features largely as in section *Calodontes,* but lamellae with
the edge concolorous with the sides or paler. Spores amyloid. Pleurocystidia
with colourless contents, if present.

1. Lamellae conspicuously reticulately intervenose. Pleurocystidia absent.
   2. Cheilocystidia 3.5–7 µm broad, cylindrical. Caulocystidia scarce, 6.5–8 µm broad, apically
   rounded: . . . . *M. fenestrata*
   2. Cheilocystidia 8–15 µm broad, subclavate. Caulocystidia numerous, 2–5.5 µm broad, api-
   cally pointed: . . . . *M. proxima*
1. Lamellae, if intervenose, not conspicuously so. Pleurocystidia present. Caulocystidia apically
   rounded: . . . . *M. pura*

Mycena fenestrata* Maas G. and de Meijer, *spec. nov.* – Fig. 40 (1–6)

Basidiomata dispersa. Pileus 15–20 mm latus, e convexo applanatus, striatus, glaber, siccus,
hygrophanus, obscure purpureobrunneus. Caro tenuis, pileo concolor, odore raphanoideo. Lamellae c. 18 stipitem attingentes, molles, adscendentes, usque ad 3 mm latae, late adnatae,
decurrentes, valde reticulatim intervenosae, griseoviolaceae, margine albidae. Stipes 30–50 × 1–
3 mm, cavus, fragilis, aequalis, cylindraceus, levis, glaber ut videtur, siccus, purpureobrunneus,
basi usque ad 4.5 mm latus, flavidus, fibrillis parcis, albis munitus.
   Basidia 19–22.5 × 5.5–6.5 µm, clavata, 4-sporigera, fibulata, sterigmatibus 4.5 µm longis
instructa. Sporae 6.7–8.1 × 3.6–4.5 µm, inaequilateraliter ellipsoideae, leves, amyloideae.
Cheilocystidia 18–35 × 8–15 µm, clavata, fusiformia, subcylindracea, fibulata, apice obtusa,
levia. Pleurocystidia nulla. Trama lamellarum iodi ope vinescens. Hyphae pileipellis 2.5–3.5 µm
latae, fibulatae, leves, parum gelatinosae. Hyphae stipitis corticales 1.8–2.5 µm latae, fibulatae,
leves, cellulae terminales 24–27 × 6.5–8 µm, subclavatae, leves.
   Humicola.
   Holotypus: A.A.R. de Meijer-GUa 3109 (No. 991.343–730; L); notulae: MBM 188516.

Basidiomata scattered. Pileus 15–20 mm across, convex, flattening with age,
translucent-striate, glabrous, appearing dry, strongly hygrophanous, the
centre and striae very dark purplish brown (10F4–11E4), between the striae

---

*Etymology: fenestratus, furnished with apertures, referring to the reticulate intervenation of the
lamellae, simulating rows of holes.

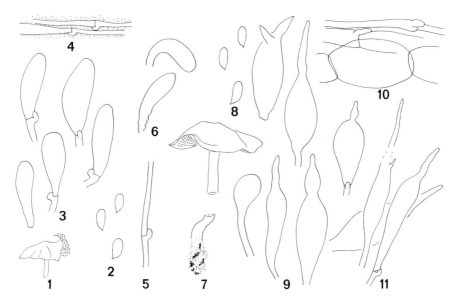

Fig. 40 (1–6) *Mycena fenestrata* (de Meijer Gua-3109). – 1. Habitus. – 2. Spores. – 3. Cheilocystidia. – 4. Hyphae of the pileipellis. – 5. Hypha of the cortical layer of the stipe. – 6. Terminal cells. (7–11) *Mycena insolita* (de Meijer TU-3065). – 7. Habitus and basal part of the stipe. – 8. Spores. – 9. Cheilocystidia. – 10. Hypha of the pileipellis. – 11. Terminal cells (caulocystidia). Fig. 1, × 2; fig. 7, × 1; all others, × 700.

fairly pale greyish violet (11C3). Context fresh concolorous with the pileus. Odour strongly raphanoid. Taste not recorded. Lamellae c. 18 reaching the stipe, tender, ascending, up to 3 mm broad, broadly adnate, decurrent, densely reticulately intervenose, fairly pale greyish violet (11D3), with whitish edge. Stipe 30–50 × 1–3 mm, hollow, fragile, equal, terete, smooth, appearing glabrous, dry, dark purplish brown (11E3–5), at the base up to 4.5 mm broad, yellowish (4AB4–5AB4), covered with sparse white fibrils.

Basidia 19–22.5 × 5.5–6.5 μm, clavate, 4-spored, clamped, with sterigmata 4.5 μm long. Spores 6.7–8.1 × 3.6–4.5 μm (Q = 2.1), pip-shaped, smooth, amyloid. Cheilocystidia 18–35 × 8–15 μm, forming a sterile band (lamellar edge homogeneous), clavate, fusiform, subcylindrical, clamped, thin-walled, with broadly rounded apex, smooth. Pleurocystidia absent. Lamellar trama vinescent in Melzer's reagent. Pileipellis a cutis of repent, radiately aligned hyphae which are 2.5–3.5 μ wide, clamped, smooth, somewhat gelatinizing. Hypoderm made up of parallel hyphae with inflated cells up to 30 μm wide. Hyphae of the cortical layer of the stipe 1.8–2.5 μm wide, clamped, smooth, the terminal cells scarce, 24–27 × 6.5–8 μm, subclavate, curved outwards, smooth, apically broadly rounded.

Growing in leaf litter in dense, ombrophilous forest, 5 m alt.

Holotype: '*Mycena fenestrata* Maas G. and de Meijer / 5 July 1995 / Paraná: Guaraqueçaba, Potinga / A.A.R. de Meijer Gua-3109' (No. 991.343–730; L); notes and drawings: MBM 188516.

In the South American region, *Mycena holoporphyra* (Berk. and Curt.) Sing. is another member of subsection *Purae* which shares the following characters with *M. fenestrata*: pileus glabrous, coloured some shade of purple ['sordide purpureo' according to the collector's notes (Pegler, 1987: 520)]; lamellae adnate, transversely intervenose; stipe with yellowish base (Dennis, 1951: 475); spores of the same size (6–9 × 3.5–5 μm in *M. holoporphyra* according to Pegler, l.c.). Since Pegler stated that *M. holoporphyra* is a 'widely distributed tropical species,' collection de Meijer 3109 was originally suspected to belong to this species, although some discrepancies were noticed. Unfortunately, there exists no truly 'full description' of *M. holoporphyra*, but the following differences between *holoporphyra* and *fenestrata* are now considered sufficient for specific separation.

	pileus	cheilocystidia	odour	habit
M. fenestrata	very dark purplish brown	forming a sterile band	strongly raphanoid	growing in leaf litter
M. holoporphyra	pale purplish blue to deep violaceous (Pegler, l.c.) vinaceous-lilac (Dennis, l.c.)	scattered (Pegler, l.c.)	not mentioned	growing on logs

Métrod (1949: 80–82) described three species of *Mycena* from Madagascar, belonging to group *Ianthinae* Kühn., a synonym of sect. *Calodontes* subsect. *Purae*, characterized by their lamellae being 'très interveinées' or the hymenium being 'plus ou moins poré.' These species, *M. decipiens* (Overeem) Métrod, *M. madecassensis* (Heim) Métrod and *M. manipularis* (Berk.) Métrod, apart from being differently coloured, all have anatomical characters which are different from those of *Mycena fenestrata*.

Mycena proxima* Maas G. and de Meijer, *spec. nov.* – Fig. 41 (1–6)

Basidiomata dispersa. Pileus 15–16 mm latus, usque ad 5 mm altus, convexus, parum sulcatus, striatus, glaber, siccus, hygrophanus, atrobrunneus. Caro tenuis, pileo concolor, odore raphanoideo. Lamellae c. 14 stipitem attingentes, molles, adscendentes, usque ad 2 mm latae, late adnatae, dente decurrentes, valde reticulatim intervenosae, subviolaceae, margine albae. Stipes 35–50 × 1.5–3 mm, fragilis, aequalis, cylindraceus, levis, puberulus, siccus, purpureobrunneus, deorsum griseobrunneus, basi albotomentosus.

Basidia 28–33 × 7 μm, anguste clavata, 4-sporigera, fibulata, sterigmatibus 4.5 μm longis instructa. Sporae 7.6–9.4 × 4.5 μm, inaequilateraliter ellipsoideae, leves, amyloideae. Cheilocystidia 27–36 × 3.5–7 μm, cylindracea vel subclavata, fibulata, apice obtusa, levia. Pleurocystidia nulla. Trama lamellarum iodi ope vinescens. Hyphae pileipellis 2.7–3.5 μm latae, fibulatae, leves, parum gelatinosae. Hyphae stipitis corticales 2.7 μm latae, fibulatae, leves, cellulae terminales 50–85 × 2–5.5 μm, vulgo anguste conicae, leves.

Humicola.

Holotypus: A.A.R. de Meijer ALAa-3201 (No. 991.343–761; L); notulae: MBM 190340.

*Etymology: proximus, very close (to *M. fenestrata*).

106

Basidiomata scattered. Pileus 15–16 mm across, up to 5 mm high, convex, flattened with age, somewhat sulcate, translucent-striate, glabrous, appearing dry, strongly hygrophanous, the striae black-brown (9F5), between the striae purplish grey-brown (9D4) drying grey-brown (6D4) at the centre, dingy pink (9A3–9B3) farther outwards. Context fresh concolorous with the pileus, drying white. Odour strongly raphanoid. Taste not recorded. Lamellae c. 14 reaching the stipe, tender, ascending, up to 2 mm broad, broadly adnate, decurrent with a tooth, densely reticulately intervenose, violet-tinted, with convex, white edge. Stipe 35–50 × 1.5–3 mm, fragile, equal, terete, smooth, puberulous, dry, fairly pale purplish brown (9D4) above, paler (9C3) to fairly pale grey-brown (5C3) below, the base in one specimen white, covered with short, white tomentum.

Basidia 28–33 × 7 μm, slender-clavate, 4-spored, clamped, with sterigmata 4.5 μm long. Spores 7.6–9.4 × 4.5 μm (Q = 2.1), pip-shaped, smooth, amyloid. Cheilocystidia 27–36 × 3.5–7 μm, forming a sterile band (lamellar edge homogeneous), cylindrical, slender-clavate, clamped, thin-walled, smooth, with broadly rounded apex. Pleurocystidia absent. Lamellar trama vinescent in Melzer's reagent. Pileipellis a cutis of repent, radiately aligned hyphae which are 2.7–3.5 μm wide, clamped, smooth, somewhat gelatinizing. Hypoderm made up of parallel hyphae with inflated cells c. 15 μm wide. Hyphae of the cortical layer of the stipe 2.7 μm wide, clamped, smooth, with

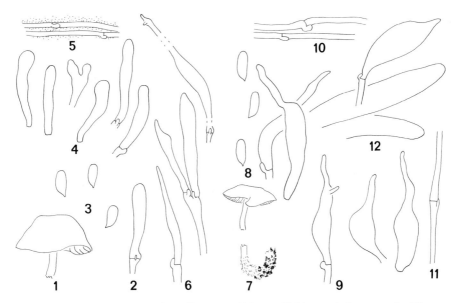

Fig. 41 (1–6) *Mycena proxima* (de Meijer ALAa-3201). – 1. Habitus. – 2. Immature basidium. – 3. Spores. – 4. Cheilocystidia. – 5. Hyphae of the pileipellis. – 6. Terminal cells (caulocystidia). (7–12) *Mycena generosa* (de Meijer RSB-3068). – 7. Habitus and basal part of the stipe. – 8. Spores. – 9. Cheilocystidia. – 10. Hypha of the pileipellis. – 11. Hypha of the cortical layer of the stipe. – 12. Terminal cells (caulocystidia).
Fig. 1, × 2; fig. 7, × 1; all others, × 700.

numerous terminal cells which are $50-85 \times 2-5.5\,\mu m$, mostly narrowly conical, smooth, apically tapering to a point.

On forest humus, in seasonal semideciduous submontane forest, 250 m alt.

Holotype: '*Mycena proxima* Maas G. and de Meijer / 17 January 1996 / Paraná: Altonia, forest at Estrada do Amendoim, 2 km N of Jardim Paredão / A.A.R. de Meijer ALAa-3201' (No. 991.343–761; L); notes and drawings: MBM 190340.

The specific epithet reflects the close proximity of the present species to *Mycena fenestrata*. Judging from the macrodescriptions of the holotypes, it may be practically impossible to tell the two species apart in the field. The differences are to be found in the microscopic details.

MYCENA PURA (Pers.: Fr.) Kummer – Fig. 39 (7–10)

Agaricus purus Pers., Neues Mag. Bot.: 101. 1794; Fr., Syst. mycol. **1**: 151. 1821. – *Mycena pura* (Pers.: Fr.) Kummer, Führ. Pilzk.: 107, 110. 1871. – Type locality: Germany.
For further literature, see Maas Geesteranus (1992: 414).

Basidiomata scattered. Pileus 18–32 mm across, hemispherical to convex, with small umbo, dry, smooth (collection COa-2827 already dried and estriate when collected), glabrous, reddish grey-violet (12 C4). Context very thin, white. Odour strongly raphanoid. Lamellae 20–22 reaching the stipe, tender, up to 5 mm broad, adnexed to sinuate-adnate and some decurrent with a tooth, smooth to veined, dorsally intervenose, whitish to greyish pink with convex, white edge. Stipe $45-60 \times 2.5-4$ mm, hollow, fragile, equal or somewhat attenuated from base upwards, terete, dry, smooth, glabrous, grey-violet (12C3), pale yellowish (4A3) at the base which is more or less densely covered with fine white fibrils.

Basidia (not fully mature) $30-35 \times 7-8\,\mu m$, slender-clavate, 4-spored, clamped, with sterigmata up to $6.5\,\mu m$ long. Spores $9.0-10.7 \times 4.3-4.8\,\mu m$ (Q = 2.2), pip-shaped, smooth, amyloid. Cheilocystidia $35-68 \times 9-18\,\mu m$, forming a dense sterile band (lamellar edge homogeneous), clavate to sub-cylindrical, short- to long-stalked, clamped, smooth, apically broadly rounded or occasionally somewhat attenuated. Pleurocystidia similar. Lamellar trama vinescent in Melzer's reagent. Pileipellis a cutis of repent, radiately aligned hyphae which are $1.8-2.7\,\mu m$ wide, clamped, smooth or rarely showing a single cylindrical excrescence. Hyphae of the cortical layer of the stipe $2-2.7\,\mu m$ wide, clamped, smooth, the terminal cells hard to find, $5.5-8\,\mu m$ wide, smooth.

On humus in mixed ombrophilous forest, 900 m alt.

Material examined: '*Mycena pura* (Pers.: Fr.) Kummer / 26 June 1993 / Paraná: Colombo, EMBRAPA – Florestal / A.A.R. de Meijer COa-2827' (No. 988.233–090; L; duplicate: MBM 190341.

Going by the colouration of the present collection, this is a form of *Mycena pura* which seems intermediate between f. *pura* and European f. *ianthina* (Gillet) Maas G. (1992: 419).

The following collections equally represent *Mycena pura* but have much darker pilei, e.g. dark purplish brown (10E4) and (8E4). Varietal names have not been given.

Material examined: '27 June 1995 / Paraná: Morretes, Porto de Cima, Parque Marumbi, near Nhundiaquara River / on leaf litter in dense ombrophilous forest, 20 m alt. / A.A.R. de Meijer MA 3089' (No. 991. 343–732; L); notes and drawings: MBM 190342.

'25 July 1995 / Paraná: Piraquara, Mananciais da Serra / on humus, in dense ombrophilous forest, 900 m alt. / A.A.R. de Meijer MA-3150' (991.343–818; L); duplicate: MBM 190343.

22.2. Subsect. **Generosae** Maas G. and de Meijer, *subsect. nov.*

Haec subsectioni *Purae* similis sed cheilocystidiorum collo forte coarctato atque apice haud late rotundato praecipue differt.

Species typica: *Mycena generosa.*

KEY TO THE SPECIES

1. Pileus pale greyish pink to greyish violet. Lamellae up to 15 mm broad. Caulocystidia mostly apically obtuse. Growing on fallen *Pinus* needles: .... *M. generosa*
1. Pileus dark purple to almost black. Lamellae up to 8 mm broad. Caulocystidia rostrate or apically passing into a long neck. Growing among leaf litter of a dicotyledonous tree:
.... *M. insolita*

Mycena generosa* Maas G. and de Meijer, *spec. nov.* – Fig. 41 (7–12)

Basidiomata dispersa. Pileus 20–55 mm latus, usque ad 28 mm altus, e campanulato plano-convexus, centro interdum perforatus, levis vel sulcatus, striatus, glaber, siccus, pallide purpureus vel griseoviolaceus, centro brunneolo vel griseo. Caro usque ad 2 mm lata, odore forsan raphanoideo. Lamellae 32–34 stipitem attingentes, molles, adscendentes, usque ad 15 mm latae, ventricosae, late adnatae, dente decurrentes, intervenosae, albae, interdum basi pallide griseo-purpureae, margine albae. Stipes 55–100 × 2–7 mm, cavus, haud fragilis, aequalis, cylindraceus, levis, siccus, sparse albopruinosus, sursum griseoviolaceus, deorsum pallide flavus, basi pallide griseobrunneus, tomento fibrillisque albis munitus.

Basidia c. 30 × 7–9 μm, clavata, 4-sporigera, fibulata. Sporae 8.1–10.7 × 3.4–4.5 μm, cylindraceae, leves, amyloideae. Cheilocystidia 45–55 × 7–10 × 2.5–4.5 μm, subfusiformia, sublageniformia, fibulata, levia. Pleurocystidia nulla. Trama lamellarum iodi ope vinescens. Hyphae pileipellis 2.5 μm latae, fibulatae, leves. Hyphae stipitis corticales 2.5 μm latae, fibulatae, leves, cellulae terminales 36–80 × 10–12.5 μm, fusiformes vel subcylindraceae, leves.

Humicola.

Holotypus: A.A.R. de Meijer RSB-3068 (No. 991.343–804; L); isotypus: MBM 188521.

Basidiomata scattered. Pileus 20–55 mm across, up to 28 mm high, at first

_____
*Etymology: generosus, noble, exquisite, referring to the beautiful colour of the pileus.

campanulate, later planoconvex, in some specimens with perforate centre, fairly smooth to sulcate, translucent-striate, glabrous, dry, pale greyish pink to greyish violet (13AB3 to 13CD3), centrally grey-brown (7D4) to pale reddish grey (8B2). Context up to 2 mm thick, concolorous with the pileus, drying white. Odour possibly raphanoid (a bad cold prevented the collector from correctly judging the odour). Taste not recorded. Lamellae 32–34 reaching the stipe, tender, ascending, up to 15 mm broad, ventricose, broadly adnate, decurrent with a small tooth, distinctly intervenose, white or pale greyish pink towards the base, with white edge. Stipe 55–100 × 2–7 mm, hollow, rather firm, equal, terete, smooth, innately white-striate, dry, sparsely white-pruinose, greyish violet above, pale yellow (4A3) below, the base turning rather pale grey-brown, covered with white tomentum and coarse fibrils.

Basidia c. 30 × 7–9 μm, slender-clavate, 4-spored, clamped, with sterigmata up to 5.5 μm long. Spores 8.1–10.7 × 3.4–4.5 μm (Q = 2.6), almost cylindrical, smooth, amyloid. Cheilocystidia 45–55 × 7–10 × 2.5–4.5 μm, forming a sterile band (lamellar edge homogeneous), subfusiform, sublageniform, clamped, with much narrowed neck and apically not broadly rounded, more or less curved, smooth. Pleurocystidia absent. Lamellar trama vinescent in Melzer's reagent. Pileipellis a cutis of repent, radiately aligned hyphae which are 2.5 μm wide, clamped, smooth. Hypoderm made up of parallel, inflated hyphae 20 μm wide. Hyphae of the cortical layer of the stipe 2.5 μm wide, clamped, smooth, terminal cells 36–80 × 10–12.5 μm, fusiform to cylindrical, smooth.

Growing on fallen needles in *Pinus* plantation, 900 m alt.

Holotype: '*Mycena generosa* Maas G. and de Meijer / 28 May 1995 / Paraná: Rio de Branco do Sul, Tranqueira Distr. / A.A.R. de Meijer RSB-3068' (No. 991.343–804; L); isotype: MBM 188521.

Mycena generosa could be mistaken for some member of the *M. pura* group, especially in the field, although the yellow lower part of the stipe (known e.g. in *M. pura* f. *multicolor* and *M. rosea*) should raise a signal. Microscopically, the difference is clear. All members of subsection *Purae* have cheilocystidia with broadly rounded apices; pleurocystidia, if sometimes scarce, are present; the spores tend to be somewhat shorter than those of *M. generosa*. It is equally clear, however, that *M. generosa* belongs to none other than section *Calodontes* (Fr. ex Berk.) Quél., but seems best accommodated in a new subsection.

Mycena porphyrocephala, described by Singer (1989: 84), could, superficially seen, be taken to be near *M. generosa* on account of the colours of the pileus and lamellae, and the size of its spores. But Singer described the cheilocystidia as much covered with 1–1.5 μm long processes and the hyphae of the pileipellis as densely diverticulate.

Mycena insolita* Maas G. and de Meijer, *spec. nov.* – Fig. 40 (7–11)

Basidiomata gregaria. Pileus 8–60 mm latus, e hemisphaerico convexus vel subplanus, interdum umbonatus, siccus, striatus, glaber, atropurpureus, hygrophanus, exsiccatus roseogriseus. Caro obscure grisea, odore saporeque raphanoideis. Lamellae 23–25 stipitem attingentes, molles, subadscendentes, usque ad 8 mm latae, adnatae, intervenosae, e albo pallide griseae, margine concolore. Stipes 40–90 × 3–6 mm, cavus, firmus, aequalis, cylindraceus, siccus, levis, pruinosus vel minute puberulus, pallide brunneogriseus, apice albus, basi tomento albo obtectus.

Basidia 27–30 × 5.5–6.5 μm, clavata, 4-sporigera, fibulata, sterigmatibus 5.5 μm longis praedita. Sporae 7.4–8.9 × 3.5–4.3 μm, subcylindraceae, leves, amyloideae. Cheilocystidia 30–65 × 9–13.5 × 1.8–6.5 μm, fusiformia vel subclavata, fibulata, levia, rostrata vel collo longo instructa. Pleurocystidia non visa. Trama lamellarum iodi ope rubrobrunnea. Hyphae pileipellis 2.7–3.5 μm latae, fibulatae, leves. Hyphae stipitis corticales 1.8–2.5 μm latae, fibulatae, leves, caulocystidia 60–110 × 4.5–14.5 × 1–2.5 μm, fusiformia, fibulata, levia, rostrata vel collo longo munita.

Humicola.

Holotypus: A.A.R. de Meijer TU-3065 (No. 990.200–188; L); isotypus: MBM 188529.

Basidiomata densely gregarious. Pileus 8–60 mm across, at first hemispherical, then convex to nearly plane, with or without broad umbo, more rarely becoming somewhat depressed, dry, smooth, translucent-striate, glabrous, the centre and striae very dark purple, almost black (11F5), between striae fairly dark purple (11D5), hygrophanous, drying darkish grey with some purplish shade (7D3) at the centre and pale pinkish grey (10B2) farther outwards. Context dark grey with some brownish tint (5E3) in the pileus and drying pure white, in the stipe pale yellowish grey (3B2) above, very pale yellow below. Odour and taste raphanoid. Lamellae 23–25 reaching the stipe, tender, somewhat ascending, up to 8 mm broad, narrowly to broadly adnate, decurrent with a tooth or not, very strongly intervenose, at first white, turning pale to somewhat darker grey (4B2–4B3), with convex to straight, concolorous edge. Stipe 40–90 × 3–6 mm, hollow, firm, equal, terete, dry, smooth, sparsely to more densely pruinose all over, apically sometimes more puberulous, fairly pale brownish grey (5C3), white above, frequently white translucent-striate in the lower part, the base covered with white tomentum and fibrils.

Basidia 27–30 × 5.5–6.5 μm, slender-clavate, 4-spored, clamped, with sterigmata 5.5 μm long. Spores 7.4–8.9 × 3.5–4.3 μm (Q = 2.3), almost cylindrical, smooth, amyloid. Cheilocystidia 30–65 × 9–13.5 × 1.8–6.5 μm, forming a sterile band (lamellar edge homogeneous), fusiform to subclavate, clamped, with colourless contents, smooth, rostrate or apically more or less abruptly passing into a much narrower, long neck. Pleurocystidia not observed (absent?). Lamellar trama staining reddish brown in Melzer's reagent. Pileipellis a cutis of repent hyphae which are 2.7–3.5 μm wide, clamped, smooth. Hypoderm made up of parallel hyphae with inflated cells up to c. 30 μm wide. Hyphae of the cortical layer of the stipe 1.8–2.5 μm wide, clamped, smooth, the caulocystidia 60–110 × 4.5–14.5 × 1–2.5 μm, fusi-

*Etymology: insolitus, unusual, referring to the unusual shape of the cheilocystidia.

111

form, clamped, smooth, rostrate or apically gradually passing into a long neck.

Among leaf litter, with the bases of the stipes appressed to decayed wood of a dicotyledonous tree in mixed ombrophilous forest, 900 m alt.

Holotype: '*Mycena insolita* Maas G. and de Meijer / 30 April 1995 / Paraná: Tunas do Paraná, Parque Estadual de Campinhos / A.A.R. de Meijer TU-3065' (No. 990.200–188; L); isotype: MBM 188529.

Raithelhuber (1980: 38; 1985: 31) described a variety of *Mycena pura* (Pers.: Fr.) Kummer, var. *marplatensis* Raith., along with an illustration of two cheilocystidia which look rather similar to those of *M. insolita*. However, his variety has the pileus 'rugoso-striato' and its spores were measured (3.5–)5– 5.5 × (2.5–)2.75–3.75 μm.

Mycena vinosella Speg. (1926: 285) is a South American species with some features not unlike those of *M. insolita*, but it differs in its narrower lamellae (1–1.5 mm) from white turning flesh-colour, and its lack of odour. The species may not even be a member of section *Calodontes* on account of its lack of cheilocystidia ('lamellis . . . acie integerrimis . . . semper trabeculis destitutis').

From Madagascar, Métrod described several species in the group of *Ianthinae* Kühn., a synonym of subsection *Purae*, (1949: 79), but the one species, whose hymenophore is neither smooth to very little intervenose nor frankly alveolar to poroid, is represented by *Mycena madecassensis* (R. Heim) Métrod. It differs from *M. insolita* by its pale pileus ('gris pâle'), broader spores ('6–6.4 μm'), and differently shaped necks of the caulocystidia ('à terminaisons globuleuses').

Corner, who showed himself averse to specific segregation in the *Mycena pura* complex (1986: 62, 'I think . . . that the so-called species that have been separated are merely a few of its varieties'), said of the cheilocystidia that 'the ventricose form, be it noted, follows on the clavate by elongation of the apex' (p. 63). What he could not foresee at the time is that, based on two kinds of elongation of the cheilocystidia, two groups of species can be recognised. In subsection *Marginatae* (cheilocystidia with coloured contents) and *Purae* (cheilocystidia with colourless contents), the transition of the main body of the cheilocystidium into the neck is gradual, whereas it is abrupt in *M. insolita* (cheilocystidia with colourless contents), a species which for the time being is maintained as a member of subsection *Purae*.

22.3. Subsection VIOLACELLAE Sing. ex Maas G.

Mycena stirps *Violacella* Sing., Agar. mod. taxon., 3rd ed.: 395. 1975 (inadmissable term denoting rank). – *Mycena* sect. *Calodontes* subsect. *Violacellae* Sing. ex Maas G. in Persoonia **11**: 112. 1980. – Holotype: *Mycena violacella* (Speg.) Sing.

Basidiomata with features largely as in sect. *Calodontes*, but spores non-amyloid. Pleurocystidia absent.

MYCENA PEARSONIANA Dennis ex Sing. – Fig. 42

Mycena pearsoniana Dennis apud Pearson in Naturalist 50. 1955 (not val. publ.); ex Sing. in Sydowia **12**: 233 ('1958') 1959. – Holotype: 'Singer M 1606' (LIL, not seen).
For further synonymy, see Maas Geesteranus (1989: 500; 1992: 422).

Basidiomata scattered. Pileus 7–30 mm across, up to 7 mm high, at first conical-convex, becoming convex with broad, low umbo, finally more or less depressed, dry, smooth but somewhat sulcate on drying out, translucent-striate, glabrous, hygrophanous, centre and striae very dark purplish brown (11E4, 11F5), between the striae purplish grey-brown (9D4), occasionally even very pale orange-white (5A2), drying purplish grey-brown (9D4) or paler or darker pinkish grey (9A3–9B3) or sometimes even very pale pink. (7A2), always with some brownish yellow shade at the centre. Context soft and brittle, concolorous with surface of the pileus. Odour and taste raphanoid. Lamellae 18–28 reaching the stipe, tender, ascending, ventricose, up to 4.5 mm broad, sinuate-adnate, decurrent with a long tooth, densely intervenose, purplish grey (8B3, 11C3) to paler or darker pinkish grey (9A3–9B3), with convex, white edge. Stipe 35–70 × 2–4 mm, hollow, fragile, equal, terete, smooth, dry, glabrous, apically very little pruinose, purplish grey (8D3) to purplish brown (11D4–11E4), paler to fairly pale yellow-brown (5C4) below or entirely this colour, the base covered with fairly few, whitish fibrils.

Basidia (few seen mature) 27–30 × 5.5–6.5 μm, slender-clavate, 4-spored, clamped, with sterigmata 4.5 μm long. Spores 7.3–8.1 × 4.5 μm (Q = 2.2), pip-shaped, smooth, non-amyloid. Cheilocystidia 20–55 × 9–15 μm, forming a dense sterile band (lamellar edge homogeneous), clavate, less frequently fusiform, clamped, smooth, apically broadly rounded or occasionally mucronate. Pleurocystidia absent (or perhaps a few present near the lamellar edge?). Lamellar trama vinescent in Melzer's reagent. Pileipellis a cutis of repent, radiately aligned hyphae which are 2.7–3.5 μm wide, clamped, smooth, those nearest the hyphae of the hypoderm embedded in gelatinous matter (which readily disappears after treatment in warm, diluted KOH).

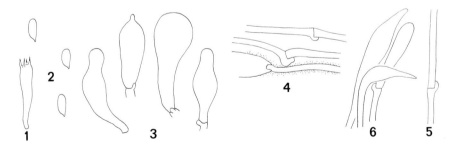

Fig. 42 (1–6) *Mycena pearsoniana* (de Meijer CUB-2933). – 1. Basidium. – 2. Spores. – 3. Cheilocystidia. – 4. Hyphae of the pileipellis. – 5. Hypha of the cortical layer of the stipe. – 6. Terminal cells (caulocystidia).
All figs., × 700.

Hyphae of the hypoderm with inflated cells up to 30 μm. Hyphae of the cortical layer of the stipe 2.7–4.5 μm wide, clamped, smooth, the terminal cells 27–65 × 4.5–8 μm, not numerous, clavate and apically obtuse, or fusiform with narrowed or acute apices.

Among leaf litter in mixed ombrophilous forest, 900 m alt.

Material examined: '*Mycena pearsoniana* Dennis ex Sing. / 14 Nov. 1994 / Paraná: Curitiba, Santo Inacío Distr., Parque Barigui / A.A.R. de Meijer cub-2933' (990.200–110; L); duplicate: mbm 190333.

Additional material: '10 July 1995 / Paraná: Rio Branco do Sul, near cemetery / A.A.R. de Meijer rsc-3132 / on forest litter in mixed ombrophilous forest, 900 m alt.' (No. 991.343–762; L); duplicate: mbm 190334.

Corner (1994: 198) described a gathering of *M. pearsoniana* from Borneo (rsnb 1901) which deviates from European and the present South American collections in having the lamellae 'adnexed' and possessing pleurocystidia. A second gathering (rsnb 5656) was stated to have 31–36 lamellae and cheilocystidia 'often with an obtuse slender appendage – 25 × 2–2.5 μm,' which is equally unusual.

23. Mycena section Adonideae (Fr.) Quél.

Agaricus (sect.) *Adonidei* Fr., Epicr. Syst. mycol.: 101. 1838 ('*Adonideae*'); Cooke, Handb. Br. Fungi **1**: 65. 1871 (formally accepted as section). – *Mycena* [sect.] *Adonideae* (Fr.) Quél. in Mém. Soc. Emul. Montbél. ii **5**: 103. 1872; Sing., Agar. mod. taxon., 3rd ed.: 395. 1975 (formally accepted as section). – *Mycena* [subsect.?] *Adonideae* (Fr.) Kühn., Genre *Mycena*: 163, 546. 1938 ('*Adonidae*'). – *Hemimycena* sect. *Adonideae* (Fr.) Sing. in Annls mycol. **41**: 120, 123. 1943 ('*Adonidae*'). – *Marasmiellus* sect. *Adonidei* (Fr.) Sing. in Lilloa **22**: 301. ('1949') 1951 ('*Adonidi*'). – Lectotype: *Agaricus adonis* Bull.: Fr.

For further synonymy, see Maas Geesteranus, 1990: 163.

Basidiomata fairly small to medium-sized. Pileus finely pruinose, often appearing glabrous, lubricous when moist or not, brightly coloured, red, orange, pink, yellow, more rarely white. Context thin, paler concolorous with the pileus. Odour and taste none or indistinctive. Lamellae tender, ascending, adnate, decurrent with a tooth, red, pink, cream or white, with paler edge. Stipe hollow, fragile, pruinose to minutely puberulous all over, pink, orange, yellowish or white, the base covered with coarse, whitish fibrils.

Basidia clavate, 2-spored and clampless or 4-spored and clamped, rarely without clamps. Spores generally pip-shaped, smooth, inamyloid. Cheilocystidia occurring mixed with basidia or forming a sterile band, mostly fusiform, clamped or clampless. Pleurocystidia similar (or absent?). Lamellar trama not vinescent in Melzer's reagent. Hyphae of the pileipellis clamped or not, (more rarely) smooth or covered with simple to much branched excrescences. Hyphae of the cortical layer of the stipe clamped or not, smooth, the terminal cells (caulocystidia) clavate or fusiform and cystidia-like.

Growing on the ground among grass and moss, on vegetable debris or on logs.

Mycena aurorea* Maas G. and de Meijer, *spec. nov.* – Fig. 43

Basidiomata dispersa. Pileus 2–7 mm latus, e hemisphaerico convexus, tenuiter sulcatus, striatus, subpruinosus, siccus, aurantiacus. Caro tenuis, odore nullo. Lamellae c. 15 stipitem attingentes, molles, adscendentes, usque ad 0.8 mm latae, ventricosae, adnatae, dente decurrentes, intervenosae, pallide roseae, margine concolore. Stipes 7–13 × 0.3–0.6 mm, cavus, fragilis, aequalis, cylindraceus, levis, supra pruinosus vel subgranulosus, deorsum glaber, pallide roseus, basi puberulus, e disco basali fibrilloso natus.

Basidia c. 27 × 7–8 μm, clavata, 4-sporigera, fibulata. Sporae 6.3–7.2 × 5.4–6.3 μm, globosae vel subglobosae, leves, inamyloideae. Cheilocystidia 30–42 × 11.5–17 × 2–3.5 μm, sublageniformia vel subfusiformia, fibulata, levia. Pleurocystidia similia. Trama lamellarum iodi ope haud vinescens. Hyphae pileipellis 2.5–7 μm latae, fibulatae, leves vel sparse diverticulatae. Hyphae stipitis corticales 2 μm latae, fibulatae, leves, cellulae terminales (caulocystidia) 13.5–35 × 6.5–9 μm, curvatae, clavatae.

Lignicola.

Holotypus: A.A.R. de Meijer MA-1992 (No. 990.200–135; L); notulae: MBM 188494.

Basidiomata scattered. Pileus 2–7 mm across, at first hemispherical, then convex, weakly sulcate, translucent-striate, somewhat pruinose, becoming scurfy on drying (especially at the centre), appearing glabrous towards the margin, dry, reddish orange (7A7). Context thin. Odour absent. Lamellae c. 15 reaching the stipe, tender, ascending, up to 0.8 mm broad, ventricose, adnate, decurrent with a tooth, dorsally intervenose, pale pink (7A2), with concolorous edge. Stipe 7–13 × 0.3–0.6 mm, hollow, fragile, equal, terete, smooth, pruinose or finely granular above, glabrous farther below, pale pink (7A2), the base somewhat puberulous and springing from a basal patch of radiating, fine to fairly coarse, woolly, white fibrils.

Basidia (none seen mature) c. 27 × 7–8 μm, clavate, 4-spored, clamped, with sterigmata c. 3.5 μm long. Spores 6.3–7.2 × 5.4–6.3 μm (Q = 1.2), globose to subglobose, smooth, inamyloid. Cheilocystidia 30–42 × 11.5–17 × 2–3.5 μm, occurring mixed with the basidia (lamellar edge heterogeneous), sublageniform to subfusiform, clamped, smooth. Pleurocystidia similar. Lamellar trama not vinescent in Melzer's reagent. Pileipellis a cutis of repent, radiately aligned hyphae 2.5–7 μm wide, clamped, smooth or sparsely covered with globose to cylindrical excrescences, the latter 2.5–13.5 × 2 μm. Hypoderm made up of parallel, thin-walled, inflated hyphae up to 30 μm wide. Hyphae of the cortical layer of the stipe 2 μm wide, clamped, smooth, the terminal cells (caulocystidia) 13.5–35 μm long, with a clavate to subglobose head 6.5–9 μm broad.

*Etymology: aureoreus, orange, the colour of the dawn.

115

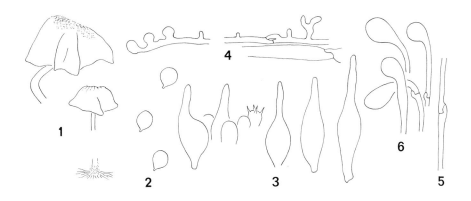

Fig. 43 (1–6) *Mycena aurorea* (de Meijer MA-1992). – 1. Habitus and basal part of the stipe. –
2. Spores. – 3. Cheilocystidia. – 4. Hyphae of the pileipellis. – 5. Hypha of the cortical layer of the
stipe. – 6. Terminal cells (caulocystidia).
Fig. 1, × 4; all others, × 700.

On a decayed branch of a dicotyledonous tree in dense ombrophilous
forest, 700 m alt.

Holotype: '*Mycena aurorea* Maas G. and de Meijer / 2 June 1991 / Paraná:
Morretes, Parque Marumbi, Estrada da Graciosa near Cascata River /
A.A.R. de Meijer MA-1992' (No. 990.200–135; L); notes and drawings: MBM
188494.

The position of *Mycena aurorea* in section *Adonideae* is not free from doubt
on account of three deviating characters. Globose spores and the presence of
a basal disc were thus far unknown in the section, while the scarcity or even
absence of ornamentation of the hyphae of the pileipellis is unusual. It should
be remembered, however, that there is a similar case in section *Hiemales*
Konr. and Maubl. This is a section predominantly with species whose spores
are pip-shaped, whereas *M. alba* (Bres. apud Sacc.) Kühn. with its globose
spores is the exception. Several other characters of *M. aurorea,* moreover,
such as the colour of the pileus, the inamyloid spores, the shape of the
cheilocystidia and caulocystidia, the smooth hyphae of the cortical layer of
the stipe, are well in accordance with those of the *Adonideae*. And it is quite
possible that the spores would have lengthened to become pip-shaped if the
type material had been collected at a somewhat older stage.

Agaricus (Mycena) alborubellus described by Montagne (1854: 96) from
Guyana is a small species with the pileus 5–10 mm across, stated to grow on
decayed fallen branches, and with a basal disc to the stipe. The overall pink
colour ('alborubellus') could be taken as the fading shade of aging specimens,
which is quite common among the *Adonideae*. Whether *A. alborubellus* is
actually a member of this section is impossible to prove without having seen
the material, but two features ('pileo . . . tandem multifisso' and 'Lamellae . . .
stipitem haud attingentes') decisively show that Montagne's species is not the
same as *M. aurorea*.

The specific epithet *aurorea* should not be confused with that of *Mycena auroricolor* (Berk. and Br.) Petch, a species of section *Calodontes* subsect. *Purae*.

Mycena chrysites* Maas G. and de Meijer, *spec. nov.* – Fig. 44 and 45 (1–6)

Basidiomata gregaria. Pileus 1–5 mm latus, convexus, siccus, levis, pruinosus, glabrescens, hygrophanus, flavus vel pallide incarnatus. Caro tenuis, odore nullo. Lamellae 7–10 stipitem attingentes, molles, arcuatae, usque ad 1.5 mm latae, decurrentes, albae, margine concolore. Stipes 3–12 × 0.3 mm, cavus, fragilis, aequalis, levis, puberulus, pileo concolor, basi fibrillis albis substrato affixus.

Basidia 23–27 × 7 μm, clavata, 4-sporigera, efibulata. Sporae 6.7–9.0 × 3.8–4.9 μm, inaequilateraliter ellipsoideae, leves, inamyloideae. Cheilocystidia 45–67 × 8–9 × 2.5–4.5 μm, graciliter lageniformia vel subcylindracea, efibulata, levia, interdum furcata. Pleurocystidia nulla. Trama lamellarum iodi ope haud vinescens. Hyphae pileipellis 2.5–6.5 μm latae, efibulatae, diverticulatae. Hyphae stipitis corticales 2–2.5 μm latae, efibulatae, leves, cellulae terminales 4.5–8 μm latae, curvatae, fusiformes.

Ramulicola.

Holotypus: A.A.R. de Meijer CUa-2123 (no. 984.162–169; L); isotypus: MBM 188500.

Basidiomata gregarious. Pileus 1–5 mm across, convex, dry, smooth, pruinose when young, glabrescent, hygrophanous, pale yellow (2A3–4A3) to pale flesh-colour (5A3), drying white. Context thin. Odour absent. Lamellae 7–10 reaching the stipe, tender, arcuate, up to 1.5 mm broad, decurrent, white with concolorous edge. Stipe 3–12 × 0.3 mm, hollow, fragile, equal, terete, smooth, puberulous, concolorous with the pileus, attached to the substratum by a dense mass of white fibrils which gradually disappear, leaving the impression that the stipe is insititious.

Basidia (none seen mature) 23–27 × 7μm, clavate, 4-spored, clampless. Spores 6.7–9.0 × 3.8–4.9 μm (Q = 1.6), pip-shaped, smooth, inamyloid. Cheilocystidia 45–67 × 8–9 × 2.5–4.5 μm, locally forming a sterile band, slender-lageniform to almost cylindrical, clampless, simple or occasionally furcate. Pleurocystidia absent. Lamellar trama not vinescent in Melzer's reagent. Pileipellis a cutis of repent, radiately aligned hyphae which are 2.5–6.5 μm wide, clampless, covered with cylindrical, curved to tortuous, simple or furcate excrescences 3.5–13.5 × 1.8–4.5 μm. Hypoderm made up of parallel, thin-walled hyphae up to 11.5 μm wide. Hyphae of the cortical layer of the stipe 2–2.5 μm wide, clampless, smooth, terminated by curved, fusiform caulocystidia 4.5–8 μm wide. Hyphae of the basal patch 7–8 μm wide, tapering to 1.8–4.5 μm, smooth, fairly thick-walled, with colourless cellwalls, rarely septate, clampless.

On decayed twigs of a dicotyledonous tree in seasonal semi-deciduous alluvial forest, 870 m alt.

Holotype: '*Mycena chrysites* Maas G. and de Meijer / 11 February 1992 / Paraná: Curitiba, Uberaba Distr., Reserva Biológica Cambuí / A.A.R. de

---

*Etymology: chrysites, denoting a yellow colour.

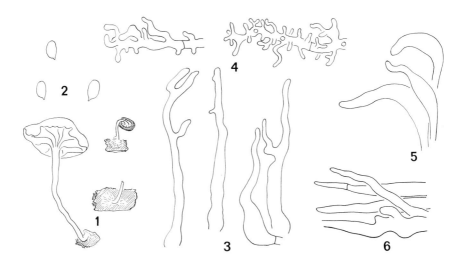

Fig. 44 (1–6) *Mycena chrysites* (de Meijer cua-2123). – 1. Habitus and basal part of the stipe. – 2. Spores. – 3. Cheilocystidia. – 4. Hyphae of the pileipellis. – 5. Terminal cells of hyphae of the stipe cortex (caulocystidia). – 6. Hyphae of the basal patch.
Fig. 1, × 4; all others, × 700.

Meijer cua-2123' (No. 984.162–169; L); isotype: mbm 188500.

The cheilocystidia of the present species do not have the shape usually found in members of section *Adonideae,* but a different disposition of the species would meet with other obstacles. As a case in point, some of the features of *M. chrysites,* such as arcuate lamellae, clampless basidia, inamyloid spores are also characteristic of section *Hiemales* subsect. *Omphaliariae* (Maas Geesteranus, 1992: 459), and one of its species, *Mycena phaeophylla* Kühn., appears to have cheilocystidia very much like those of *M. chrysites.* But *M. chrysites* is definitely not a member of subsect. *Omphaliariae,* whose species never have a yellow pileus, while their caulocystidia are differently shaped.

A further difference which separates *M. chrysites* from most species of section *Adonideae* lies in its lack of pleurocystidia, but it should be re-membered that these organs are not always present either in *Mycena lepto-phylla* (Peck) Sacc. (Maas Geesteranus, 1990: 174).

The description of a further collection is appended here, because there is some doubt as to its identity.

Basidiomata scattered. Pileus 2–5 mm across, hemispherical to campanulate, in one case with small obtuse papilla, dry, smooth, translucent-striate, min-utely pruinose, hygrophanous, yellow (3A5), the centre and striae greyish yellow. Odour absent. Lamellae c. 6 reaching the stipe, tender, arcuate, up to 1.5 mm broad, decurrent, white, with narrow, light yellow edge. Stipe 6–16 ×

0.1–0.3 mm, hollow, fragile, equal, terete, smooth, dry, yellow-puberulous all over, pale yellow (3A4), attached to the substratum by a patch of unobtrusive, radiating, whitish fibrils.

Basidia (all immature) c. 25 × 6.5–8 µm, clavate, clamped. Spores 7.2–8.9(–9.8) × 3.8–4.5 µm, pip-shaped, smooth inamyloid. Cheilocystidia at least 30 µm long × 6.5–8 × 2.5–4.5 µm, occurring mixed with basidia, presumably lageniform, simple, smooth. Pleurocystidia not observed. Lamellar trama not vinescent in Melzer's reagent. Pileipellis a cutis of repent, radiately aligned hyphae which are 1.5–4.5 µm wide, clamped, covered with simple to somewhat branched excrescences 1.8–13.5 × 1.8–2.5 µm. Hyphae of the cortical layer of the stipe 2.5–3.5 µm wide, clamped, smooth, the caulocystidia 27–60 × 6–7 × 2–3 µm, mostly simple, more rarely somewhat branched.

On dead leaves and a twig of a dicotyledonous tree in dense, ombrophilous forest, 20 m alt.

Material examined: 'Mycena cf. chrysites Maas G. and de Meijer / 27 June 1995 / Paraná: Morretes, Porto de Cima, Parque Marumbi, near Nhundiaquara river / A.A.R. de Meijer MA-3090' (No. 991.343–794; L); notes and drawings: MBM 188501.

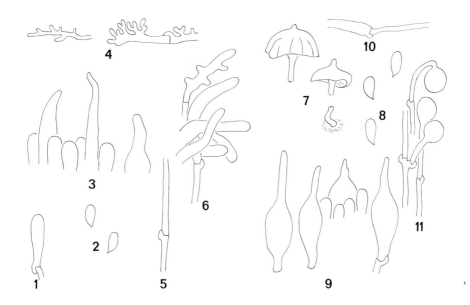

Fig. 45 (1–6) *Mycena* cf *chrysites* (de Meijer MA-3090). – 1. Immature basidium. – 2. Spores. – 3. Cheilocystidia. – 4. Hyphae of the pileipellis. – 5. Hypha of the cortical layer of the stipe. – 6. Terminal cells (caulocystidia).
(7–11) *Mycena mira* (de Meijer MA-2911). – 7. Habitus and basal part of the stipe. – 8. Spores. – 9. Cheilocystidia. – 10. Hypha of the pileipellis. – 11. Terminal cells (caulocystidia).
Fig. 7, × 5; all others, × 700.

If the present collection should prove identical with the type of *M. chrysites*, it represents the clamped condition of the species.

Mycena mira* Maas G. and de Meijer, *spec. nov.* – Fig. 45 (7–11)

Basidiomata dispersa. Pileus 0.5–4 mm latus, 0.5–2.8 mm altus, e conico convexus, umbonatus, haud sulcatus, striatus, glaber, siccus, primo totus ruber, pallescens (centro albo-aurantiacus, marginem versus albus). Caro tenuis, odore nullo. Lamellae 8–11 stipitem attingentes, molles, horizontales vel subarcuatae, usque ad 0.6 mm latae, late adnatae, dente decurrentes, haud intervenosae, albae, margine concolore. Stipes 1.2–8 × 0.2–0.6 mm, cavus, fragilis, aequalis, cylindraceus, levis, totus pruinosus, deorsum glabrescens, siccus, albus vel pallide flavo-albus vel basi nonnumquam roseotinctus, e disco basali albofibrilloso natus.

Basidia 23–27 × 6.5–7 μm, subclavata, 4-sporigera, fibulata, sterigmatibus c. 4.5 μm longis instructa. Sporae 7.2–8.6 × 4.3–4.7 μm, inaequilateraliter ellipsoideae, leves, inamyloideae. Cheilocystidia 36–50 × 9–13.5 × 1.8–2.5 μm, sublageniformia vel subfusiformia, fibulata, levia. Pleurocystidia haud numerosa, similia. Trama lamellarum iodi ope haud vinescens. Hyphae pileipellis 1.8–4.5 μm latae, fibulatae, leves. Hyphae stipitis corticales 1.8–2.7 μm latae, fibulatae, leves, cellulae terminales (caulocystidia) 16–27 × 7–10 μm, capitatae.

Lignicola et foliicola.

Holotypus: A.A.R. de Meijer MA-2911 (No. 990.200–094; L); isotypus: MBM 188532.

Basidiomata scattered. Pileus 0.5–4 mm across, 0.5–2.8 mm high, at first conical, then convex, mostly already at an early stage with a strikingly prominent, rounded umbo, not sulcate, indistinctly translucent-striate, glabrous, dry, at first entirely red (9A7), then with the centre red (9A7) and more orange-red (7A7) or pale orange-pink (7A4) towards the margin, finally pallescent, with only the centre very pale orange-white and the remainder whitish. Context very thin. Odour absent. Lamellae 8–11 reaching the stipe, tender, horizontal or subarcuate, up to 0.6 mm broad, broadly adnate, decurrent with a tooth, not intervenose, white, with concolorous edge. Stipe 1.2–8 × 0.2–0.6 mm, hollow, fragile, equal, terete, smooth, finely pruinose all over, glabrescent in the lower part, dry, white to very pale yellowish white or at the base sometimes slightly pinkish-tinted, the base springing from a basal patch of radiating, fine, silky, white fibrils.

Basidia (few seen mature) 23–27 × 6.5–7 μm, subclavate to almost cylindrical, 4-spored (a single basidium seen 2-spored with two 9 μm long sterigmata), clamped, with sterigmata c. 4.5 μm long. Spores 7.2–8.6 × 4.3–4.7 μm (Q = 2.1), pip-shaped, not infrequently somewhat curved, smooth, inamyloid. Cheilocystidia 36–50 × 9–13.5 × 1.8–2.5 μm, occurring mixed with the basidia (lamellar edge heterogeneous), sublageniform, subfusiform, clamped, smooth. Pleurocystidia scarce, similar. Lamellar trama not vinescent in Melzer's reagent. Pileipellis a cutis of repent, radiately aligned hyphae, 1.8–4.5 μm wide, clamped, smooth. Hypoderm made up of parallel, inflated hyphae up to 30 μm wide. Hyphae of the cortical layer of the stipe 1.8–2.7 μm wide, clamped, smooth, the terminal cells (caulocystidia) 16–27 μm long, made up of a straight or curved stalk 2.5–4.5 μm broad and a globose head 7–10 μm across.

*Etymology: mirus, wonderful, in reference to the striking colour of the pileus.

120

On a decayed twig and leaves of a dicotyledonous tree in dense ombrophilous forest, 300 m alt.

Holotype: '*Mycena mira* Maas G. and de Meijer / 12 June 1994 / Paraná: Morretes, Parque Marumbi, near Nhundiaquara River / A.A.R. de Meijer MA-2911' (No. 990.200–094; L); isotype: MBM 188532.

Additional material: '29 June 1995 / Paraná: Morretes, Porto de Cima, Parque Marumbi, near Nhundiaquara River / on dead twigs of a dicotyledonous tree in dense ombrophilous forest, 20 m. alt. / A.A.R. de Meijer MA-3101' (No. 991.343–791; L); duplicate: MBM 188538.

Mycenas in the South American area with a red pileus and white lamellae and/or stipe have been described by Dennis and by Singer: *Hemimycena roseipallens* (Murrill) Dennis (1961: 86), *Mycena heroica* Sing. (1960: 387) and *M. ribesina* Sing. (1969: 113). The species described by Dennis (which perhaps is not the same as *Prunulus roseipallens* originally described by Murrill [1916: 324]) differs from *M. mira* in the lack of a prominent umbo, in having adnexed, pinkish lamellae (decurrent with a tooth and white in *M. mira*), and an apparently glabrous stipe (pruinose in *M. mira*).

Singer's *Mycena heroica* is readily distinguishable from *M. mira* by its lack of an umbo, by its narrower spores (3–3.3 μm) and diverticulate hyphae of the pileipellis. The difference between *Mycena ribesina* and *M. mira* is less obvious, since both species have several characters in common, but Singer's description of the pileus of *M. ribesina* as 'convexo, obtuso vel subumbonato' conjures up a picture very different from that of the pileus of *M. mira* which 'already at an early stage [has] a strikingly prominent, rounded umbo.' Also, Singer described the lamellae of *M. ribesina* as 'angustis vel sublatis v[el] latis . . ., confertis, adnexis vel adnatis vel decurrentibus.' This does not apply to the lamellae of *M. mira* which are few in number, very narrow, broadly adnate and decurrent with a tooth. If these differences may seem rather unconvincing in the eyes of some, there is one feature that turns the scale – the stipe of *M. ribesina* is described as glabrous. Since the presence of caulocystidia is a regular feature in section *Adonideae,* it may even be asked whether *Mycena ribesina* is a member of this section.

24. MYCENA sect. **Granuliferae** Maas G. and de Meijer, *sect. nov.*

Basidiomata statura media. Pileus quasi glaber, albus vel pallidus. Caro tenuis. Lamellae molles, adnatae, dente decurrentes, albae, margine albo. Stipes fragilis, quasi glaber, albus, e disco basali fibrilloso natus.

Basidia clavata, fibulata. Sporae subcylindraceae, leves, inamyloideae. Cheilocystidia clavata, fibulata, apice surculis brevibus praedita. Pleurocystidia clavata vel subfusiformia, fibulata, levia vel nulla. Trama lamellarum iodi ope haud vinescens. Hyphae pileipellis fibulatae, surculis minutis obtectae. Hyphae stipitis corticales fibulatae, leves vel surculis sparsis munitae, cellulae terminales diverticulatae.

Foliicola.

Species typica: *Mycena granulifera.*

Section *Granuliferae* seems to have an isolated position within the genus. It may have a single character in common with other sections, but differs in most other important characters. The hyphae of the pileipellis may serve as an example. They are densely covered with small, more or less granular excrescences. Although this kind of ornamentation also occurs in species of sections *Sacchariferae* Kühn. ex Sing., *Basipedes* (Fr.) Quél., *Supinae* Konr. and Maubl., *Pterigenae* (Maas G.) Maas G., and *Polyadelphia* Sing. ex Maas G., these sections differ widely from sect. *Granuliferae* in that their species are characterized by amyloid spores, differently shaped and/or ornamented cheilocystidia and caulocystidia. A similar discussion can be applied in connection with the basal patch to the stipe or the inamyloidity of the spores or the foliicolous habit.

Section *Granuliferae* should perhaps be placed near section *Aciculae* Kühn. ex Sing. (Maas Geesteranus, 1990: 178).

KEY TO THE SPECIES

1. Lamellae ascending, lamellar edge convex. Pleurocystidia present. Hyphae of the cortical layer of the stipe diverticulate: . . . . *M. granulifera*
1. Lamellae subarcuate, lamellar edge concave. Pleurocystidia absent. Hyphae of the cortical layer of the stipe smooth: . . . . *M. sertipes*

Mycena granulifera* Maas G. and de Meijer, *spec. nov.* – Fig. 46

Basidiomata dispersa. Pileus 2–5 mm latus, convexus, siccus, levis, striatus, quasi glaber, albus vel flavo-albidus, centro interdum pallide flavobrunneus. Caro tenuis, odore nullo. Lamellae 6–14 stipitem attingentes, molles, adscendentes, 1 mm latae, adnatae, dente breviter decurrentes, albae, margine convexo, albo. Stipes 30–60 × 0.3–0.4 mm, cavus, fragilis, aequalis, cylindraceus, siccus, levis, quasi glaber vel sursum minute pruinosus, albus vel pallide flavus, e disco basali fibrilloso natus.

Basidia 14.5–15 × c. 7 μm, clavata, 4-sporigera, fibulata, sterigmatibus 3.5 μm longis instructa. Sporae 8.9–10.7 × 2.7–3.6 μm, cylindraceae, leves, inamyloideae. Cheilocystidia 14.5–30 × 5.5–11.5 μm, clavata, fibulata, apice surculis clavatis vel subcapitatis 2.5–6.3 × 1.8–3.5 μm praedita. Pleurocystidia 23–27 × 6.5–10.5 μm, clavata vel subfusiformia, levia. Trama lamellarum iodi ope haud vinescens. Hyphae pileipellis 2.5–4.5 μm latae, fibulatae, diverticulatae. Hyphae stipitis corticales 1.8–2.7 μm latae, fibulatae, sparse diverticulatae, cellulae terminales 4.5–6.5 μm latae, diverticulatae vel ramosae.

Foliicola.

Holotypus: A.A.R. de Meijer PAC-2706 (No. 988.233–091; L); isotypus: MBM 188524.

Basidiomata scattered. Pileus 2–5 mm across, convex, dry, smooth, striate, appearing glabrous, pure white or yellowish white (2A2) to pale yellowish grey (2B2), at the very centre sometimes pale yellowish brown. Context very thin. Odour absent. Lamellae 6–14 reaching the stipe, tender, ascending, 1 mm broad, adnate, some decurrent with a short tooth, pure white, the edge generally convex, white. Stipe 30–60 × 0.3–0.4 mm, hollow, fragile, equal, terete, dry, smooth, appearing glabrous or upwards minutely pruinose, pure

*Etymology: granulifera, grain-bearing, in reference to the hyphae of the pileipellis which are studded with granular or short cylindrical excrescences.

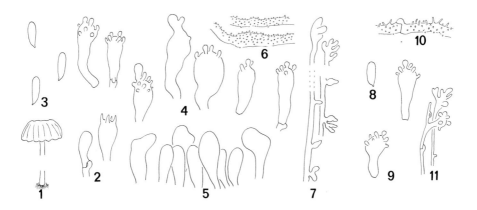

Fig. 46 (1–7) *Mycena granulifera* (de Meijer PAC-2706). – 1. Habitus and basal part of the stipe. –
2. Basidia. – 3. Spores. – 4. Cheilocystidia. – 5. Pleurocystidia and immature basidia. – 6. Hyphae of
the pileipellis. – 7. Hyphae of the cortical layer of the stipe.
(8–11) *Mycena granulifera* (de Meijer MA-3096). – 8. Spore. – 9. Cheilocystidia. – 10. Hypha of the
pileipellis. – 11. Terminal cells of hyphae of the cortical layer of the stipe.
Fig. 1, × 3; all others, × 700.

white to pale yellow (4A2–3), springing from a small patch of radiating, white
fibrils which with age tend to disappear, giving the impression of the stipe
being insititious.

Basidia (none seen fully mature) 14.5–15 × c. 7 μm, clavate, 4-spored,
clamped, with sterigmata 3.5 μm long. Spores 8.9–10.7 × 2.7–3.6 μm (Q =
3.0), almost cylindrical, smooth, inamyloid. Cheilocystidia 14.5–30 × 5.5–
11.5 μm, forming a sterile band (lamellar edge homogeneous), clavate,
clamped, apically covered with fairly few, coarse, sometimes very coarse,
clavate to more or less capitate excrescences 2.5–6.3 × 1.8–3.5 μm.
Pleurocystidia 23–27 × 6.5–10.5 μm, clavate to subfusiform, clamped,
smooth. Lamellar trama not vinescent in Melzer's reagent. Pileipellis a cutis
of repent, radiately aligned hyphae which are 2.5–4.5 μm wide, clamped,
densely covered with short-cylindrical to granular, simple excrescences 0.9–
2.7 × 0.9 μm. Hypoderm consisting of parallel hyphae up to 20 or 30 μm
wide. Hyphae of the cortical layer of the stipe 1.8–2.7 μm wide, clamped,
sparsely covered with cylindrical to utriform, simple to furcate or somewhat
branched excrescences 4.5–6.3 × 1.8–3.6 μm, the terminal cells scarce to
numerous, thin-walled, 4.5–6.5 μm broad, lobed to somewhat branched.

On fallen, dead leaves of a dicotyledonous tree in dense ombrophilous
forest, 10 m alt.

Holotype: '*Mycena granulifera* Maas G. and de Meijer / 18 May 1993 /
Paraná: Paranaguá, Alexandra, along road BR-277 / A.A.R. de Meijer PAC-
2706' (No. 988.233–091; L); isotype: MBM 188524.

Additional material: '27 June 1995 / Paraná: Morretes, Porto de Cima,
Parque Marumbi, near Nhundiaquara River / A.A.R. de Meijer MA-3096 / on

123

dead leaves of a dicotyledonous tree (including *Cecropia* sp.) in dense ombrophilous forest, 20 m alt.' (No. 991.343–750; L); duplicate: MBM 188525.

Clamp-connections proved to be very difficult to find.

Mycena sertipes* Maas G. and de Meijer, *spec. nov.* – Fig. 47

Basidiomata solitaria vel bina. Pileus 3–5 mm latus, convexus, tenuiter sulcatus, striatus, subglaber, siccus, levis, albus, centro pallide flavus, striis flavogriseis, hygrophanus, desiccatus albus.
Caro tenuis, odore nullo. Lamellae 9–11 stipitem attingentes, molles, subarcuatae, usque ad
0.8 mm latae, late adnatae, dente decurrentes, albae, margine concavo, concolore. Stipes 25–40
× 0.3–0.5 mm, cavus, fragilis, aequalis, cylindraceus, siccus, levis, subglaber, albus, basi subpuberulus, interdum pallide flavus, e disco basali c. 1 mm lato, sericeo natus.
   Basidia 17–22.5 × 6.5–8 μm, clavata, 4-sporigera, fibulata, sterigmatibus 5.5–6.5 μm longis
instructa. Sporae 8.9–10.7 × 2.7–3.6 μm, subcylindraceae, leves, inamyloideae. Cheilocystidia
c. 23 × 7–10 μm, clavata, fibulata, levia vel apice surculis paucis 1–2.7 × 1–2 μm praedita.
Pleurocystidia nulla. Trama lamellarum iodi ope haud vinescens. Hyphae pileipellis 2.5–4.5 μm
latae, fibulatae, diverticulatae. Hyphae stipitis corticales 1.8–2.7 μm latae, fibulatae, leves, cellulae terminales 11–23 × 4.5–8 μm, vulgo clavatae, surculis crassis munitae.
   Foliicola.
   Holotypus: A.A.R. de Meijer MA-2912 (No. 990.200–039; L); isotypus: MBM 190350.

Basidiomata solitary or in twos. Pileus 3–5 mm across, convex, shallowly
sulcate, translucent-striate, appearing glabrous, dry, centrally pale yellow,
striae yellowish grey, between the striae white, somewhat hygrophanous,
drying white. Context thin. Odour absent. Lamellae 9–11 reaching the stipe,
tender, subarcuate, up to 0.8 mm broad, broadly adnate, decurrent with a
tooth, white, with concave, concolorous edge. Stipe 25–40 × 0.3–0.5 mm,
hollow, fragile, equal, terete, dry, smooth, appearing glabrous, white, the
base minutely puberulous, sometimes pale yellow (4A2–3), arising from a
basal disc c. 1 mm across formed by radiating, very fine, silky fibrils.
   Basidia 17–22.5 × 6.5–8 μm, clavate, 4-spored, clamped, with sterigmata
5.5–6.5 μm long. Spores 8.9–10.7 × 2.7–3.6 μm (Q = 3.2), almost cylindrical, smooth, inamyloid. Cheilocystidia c. 23 × 7–10 μm, occurring mixed
with the basidia and hardly protruding, clavate, clamped, smooth or covered
with few, wart-like or cylindrical, obtuse excrescences 1–2.7 × 1–2 μm.
Pleurocystidia absent. Lamellar trama not vinescent in Melzer's reagent.
Pileipellis a cutis of repent hyphae which are 2.5–4.5 μm wide, clamped,
covered with simple, cylindrical excrescences 1.8–2.7 × 0.9–1.5 μm. Hypoderm consisting of parallel hyphae with inflated cells up to 20 μm. Hyphae of
the cortical layer of the stipe 1.8–2.7 μm wide, clamped, smooth, the terminal cells not numerous, 11–23 × 4.5–8 μm, straight to curved, clavate to
more or less irregularly shaped, covered with coarse, obtuse excrescences 1.5–
5.5 × 1.5–3.5 μm.
   On dead leaves of a dicotyledonous tree in dense ombrophilous forest,
300 m alt.

---

*Etymology: sertum, wreath; pes, foot, referring to the whorl of silky threads round the base of the
stipe.

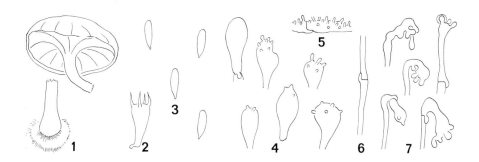

Fig. 47 (1–7) *Mycena sertipes* (de Meijer MA-2912). – 1. Habitus and basal part of the stipe. – 2. Basidium. – 3. Spores. – 4. Cheilocystidia. – 5. Fragment of a hypha of the pileipellis. – 6. Hypha of the cortical layer of the stipe. – 7. Terminal cells.
Fig. 1, × 10; all others, × 700.

Holotype: '*Mycena sertipes* Maas G. and de Meijer / 12 June 1994 / Paraná: Morretes, Parque Marumbi, near Nhundiaquara River / A.A.R. de Meijer MA-2912' (No. 990.200–039; L); isotype: MBM 190350.

The pale colour of the entire fungus and the almost cylindrical, inamyloid spores are characters rather suggestive of those found in the genus *Hemimycena* Sing. On the other hand, the cheilocystidia and caulocystidia of *M. sertipes* are widely different from those of the type species *H. lactea* (Pers.: Fr.) Sing., while they compare satisfactorily with those of *Mycena alba* (Bres. apud Sacc.) Kühn. and *M. speirea* (Fr.: Fr.) Gillet. *Mycena sertipes* may prove to be a species that will be welcomed by those who are in favour of merging the genera *Mycena* and *Hemimycena*.

25. MYCENA sect. Notabiles Maas G. and de Meijer, *sect. nov.*

Basidiomata parva. Pileus pallide flavus. Caro tenuis, odore nullo. Lamellae molles, adscendentes, late adnatae, dente decurrentes, albae, margine concolores. Stipes fragilis, siccus, pallide flavus, infra albus, basi minute puberulus, e disco basali minuto albofibrilloso natus.

Basidia clavata, fibulata. Sporae inaequilateraliter ellipsoideae, leves, inamyloideae. Cheilocystidia cylindracea, dense spinulosa. Pleurocystidia haud observata. Trama lamellarum iodi ope haud vinescens. Hyphae pileipellis diverticulatae. Hyphae stipitis corticales fibulatae, haud in materiam gelatinosam immersae, diverticulatae, caulocystidia cylindracea, dense spinulosa.

Corticola.

Species typica: *Mycena notabilis*.

This section might be placed between sections *Oregonenses* Maas G. (1990: 182) and *Hiemales* Konr. and Maubl. (Maas Geesteranus, 1991: 81).

Mycena notabilis* Maas G. and de Meijer, *spec. nov.* – Fig. 48

Basidiomata dispersa. Pileus 1–2 mm latus, 1–2 mm altus, campanulatus, centro subdepressus, siccus, tenuiter sulcatus striatusque, minute pruinosus, pallide flavus. Caro tenuis, odore nullo.

*Etymology: notabilis, remarkable, because of the cheilocystidia and caulocystidia which externally are indistinguishable from those of *Mycena aspratilis*, an altogether different species.

Lamellae 6–8 stipitem attingentes, molles, adscendentes, parum ventricosae, usque ad 0.6 mm latae, late adnatae, dente decurrentes, albae, margine concolores. Stipes 8–18 × 0.1–0.2 mm, fistulosus, fragilis, aequalis, cylindraceus, siccus, levis, pallide flavus, deorsum albus, e disco basali minuto albo-fibrilloso natus.

Basidia c. 18 × 7 μm, 2-sporigera?, fibulata. Sporae 9.0–10.3 × 4.3–5.4 μm, inaequilateraliter ellipsoideae, leves, inamyloideae. Cheilocystidia 21.5–30 × 4.5–6 μm, cylindracea, tenuitunicata, surculis cylindraceis 0.9–1.8 × 0.5 μm dense instructa. Pleurocystidia haud visa. Trama lamellarum iodi ope haud vinescens. Hyphae pileipellis 2.5–3.5 μm latae, subgelatinosae?, surculis 0.9–1.8 × 0.5–0.9 μm munitae. Hyphae stipitis corticales 0.9–1.8 μm latae, fibulatae, haud in materiam gelatinosam immersae, diverticulatae, caulocystidia 16–30 × 6–8 μm, cylindracea, subclavata, tenuitunicata, surculis cylindraceis 0.9–1.8 × 0.5–0.9 μm praedita.

Corticola.

Holotypus: A.A.R. de Meijer PAf-3077 (No. 995.187–514; L); notulae: MBM 190325.

Basidiomata scattered. Pileus 1–2 mm across, 1–2 mm high, campanulate, centrally flattened or somewhat depressed, dry, delicately sulcate-striate, minutely pruinose, more pronouncedly so towards the margin, fairly pale yellow (4A4). Context very thin. Odour absent. Lamellae 6–8 reaching the stipe, tender, ascending, little ventricose to equal, up to 0.6 mm broad, broadly adnate, decurrent with a tooth, white, with almost straight, concolorous edge. Stipe 8–18 × 0.1–0.2 mm, fistulose, fragile, equal, terete, dry, smooth, appearing glabrous, minutely puberulous near the base, pale yellow (4A3), white farther down, springing from a very small patch made up of minute, white fibrils (possibly detectable only when dried).

Basidia immature, c. 18 × 7 μm, clavate, one seen with two incipient sterigmata, clamped. Spores 9.0–10.3 × 4.3–5.4 μm (Q = 2.0), pip-shaped, smooth, inamyloid. Cheilocystidia 21.5–30 × 4.5–6 μm, forming a sterile band (lamellar edge homogeneous), cylindrical, few observed to have a clamp, thin-walled (0.9 μm), densely covered with cylindrical excrescences 0.9–1.8 × 0.5 μm. Pleurocystidia not observed. Lamellar trama not vinescent in Melzer's reagent. Pileipellis a cutis of one or two repent, radiately aligned hyphae which are 2.5–3.5 μm wide, probably somewhat gelatinizing, covered

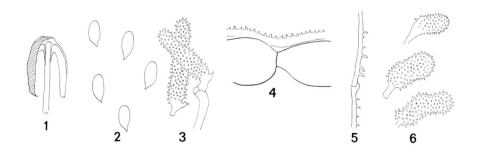

Fig. 48 (1–6) *Mycena notabilis* (de Meijer PAf-3077). – 1. Habitus. – 2. Spores. – 3. Cheilocystidia. – 4. Hypha of the pileipellis. – 5. Hypha of the cortical layer of the stipe. – 6. Caulocystidia. Fig. 1, × 10; all others, × 700.

with simple excrescences 0.9–1.8 × 0.5–0.9 μm. Hypoderm made up of inflated hyphae up to 30 μm wide. Hyphae of the cortical layer of the stipe 0.9–1.8 μm wide, clamped, not embedded in gelatinous matter, covered with cylindrical, simple, straight to somewhat curved excrescences 2.7–3.5 × 0.9–1.5 μm, the caulocystidia 16–30 × 6–8 μm, cylindrical to somewhat ellipsoid, thin-walled, densely covered with cylindrical excrescences 0.9–1.8 × 0.5–0.9 μm.

On bark of twigs and on leaf petioles of a dicotyledonous tree in dense ombrophilous forest, 20 m alt.

Holotype: '*Mycena notabilis* Maas G. and de Meijer / 22 June 1995 / Paraná: Paranaguá, 5 km W of Saquarema / A.A.R. de Meijer PAf-3077' (No. 995.197–514; L); notes and drawings: MBM 190325.

The two most outstanding features of the present species are the densely spinulose cheilocystidia and caulocystidia, and the surprising thing is that these are indistinguishable externally from their counterparts in *Mycena aspratilis*. However, the latter species is not even remotely related, differing in having a viscid stipe, amyloid spores, and strikingly thick-walled cheilo- and caulocystidia.

26. MYCENA section HIEMALES Konr. and Maubl.

Mycena [sect.] *Hiemales* Konr. and Maubl., Ic. sel. Fung. **6**: 274. 1934; Sing., Agar. mod. taxon., 3rd ed.: 396. 1975 (formally accepted as section). – *Marasmiellus* sect. *Hiemales* (Konr. and Maubl.) Sing. in Lilloa **22**: 302. ('1949') 1951. – Lectotype (Sing., 1951: 302): *Marasmiellus hiemalis* (Osb. apud Retz.: Fr.) Sing.

Mycena [subsect.?] *Hiemales* Kühn., Genre *Mycena*: 164, 564. 1938 (no reference to Konr. and Maubl.) – *Hemimycena* sect. *Hiemales* (Kühn.) Sing. in Annls mycol. **41**: 120, 121, 123. 1943. – Lectotype (Donk, unpublished): *Mycena hiemalis*.

Basidiomata fairly small to medium-sized. Pileus glabrous to pruinose, lubricous or not, grey-brown to white, darker at the centre to black-brown. Context thin. Odour absent or of little importance. Lamellae tender, white to greyish. Stipe hollow, pruinose to glabrous, white, pallid or brownish, rarely bright yellow above when young, the base as a rule covered with coarse fibrils.

Basidia clavate, 2-spored and clampless or 4-spored and clamped. Spores pip-shaped to globose, smooth, non-amyloid. Cheilocystidia forming a sterile band or occurring mixed with basidia, variously shaped, generally simple or apically somewhat branched, clamped or not. Pleurocystidia similar or absent. Lamellar trama usually not staining in Melzer's reagent. Hyphae of the pileipellis clamped or not, diverticulate or, more rarely, smooth. Hyphae of the cortical layer of the stipe clamped or not, smooth or diverticulate, caulocystidia generally present.

Growing among moss or vegetable debris, on wood or moss-covered treetrunks.

1. Lamellae ascending, edge convex: . . . . 26.1. subsect. *Hiemales*
1. Lamellae horizontal to arcuate, edge straight or concave: . . . . . . 26.2. subsect. *Omphaliariae*

26.1. Subsection HIEMALES Maas G.

Mycena subsect. *Hiemales* Maas G. in Persoonia **11**: 114. 1980. – Type species: *Mycena hiemalis*.
    For further synonymy, see Maas Geesteranus, l.c.

Basidiomata with features as in sect. *Hiemales*, but lamellae ascending and the edge convex.

KEY TO THE SPECIES

1. Cheilocystidia 16–24 μm long. Pleurocystidia absent. Hyphae of the pileipellis diverticulate:
. . . . *M. exigua*
1. Cheilocystidia 30–65 μm long. Pleurocystidia present. Hyphae of the pileipellis smooth:
. . . . *M. globata*

Mycena exigua* Maas G. and de Meijer *spec. nov.* – Fig. 49 (1–7)

Basidiomata dispersa. Pileus 1–3 mm latus, 0.8–2 mm altus, convexus, siccus, sulcatus, striatus, pruinosus, albus. Caro tenuis, alba, odore indistincto. Lamellae 12–16 stipitem attingentes, molles, adscendentes, usque ad 1 mm latae, adnatae, interdum dente decurrentes, albae, margine concolores. Stipes 10–30 × 0.2–0.5 mm, fistulosus, fragilis, aequalis, cylindraceus, siccus, levis, pruinosus, basin versus albo-puberulus, albus, basi fibrillis radiantibus, albis substrato affixus.
    Basidia c. 15 × 5.5 μm, subclavata, 2-sporigera, efibulata, sterigmatibus 4.5 μm longis praedita. Sporae 8.1–10.3 × 3.6–4.4 μm, inaequilateraliter ellipsoideae, interdum subcurvatae, leves, inamyloideae. Cheilocystidia 16–24 × 3.5–6.5 × 2.5–3.5 μm, cylindracea, sublageniformia, efibulata, levia, apice obtusa. Pleurocystidia nulla. Trama lamellarum iodi ope haud vinescens. Hyphae pileipellis 1.8–2.5 μm latae, efibulatae, diverticulatae, subgelatinosae. Hyphae stipitis corticales 1.8–2.5 μm latae, efibulatae, pro majore parte leves, haud in materiam gelatinosam immersae, caulocystidia 2.5–18 × 4.5–6.5 × 2.5–3.5 μm, subcylindracea.
    Ramulicola.
    Holotypus: A.A.R. de Meijer RS-3021 (No. 990.200–056; L); notulae: MBM 188515.

Basidiomata scattered. Pileus 1–3 mm across, 0.8–2 mm high, convex, dry (presumably somewhat glutinous when wet), sulcate, striate, pruinose, white. Context thin, white. Odour indistinct. Lamellae 12–16 reaching the stipe, tender, ascending, up to 1 mm broad, straight to somewhat ventricose, adnate, some decurrent with a short tooth, white, with horizontal to slightly convex, concolorous edge (which when dried is covered with orange oily droplets). Stipe 10–30 × 0.2–0.5 mm, fistulose, fragile, equal, terete, dry, smooth, pruinose, towards the base white-puberulous, white, springing from a basal patch, about 1 mm across, made up of radiating white fibrils.
    Basidia (none seen mature) c. 15 × 5.5 μm, subclavate, 2-spored, clampless, with sterigmata 4.5 μm long. Spores 8.1–10.3 × 3.6–4.4 μm (Q = 2.5), elongate pip-shaped, not infrequently somewhat curved, smooth, inamyloid. Cheilocystidia 16–24 × 3.5–6.5 × 2.5–3.5 μm, forming a dense sterile band

*Etymology: exiguus, small.

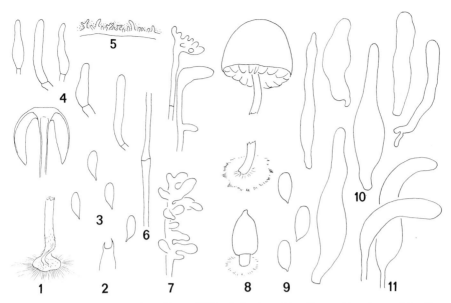

Fig. 49 (1–7) *Mycena exigua* (de Meijer RS-3021). – 1. Section of the pileus and basal part of the stipe. 2. – Immature basidium. – 3. Spores. – 4. Cheilocystidia. – 5. Hypha of the pileipellis. – 6. Hypha of the cortical layer of the stipe. – 7. Terminal cells (caulocystidia).
(8–11) *Mycena globata* (de Meijer CUa-291). – 8. Habitus and basal part of the stipe. – 9. Spores. – 10. Cheilocystidia. – 11. Terminal cells (caulocystidia).
Fig. 1, × 15; fig. 8, × 7; all others, × 700.

(lamellar edge homogeneous), cylindrical, sublageniform, clampless, with obtuse apex. Pleurocystidia absent. Lamellar trama not vinescent in Melzer's reagent. Pileipellis a cutis of repent, radiately aligned hyphae which are 1.8 – 2.5 μm wide, clampless, covered with simple to somewhat furcate, cylindrical, straight to curved excrescences 1.8–4.5 × 0.9–1.8 μm, which appear somewhat gelatinized under the microscope. Hyphae of the hypoderm with much inflated cells. Hyphae of the cortical layer of the stipe 1.8–2.5 μm wide, clampless, not gelatinized, smooth for the greater part, sparsely diverticulate towards their tips, caulocystidia 2.5–18 × 4.5–6.5 × 2.5–3.5 μm, subcylindrical.

On decayed twigs of a dicotyledonous tree in secondary mixed ombrophilous forest, 900 m alt.

Holotype: '*Mycena exigua* Maas G. and de Meijer / 11 Feb. 1995 / Paraná: Rio Branco do Sul, Areias Distr. / A.A.R. de Meijer RS-3021' (No. 990.200–056; L); notes and drawings: MBM 188515.

Mycena globata* Maas G. and de Meijer, *spec. nov.* – Fig. 49 (8–11)

Basidiomata dispersa. Pileus usque ad 8 mm latus, e campanulato convexus, siccus, levis, substriatus, glaber, albidus. Caro tenuis, odore ignoto. Lamellae c. 16 stipitem attingentes, molles, adscendentes, usque ad 2 mm latae, minime adnatae, albae, margine concolores. Stipes 8–17 ×

*Etymology: globatus, rounded, referrring to the rounded shape of the pileus.

0.5–1.2 mm, fistulosus, fragilis, aequalis, cylindraceus, siccus, levis, totus albo-puberulus, griseo-albus, e disco basali c. 1.5 mm lato, albo natus.

Basidia 27–30 × 8–9 μm, subclavata, 4-sporigera, fibulata, sterigmatibus c. 4.5 μm longis instructa. Sporae 9.2–11.2 × 4.9–5.8 μm, inaequilateraliter ellipsoideae, leves, inamyloideae. Cheilocystidia 30–65 × 6.5–11.5 × 4.5–7 μm, cylindracea, subfusiformia, sublageniformia, fibulata, levia, apice vulgo rotundata. Pleurocystidia similia. Trama lamellarum iodi ope haud vinescens. Hyphae pileipellis c. 2.7 μm latae, leves, haud in materiam gelatinosam immersae. Hyphae stipitis corticales 1.8–2.7 μm latae, leves, haud in materiam gelatinosam immersae, caulocystidia 40–75 × 6.5–12.5 μm, numerosa, cylindracea, curvata, tenuitunicata.

Lignicola.

Holotypus: A.A.R. de Meijer cua-291 (No. 990.200–024; L); isotypus: mbm 188522.

Basidiomata scattered. Pileus up to 8 mm across, at first campanulate, with or without a small umbo, then convex, flattening with age, dry, smooth, vaguely striate, glabrous, whitish. Context thin. Odour not recorded. Lamellae c. 16 reaching the stipe, tender, ascending, up to 2 mm broad, adnexed, white, with concolorous edge. Stipe 8–17 × 0.5–1.2 mm, fistulose, fragile, equal, terete, dry, smooth, white-puberulous all over, greyish white, very pale brownish towards the base, springing from a c. 1.5 mm broad, white basal disc which is made up of radiating, fine, silky fibrils.

Basidia (none seen fully mature) 27–30 × 8–9 μm, subclavate, 4-spored, clamped, with sterigmata 4.5 μm long. Spores 9.2–11.2 × 4.9–5.8 μm (Q = 2.1), pip-shaped, smooth, inamyloid. Cheilocystidia 30–65 × 6.5–11.5 × 4.5–7 μm, forming a sterile band (lamellar edge homogeneous), cylindrical, subfusiform, sublageniform, clamped, smooth, thin-walled (one observed with thickened cell-walls), apically generally broadly rounded. Pleurocystidia similar, frequently somewhat broader. Lamellar trama not vinescent in Melzer's reagent. Pileipellis a cutis of repent, radiately aligned hyphae which are c. 2.7 μm wide, smooth, not immersed in gelatinous matter. Hypoderm consisting of parallel hyphae with inflated cells. Hyphae of the cortical layer of the stipe 1.8–2.7 μm wide, smooth, not immersed in gelatinous matter; caulocystidia 40–75 × 6.5–12.5 μm, numerous, cylindrical, curved, thin-walled.

Found on dead branch of a dicotyledonous tree in seasonal semi-deciduous alluvial forest.

Holotype: 'Mycena globata Maas G. and de Meijer / 16 Dec. 1979 / Paraná: Curitiba, Uberaba Distr., Reserva Biológica Cambuí / A.A.R. de Meijer cua-291' (No. 990.200–024; L); isotype: mbm 188522.

Owing to the poor condition of the type material, it was not possible to find clamp-connections except at the base of a few basidia and remnants of clamps at the base of some of the cheilocystidia.

Species with smooth hyphae of the pileipellis and of the cortical layer of the stipe are rare in section Hiemales, the best known European example being Mycena olida Bres. (Maas Geesteranus, 1991: 86). The spores of the latter species, which is generally found two-spored, are rather shorter (6.5–

130

8.8 μm) than those of *M. globata,* its caulocystidia are differently shaped and, strikingly different, its stipe does not spring from a basal disc.

Raithelhuber described from Brazil a *Mycena perturbata* (1984: 30; 1991: 133) which is entirely white and characterized by its growth on wood, hardly amyloid spores, and smooth, fusiform to lageniform cheilocystidia. Raithelhuber published this as a new name to replace *Mycena nivea* Pers. sensu Rick but his failure to give a Latin diagnosis renders the publication invalid. Although its new name may be ignored, the species is a reality and requires attention. It differs from *M. globata* in having a somewhat pruinose pileus ('Hut . . . etwas bereift'), adnate lamellae ('Lamellen . . . angewachsen'), glabrous stipe ('Stiel . . . glatt, auch an der Basis nicht haarig'), apparent lack of a basal disc, and somewhat shorter spores ('Sporen . . . 7.5–8 μm').

26.2. Subsection OMPHALIARIAE Kühn. ex Maas G.

Mycena [subsect.?] *Omphaliariae* Kühn., Genre *Mycena*: 164, 582. 1938 (not val. publ.: no Latin descr.). – *Marasmiellus* subsect. *Omphaliarii* (Kühn.) Sing. in Lilloa **22**: 302. ('1949') 1951 (not val. publ.: no Latin descr.). – *Mycena* subsect. *Omphaliariae* (Kühn.) Sing., Agar. mod. taxon., 3rd ed.: 396. 1975 (not val. publ.: no Latin descr.). – *Mycena* subsect. *Omphaliariae* Kühn. ex Maas G. in Persoonia **11**: 115. 1980. – Holotype: *Mycena speirea* (Fr.: Fr.) Gillet.

For further synonymy, see Maas Geesteranus, l.c.

Basidiomata with features as in sect. *Hiemales,* but lamellae horizontal to arcuate and the edge straight to concave.

KEY TO THE SPECIES

1. Cheilocystidia apically ornamented. Hyphae of the cortical layer of the stipe sparsely covered with excrescences: . . . . *M. lepida*
1. Cheilocystidia smooth. Hyphae of the cortical layer of the stipe smooth: . . . *M. straminella*

Mycena lepida* Maas G. and de Meijer, *spec. nov.* – Fig. 50 (1–5)

Basidiomata solitaria vel dispersa. Pileus 0.8–5 mm latus, usque ad 4 mm altus, campanulatus vel convexus, siccus, levis vel subsulcatus, striatus, glaber, hygrophanus, pallide flavo-albus. Caro tenuis, alba, odore nullo. Lamellae 7–15 stipitem attingentes, molles, arcuatae, usque ad 0.5 mm latae, late adnatae, longe decurrentes, albae, margine concolore. Stipes 5–40 × 0.5–1 mm, cavus, fragilis, aequalis, cylindraceus, siccus, levis, minute puberulus, albus, basi fibrillis radiantibus, albis substrato affixus.

Basidia c. 18 × 7 μm, immatura, fibulata. Sporae 6.7–7.2 × 4.0–4.5 μm, immaturae?, inaequilateraliter ellipsoideae, leves, inamyloideae. Cheilocystidia 16–27 × 4.5–6.5 μm, subclavata vel subcylindracea, fibulata, apice diverticulata vel furcata. Pleurocystidia nulla. Trama lamellarum iodi ope haud vinescens. Hyphae pileipellis 2.5 μm latae, fibulatae, sparse diverticulatae. Hyphae stipitis corticales 1.8–2.5 μm latae, fibulatae, sparse diverticulatae, cellulae terminales (caulocystidia) 12.5–27 × 5.5–11.5 μm, crasse lobatae.

Foliicola vel raro ramulicola.

Holotypus: A.A.R. de Meijer MA-2999 (No. 990.200–057; L); isotypus: MBM 188530.

Basidiomata solitary or scattered. Pileus 0.8–5 mm across, up to 4 mm high,

*Etymology: lepidus, pretty.

campanulate to convex, dry, smooth to delicately sulcate, translucent-striate, appearing glabrous, hygrophanous, the centre and striae very pale yellowish white (2A2), between the striae white. Context thin, white. Odour absent. Lamellae 7–15 reaching the stipe, tender, arcuate, up to 0.5 mm broad, broadly adnate, far decurrent down the stipe, white, with concave, concolorous edge. Stipe 5–40 × 0.5–1 mm, hollow, fragile, equal, terete, dry, smooth, minutely puberulous, white, the base attached to the substratum by a whorl of radiating, fine, white fibrils.

Basidia (none seen mature) c. 18 × 7 μm, clavate, sterigmata not observed, clamped. Spores (very few observed, immature?) 6.7–7.2 × 4.0–4.5 μm (Q = 1.8), pip-shaped, smooth, non-amyloid. Cheilocystidia 16–27 × 4.5–6.5 μm, subclavate, subcylindrical, clamped, apically with a few coarse excrescences or somewhat lobed-furcate, more rarely smooth. Pleurocystidia absent. Lamellar trama not vinescent in Melzer's reagent. Pileipellis a cutis of repent, radiately aligned hyphae which are 2.5 μm wide, clamped, not very densely covered with (somewhat gelatinizing?) simple excrescences 1.8–4.5 × 1–1.8 μm. Hypoderm consisting of parallel hyphae with inflated cells 25 μm wide. Hyphae of the cortical layer of the stipe 1.8–2.5 μm wide, clamped, sparsely covered with simple to lobed-furcate excrescences 3.6–6.5 × 2.7–3.6 μm, the terminal cells (caulocystidia) 12.5–27 × 5.5–11.5 μm, apically variously lobed.

Mostly on decayed leaves of a dicotyledonous tree, rarely on decayed branches, in dense, ombrophilous forest, 450 m alt.

Holotype: 'Mycena lepida Maas G. and de Meijer / 28 Dec. 1994 / Paraná:

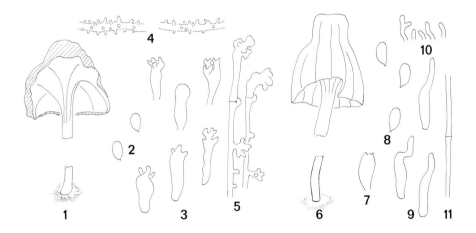

Fig. 50 (1–5) *Mycena lepida* (de Meijer MA-2999). – 1. Habitus and basal part of the stipe. – 2. Spores. – 3. Cheilocystidia. – 4. Hyphae of the pileipellis. – 5. Hyphae of the cortical layer of the stipe and terminal cells.

(6–11) *Mycena straminella* (de Meijer RSC-3134). – 6. Habitus and basal part of the stipe. – 7. Immature basidium. – 8. Spores. – 9. Cheilocystidia. – 10. Excrescences of a hypha of the pileipellis. – 11. Hypha of the cortical layer of the stipe.

Fig. 1, × 7.5; fig. 6, × 10; all others, × 700.

Morretes, Parque Marumbi, Estação Marumbi / A.A.R. de Meijer MA-2999' (No. 990.200–057; L); isotype: MBM 188530.

Mycena lepida is obviously related to *M. speirea* (Fr.: Fr.) Gillet, from which it differs in narrower lamellae, consistently unbranched and shorter excrescences of the hyphae of the pileipellis, and differently shaped caulocystidia.

Mycena minutuliaffinis described by Singer (1969: 131) from Chile has, like the present species, a whitish pileus not more than 10 mm across, decurrent lamellae, a stipe which springs from a basal patch of radiating fibrils, pip-shaped spores, apically ornamented cheilocystidia, and diverticulate hyphae of both the pileipellis and the cortical layer of the stipe. But the differences (*minutuliaffinis*: weakly amyloid spores; pseudoamyloid hyphae; vesiculose cheilocystidia apically with fine excrescences $1-6 \times 0.7-1$ μm) clearly show the two species distinct.

Raithelhuber (1984: 7) placed *Mycena minutuliaffinis* in the synonymy of *M. basibarbis* Rick, a species of which he had seen the original collection No. 14237, and of which he described the lectotype. His description, however, clearly establishes that the two species have nothing to do with each other (*basibarbis*: pileus pale grey; lamellae subdecurrent; stipe strongly hairy-felted below; cheilocystidia up to 85 μm long, smooth; occurrence in humus). Neither is there any close relation of *M. basibarbis* to *M. lepida*.

Mycena straminella* Maas G. and de Meijer, *spec. nov.* – Fig. 50 (6–10)

Basidiomata dispersa. Pileus 1.5–5 mm latus, usque ad 4 mm altus, e conico convexus, e leve sulcatus, striatus, glaber ut videtur, siccus, pallide stramineus. Caro tenuis, odore nullo. Lamellae 9–10 stipitem attingentes, molles, arcuatae, c. 1.5 mm latae, late adnatae decurrentesque, albae, margine concavae, concolores. Stipes 13–35 × 0.1–0.3 mm, cavus, fragilis, aequalis, cylindraceus, levis, siccus, glaber, albus, basi pallide stramineus, e disco basali fibrilloso, albo natus.

Basidia 18–21.5 × 6.5–7 μm, clavata, 2-sporigera, haud fibulata. Sporae 7.3–8.8 × 3.6–4.7 μm, inaequilateraliter ellipsoideae, leves, haud amyloideae. Cheilocystidia c. 22 × 3.5–4.5 × 2.5 μm, sublageniformia, subcylindracea, haud fibulata, levia. Pleurocystidia nulla. Trama lamellarum iodi ope haud vinescens. Hyphae pileipellis c. 3.5–4.5 μm latae, diverticulatae. Hyphae stipitis corticales 1.5–3.5 μm latae, haud fibulatae, leves, cellulae terminales haud visae.

Ramulicola.

Holotypus: A.A.R. de Meijer RSC-3134 (No. 991.343–778; L); notulae: MBM 190351.

Basidiomata scattered. Pileus 1.5–5 mm across, up to 4 mm high, conical, then convex, at first smooth, then sulcate, translucent-striate, appearing glabrous, dry, the centre and striae pale yellowish white (3A2), between the striae white. Context thin, white. Odour absent. Lamellae 9–10 reaching the stipe, tender, arcuate, c. 1.5 mm broad, broadly adnate and decurrent, not intervenose, white, with concave, concolorous edge. Stipe 13–35 × 0.1–0.3 mm, hollow, fragile, equal, terete, smooth, dry, glabrous, white, near the

---

*Etymology: straminellus, diminutive form of stramineus, straw-coloured, denoting the very pale yellowish white colour of the pileus.

base yellowish white (4A2), springing from a very finely fibrillose, somewhat gelatinized (?), whitish basal patch.

Basidia (immature) $18-21.5 \times 6.5-7$ µm, clavate, one seen with two incipient sterigmata, clampless. Spores $7.3-8.8 \times 3.6-4.7$ µm (Q = 2.0), pipshaped or slightly amygdaliform, smooth, not amyloid. Cheilocystidia c. $22 \times 3.5-4.5 \times 2.5$ µm, forming a sterile band, sublageniform to subcylindrical, clampless, more or less flexuous, smooth. Pleurocystidia absent. Lamellar trama not vinescent in Melzer's reagent. Pileipellis a cutis of repent, radiately aligned hyphae which are c. $3.5-4.5$ µm wide, covered with cylindrical, simple to furcate excrescences $7-11 \times 1.5-2.5$ µm. Hypoderm made up of hyphae with much inflated cells. Hyphae of the cortical layer of the stipe $1.5-3.5$ µm wide, clampless, smooth, terminal cells not seen (but see remark).

On decayed twigs of dicotyledonous trees in mixed ombrophilous forest, 900 m alt.

Holotype: 'Mycena straminella Maas G. and de Meijer / 10 July 1995 / Paraná: Rio Branco do Sul, near cemetry / A.A.R. de Meijer RSC-3134 (No. 991.343-778; L); notes and drawings: MBM 190351.

Among the members of subsection Omphaliariae, Mycena straminella and equally pale yellowish M. alba (Bres. apud Sacc.) Kühn. stand out on account of their hyphae of the stipe cortex being smooth. Otherwise the two species have little in common, M. alba differing from M. straminella in having almost globose spores, inflated excrescences of the hyphae of the pileipellis, and well developed caulocystidia.

Apart from being rather meagre, the type collection is in poor condition; it proved very difficult to see details of the hymenial elements and the pileipellis.

One specimen of the type has been entirely sacrificed for microscopic analysis and, although inspection under the dissecting microscope suggested the presence of caulocystidia, none were found. The stipe turned out to be covered with spores, instead. However, the possibility cannot be excluded that caulocystidia may have been present in other specimens.

27. MYCENA sect. **Nodosae** Maas G. and de Meijer, *sect. nov.*

Basidiomata parva. Pileus minute puberulus, obscure brunneus. Caro tenuis. Lamellae molles, pallidae, margine concolores. Stipes fragilis, glaber, (saltem pro maxima parte) albus.

Basidia clavata, fibulata. Sporae inaequilateraliter ellipsoideae, leves, amyloideae. Cheilocystidia clavata, fibulata, apice vulgo surculis crassis munita. Pleurocystidia nulla. Trama lamellarum (statu siccato) iodi ope haud vel tenuiter vinescens. Hyphae pileipellis haud in materiam gelatinosam immersae, fibulatae, diverticulatae. Hyphae stipitis corticales haud in materiam gelatinosam immersae, fibulatae, leves, cellulis terminalibus destitutae.

Lignicola.

Species typica: *Mycena nodosa.*

Section *Nodosae*, along with section *Diversae* Maas G. and de Meijer, should be placed near section *Exornatae* Maas G. (1982: 538).

134

Mycena nodosa* Maas G. and de Meijer, *spec. nov.* – Fig. 51 (1–4)

Basidiomata gregaria. Pileus 6.5–13 mm latus, hemisphaericus, demum applanatus, siccus, tenuiter sulcatus, striatus, minute puberulus, glabrescens, obscure brunneus, margine albus. Caro tenuis, odore indistincto. Lamellae c. 16 stipitem attingentes, molles, adscendentes, c. 2 mm latae, adnexae, pallide griseo-albae, margine convexo, concolore. Stipes 5–25 × 1–1.3 mm, cavus, fragilis, aequalis, cylindraceus, siccus, levis, glaber, sursum albus, deorsum obscure flavo-brunneus, basi e disco usque ad 3 mm lato, albo-fibrilloso natus.

Basidia c. 16 × 8–9 μm, clavata, 4-sporigera, fibulata. Sporae 7.6–9.8 × 4.5–5.4 μm, inaequilateraliter ellipsoideae, leves, amyloideae. Cheilocystidia 30–50 × 7–13.5 μm, clavata, fibulata, apice vulgo crasse diverticulata. Pleurocystidia nulla. Trama lamellarum (statu siccato) iodi ope haud vinescens. Hyphae pileipellis 1.5–4 μm latae, fibulatae, diverticulatae. Hyphae stipitis corticales 1.8–2.5 μm latae, fibulatae, leves, cellulis terminalibus destitutae.

Truncicola.

Holotypus: A.A.R. de Meijer cua-286b (No. 988.233–087; L); isotypus: mbm 190324.

Basidiomata gregarious. Pileus 6.5–13 mm across, hemispherical, flattening with age, dry, shallowly sulcate, translucent-striate, minutely puberulous, glabrescent, hygrophanous, dark brown or dark brown with a slight yellowish tint (Munsell 10 YR 4/3–4), the extreme margin white. Context thin. Odour indistinct. Lamellae c. 16 reaching the stipe, tender, ascending, up to 2 mm broad, adnexed, pale greyish white, with convex, concolorous edge. Stipe 5–25 × 1–1.3 mm, hollow, fragile, equal, terete, dry, smooth, glabrous, white above, dark yellowish brown below, the base arising from a disc which is up to 3 mm across, finely radiately grooved, white-tomentose.

Basidia (none seen mature) c. 16 × 8–9 μm, clavate, with four incipient sterigmata, clamped. Spores 7.6–9.8 × 4.5–5.4 μm (Q = 1.9), pip-shaped, smooth, rather weakly amyloid. Cheilocystidia 30–50 × 7–13.5 μm, forming a sterile band (lamellar edge homogeneous), clavate, clamped, mostly apically covered with a few small cylindrical excrescences and some very coarse ones, 5–12 × 3–8 μm. Pleurocystidia not observed. Lamellar trama (dried) not vinescent in Melzer's reagent. Pileipellis a cutis of repent, very much branched and anastomosing hyphae which are not embedded in gelatinous matter, 1.5–4 μm wide, clamped, and covered with simple to much branched, cylindrical excrescences 1.5–9 × 0.9–1.5 μm (eventually forming dense masses). Hyphae of the cortical layer of the stipe not embedded in gelatinous matter, 1.8–2.5 μm wide, clamped, smooth, terminal cells absent.

On fallen trunk of a dicotyledonous tree in seasonal semi-deciduous alluvial forest, 870 m alt.

Holotype: '*Mycena nodosa* Maas G. and de Meijer / 19 March 1980 /

---

*Etymology: nodosus, knobby, referring to the coarse excrescences of the cheilocystidia.

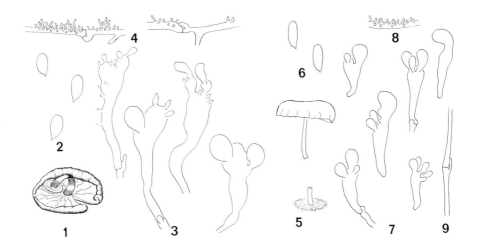

Fig. 51 (1–4) *Mycena nodosa* (de Meijer cua-286b). – 1. Habitus. – 2. Spores. – 3. Cheilocystidia. – 4. Hyphae of the pileipellis.
(5 – 9) *Mycena deformis* (de Meijer ma-2909). – 5. Habitus and basal part of the stipe. – 6. Spores. – 7. Cheilocystidia. – 8. Hypha of the pileipellis. – 9. Hypha of the cortical layer of the stipe.
Fig. 1, × 3; fig. 5, × 10; all others, × 700.

Paraná: Curitiba, Uberaba Distr., Reserva Biológica Cambuí / A.A.R. de Meijer cua-286b' (No. 988.233–087; L); isotype: mbm 190324.

Additional material: '14 Dec. 1979 / same region / A.A.R. de Meijer cua 286 / on dead branches, in seasonal semideciduous alluvial forest, 870 m alt.' (Herb. de Meijer).

Using the key to the sections of *Mycena* (Maas Geesteranus, 1992: 1), one is led to take *M. nodosa* for a member of section *Insignes*, which it is certainly not. The hyphae of the pileipellis as well as of the cortical layer of the stipe of *M. nodosa* are not embedded in gelatinous matter, and the clamp connections in the hyphae of the pileipellis, although not as strikingly loop-like as those in section *Ingratae*, look different from those of several of the *Insignes*-members. An additional difference, albeit perhaps of lesser importance, is the absence of caulocystidia. The differences mentioned would seem to be ample justification for the erection of a new section.

The specific epithet should not be confused with that of *Mycena nodulosa* A.H. Smith (1947: 446) which is a species with tuberculate spores and not a member of the genus *Mycena*.

Mycena deformis* Maas G. and de Meijer, *spec. nov.* – Fig. 51 (5 – 9)

Basidiomata dispersa. Pileus 0.3 – 2.2 mm latus, 0.3 – 1 mm altus, e hemisphaerico planoconvexus, deinde applanatus vel centro interdum subdepressus, tenuiter sulcatus, striatus, pruinosus, siccus, brunneologriseus, hygrophanus, desiccatus albus. Caro tenuis, odore nullo. Lamellae 8 – 11 sti-

*Etymology: deformis, misshapen, referring to the coarse excrescences of the cheilocystidia.

pitem attingentes, molles, adscendentes, c. 0.4 mm latae, adnatae vel pseudocollario affixae, albae, margine convexo, concolore. Stipes 1.5–20 × 0.3 mm, cavus, fragilis, aequalis, cylindraceus, siccus, levis, glaber, albidus, e disco basali c. 1 mm lato, albo-fibrilloso natus.

Basidia 15–18 × 5–6.5 μm, subclavata, 4-sporigera, fibulata, sterigmatibus c. 2.7 μm longis praedita. Sporae 7.2–9.8 × 3.6–4.5 μm, inaequilateraliter ellipsoideae, leves, amyloideae. Cheilocystidia 13.5–30 × 4.5–7 μm, clavata, fibulata, apice vulgo surculis crassis obtusisque 3.5–7 × 2.7–5.5 μm instructa. Pleurocystidia nulla. Trama lamellarum iodi ope tenuiter brunneovinescens. Hyphae pileipellis 1.8–3.5 μm latae, fibulatae, diverticulatae. Hyphae stipitis corticales 1.5–1.8 μm latae, fibulatae, leves, cellulis terminalibus destitutae.

Ad palmarum folia.

Holotypus: A.A.R. de Meijer MA-2909 (No. 990.200–093; L); isotypus: MBM 188504.

Basidiomata scattered. Pileus 0.3–2.2 mm across, 0.3–1 mm high, at first hemispherical, then planoconvex, finally flattened or sometimes with slightly depressed centre, shallowly sulcate, translucent-striate, pruinose, dry, fairly dark grey with some brownish shade (6D2), hygrophanous, drying white. Context thin. Odour absent. Lamellae 8–11 reaching the stipe, tender, ascending, c. 0.4 mm broad, adnate or attached to a pseudocollarium, white, with convex, concolorous edge. Stipe 1.5–20 × 0.3 mm, hollow, fragile, equal, terete, dry, smooth, glabrous, watery-whitish, arising from a basal disc which is c. 1 mm across, radiately fibrillose, white.

Basidia (none seen mature) 15–18 × 5–6.5 μm, subclavate, 4-spored, clamped, with sterigmata c. 2.7 μm long. Spores 7.2–9.8 × 3.6–4.5 μm (Q = 2.1), pip-shaped, smooth, amyloid. Cheilocystidia 13.5–30 × 4.5–7 μm, forming a sterile band (lamellar edge homogeneous), clavate, clamped, apically and/or laterally covered with very coarse, obtuse excrescences 3.5–7 × 2.7–5.5 μm, more rarely smooth. Pleurocystidia absent. Lamellar trama weakly brownish vinescent in Melzer's reagent. Pileipellis a cutis of repent hyphae which are not embedded in gelatinous matter, 1.8–3.5 μm wide, clamped, covered with simple, cylindrical excrescences 1.8–3.5 × 0.9–1.5 μm. Hyphae of the cortical layer of the stipe not embedded in gelatinous matter, 1.5–1.8 μm wide, clamped, smooth, terminal cells absent.

On decayed fronds of a palm, *Euterpe edulis* Mart., in dense ombrophilous forest, 300 m alt.

Holotype: '*Mycena deformis* Maas G. and de Meijer / 12 June 1994 / Paraná: Morretes, Parque Marumbi, Estação Engenheiro Lange, near Nhundiaquara River / A.A.R. de Meijer MA-2909' (No. 990.200–093; L); isotype: MBM 188504.

Singer (1978: 31) described a *Mycena papilligera* which seems not unlike *M. deformis* and which was stated to have a grey pileus, white lamellae, a glabrous stipe, amyloid spores, and cheilocystidia 'with or more rarely without apical (more rarely also lateral) bulges . . .' Singer's species has been found only once and the same, thus far, is true of *M. deformis* so, with the variability of both species being unknown, it is advisable to compare their remaining characters more closely. In *M. papilligera*, the pileus is said to be strongly papillate, the lamellae arcuate and decurrent, the hyphae of the pileipellis 'beset with low, rounded diverticula (. . . 3 × 3 μ) . . .' These characters clearly distinguish *M. papilligera* from *M. deformis*.

Singer thought his species to be a member of his stirps *Cinerella,* but this seems doubtful. Unlike *M. papilligera,* species of stirps *Cinerella* (later raised to section) have their pilei without a papilla, the lamellae somewhat concolorous with the pileus, and the stipes pruinose.

28. MYCENA sect. EXORNATAE Maas G.

Mycena sect. *Exornatae* Maas G. in Proc. K. Ned. Akad. Wet. (C) **85**: 538. 1982. – Type species: *Hiatula boninensis* Berk. and Curt. = *Agaricus chlorophos* Berk. and Curt.

? *Mycena* sect. *Ingratae* Maas G. in Proc. K. Ned. Wet. (C) **92**: 353. 1989. – Type species: *Mycena chlorinosma* Sing.

Basidiomata medium-sized. Pileus viscid, covered with a separable, gelatinous pellicle, brown. Context thin. Odour strong (variously experienced). Lamellae tender, ascending, free or attached to a slight collar, white, the edge not gelatinized. Stipe puberulous, not viscid, whitish to greyish, springing from a white-pubescent basal disc.

Basidia 4-spored, clamped. Spores pip-shaped, smooth, amyloid. Cheilocystidia not embedded in gelatinous matter, fusiform, clamped, simple to somewhat branched apically. Pleurocystidia absent. Lamellar trama vinescent in Melzer's reagent. Pileipellis an ixocutis of hyphae which are partly smooth, partly covered with slender excrescences, clamped, and terminated by long-stalked, clavate, densely diverticulate pileocystidia. Hyphae of the cortical layer of the stipe not embedded in gelatinous matter, smooth, clamped, with smooth caulocystidia.

Lignicolous.

MYCENA CHLOROPHOS (Berk. and Curt.) Sacc. – Fig. 52

Agaricus chlorophos Berk. and Curt. in Proc. Amer. Acad. Arts Sci. **4**: 113. 1860. – *Mycena chlorophos* (Berk. and Curt.) Sacc., Syll. Fung. **5**: 301. 1887. – Holotype (Maas Geesteranus, 1982: 276): 'Herbarium Mycologicum Berkeleyanum / 502. *Agaricus chlorophos,* B. and C. / Bonin Isles. U.S.E.E.' (K).

Prunulus subepipterygius Murrill in Bull. Torrey bot. Club **67**: 233. 1940. – *Mycena subepipterygia* (Murrill) Murrill in Bull. Torrey bot. Club **67**: 235. 1940. – Holotype (Maas Geesteranus, 1989: 353): '*Prunulus subepipterygius* sp. n. / Dead hardwood log / Planera Hammock, Fla. / West and Murrill 7–20–38 / slimy viscid' (FLAS).

For further synonymy, see Maas Geesteranus, 1991: 98.

Basidiomata scattered. Pileus 5–22 mm across, at first subglobose to campanulate, 3.5–5 mm high, then flattening and becoming plano-convex with depressed centre, sulcate, translucent-striate, covered with a separable, gelatinous pellicle, viscid, hygrophanous, centre and striae fairly dark brown (Munsell 10 YR 4/3–4, corresponding more or less with 5E6), turning greyish (4C3) with age, paler to almost white between the striae and towards the margin. Context thin, grey (Munsell 10 YR 6/1, more or less corresponding with 4C2). Odour strong, of chlorine. Lamellae 25–32 reaching the stipe, tender, ascending, up to 4 mm broad, free, pure white, the edge convex, concolorous. Stipe $7-40 \times 1-2$ mm, hollow, equal, terete, puberulous to almost flocculose above, glabrous farther below, shining in dried condition, dry, greyish (4C2) with or without a slight bluish tinge, arising from a small, white–pubescent basal disc.

Basidia $18-29 \times 9-11$ μm, clavate, 4-spored, clamped, with sterigmata up to 6.5 μm long. Spores $7.2-9.0 \times 4.9-5.4$ μm (Q = 1.5), pip-shaped, smooth, weakly amyloid. Cheilocystidia $30-65 \times 9-22.5 \times 2.5-6.5$ μm, forming a sterile band (lamellar edge homogeneous), not embedded in gelatinous matter, fusiform or broadly lageniform, clamped, with a narrow stalk, apically narrowed or acute near the middle of the lamella, producing one or two, simple to branched excrescences $4.5-27 \times 1-2.5$ μm near the pileus margin. Pleurocystidia absent. Lamellar trama vinescent in Melzer's reagent. Pileipellis an ixocutis of repent, radiately aligned hyphae which are $1.8-2.7$ μm wide, clamped, in part smooth, in part sparsely covered with simple to somewhat branched, cylindrical, curved excrescences $3.5-22.5 \times 0.9$ μm, and terminated by long-stalked, clavate pileocystidia $30-110 \times 8-18$ μm which are more or less densely covered with warts and cylindrical excrescences 0.9 –

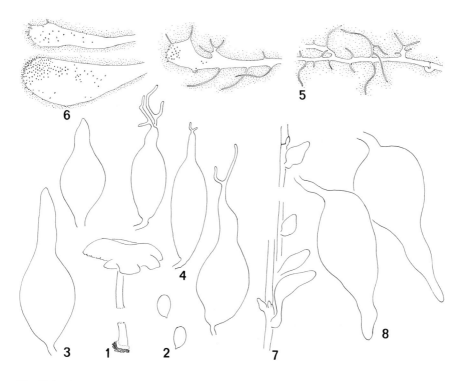

Fig. 52 (1–8) *Mycena chlorophos* (de Meijer cua-87c). – 1. Habitus and basal part of the stipe. – 2. Spores. – 3. Cheilocystidia near the middle of the lamella. – 4. Cheilocystidia near the pileus margin. – 5. Hyphae of the pileipellis. – 6. Terminal cells of hyphae of the pileipellis (pileocystidia). – 7. Hyphae of the cortical layer of the stipe. – 8. Caulocystidia.
Fig. 1, × c. 1.5; all others, × 700.

4.5 × 0.9 μm. Hyphae of the cortical layer of the stipe 2.5–3 μm wide, clamped, smooth, not visibly embedded in gelatinous matter, covered with fusiform to broadly lageniform, smooth caulocystidia, the larger of which measure 70–80 × 20–27 × 4.5–7 μm.

In frondose forest, on decaying stump in seasonal semi-deciduous alluvial forest, 870 m alt.

Material examined: '*Mycena chlorophos* (Berk. and Curt.) Sacc. / 19 Oct. 1979 / Paraná: Curitiba, Uberaba Distr., Reserva Biológica Cambuí / A.A.R. de Meijer CUa-87c' (No. 990.200–161; L); duplicate: MBM 188497.

Additional material: '5 July 1995 / Paraná: Guaraqueçaba, Potinga / A.A.R. de Meijer GUa-3113, on decayed wood of a dicotyledonous tree in dense ombrophilous forest, 5 m alt.' (No. 990.200–127; L); notes and drawings: MBM 188498.

'10 July 1995 / Paraná: Rio Branco do Sul, near cemetery / A.A.R. de Meijer RSc-3135, on decayed branch of a dicotyledonous tree in mixed ombrophilous forest 900 m alt.' (No. 991.343–766; L); duplicate: MBM 1888499.

A species that is known from the Bonin Islands (the type locality) and has been recorded from places as far apart as Borneo, Sri Lanka and Brazil (Corner, 1954: 262) is bound to show some variation, but this concerns only the details. Corner correctly decided that the fungus he had collected 'on numerous occasions' in Brazil would at most 'seem to be a variety of *M. chlorophos*.' Collection CUa-87c described above matches very well the descriptions of *M. chlorophos* given earlier (Maas Geesteranus, 1982: 276 and 1991: 98), somewhat less that of *Mycena subepipterygia* (Murrill) Murrill (Maas Geesteranus, 1989: 354, figs. 102–107), the difference being that the stipe of *subepipterygia* was said to be viscid, while the clamps in the hyphae of the pileipellis are strikingly loop-like. There is no explanation for the latter phenomenon, but it should not be excluded that the viscidity of the stipe may prove to be a variable character. The fact that the stipe of collection CUa-87c has a shining surface in dried condition, while the hyphae of its cortical layer prove to be loosely arranged when seen under the microscope, definitely point to the presence of at least a certain amount of gelatinous matter. Moreover, all other microscopic details correspond very well with those of *M. chlorophos*. It is plausible, therefore, that viscid-stemmed *M. subepipterygia*, found in Florida, is just another name of this wide-spread species.

Whether *Mycena chlorinosma* Singer belongs here is uncertain. Singer considered *chlorinosma* and *subepipterygia* to be the same species (Maas Geesteranus, 1989: 354), but there are differences, both macro- and microscopically.

29. MYCENA sect. **Adornatae** Maas G. and de Meijer, *sect. nov.*

Basidiomata parva. Pileus siccus, pallide griseoflavus. Caro odore nullo. Lamellae molles, arcuatae, albae, margine concolores. Stipes fragilis, siccus, puberulus, obscurus, apice pallidior, insititius.

Basidia clavata, 4-sporigera, fibulata. Basidiola numerosa. Sporae inaequilateraliter ellipsoideae, leves, amyloideae. Cheilocystidia clavata, fibulata, apice surculis crassis instructa. Pleurocystidia nulla. Trama lamellarum iodi ope brunneovinescens. Hyphae pileipellis fibulatae, leves, reticulum formantes, in materiam gelatinosam immersae. Pileocystidia supra dilatata atque diverticulata. Hyphae stipitis corticales fibulatae, haud in materiam gelatinosam immersae, leves; caulocystidia fusiformia, levia.

Foliicola.

Species typica: *Mycena adornata.*

This section is possibly best placed after section *Exornatae* Maas G. (1982: 538).

Mycena adornata* Maas G. and de Meijer, *spec. nov.* – Fig. 53

Basidiomata dispersa. Pileus 0.7–3.5 mm latus, usque ad 3 mm altus, hemisphaericus, centro aetate depresssus, sulcatus, striatus, tenuiter pruinosus, siccus, pallide griseoflavus, centro albidoflavus. Caro tenuis, odore nullo. Lamellae 11–14 stipitem attingentes, molles, arcuatae, usque ad 1.3 mm latae, decurrentes, albae, margine concavo, concolore. Stipes 10–50 × 0.2–0.5 mm, cavus, fragilis, aequalis, cylindraceus, siccus, levis, totus puberulus, rubrobrunneus, apice pallide ochraceus, insititius.

Basidia c. 20 × 8–9 μm, clavata, 4-sporigera, fibulata. Basidiola 22.5–23 × 5.5–8 μm, fusiformia, fibulata. Sporae 8.2–9.6 × 3.8–4.5 μm, inaequilateraliter ellipsoideae, leves, amyloideae. Cheilocystidia 14.5–30 × 7–12.5 μm, clavata, fibulata, apice surculis crassis munita. Pleurocystidia nulla. Trama lamellarum iodi ope brunneovinescens. Hyphae pileipellis 1.8–3.5 μm latae, fibulatae, leves, reticulum formantes, in materiam gelatinosam immersae. Pileocystidia 14.5–36 × 7–15 μm, clavata, fibulata, apice diverticulata. Hyphae stipitis corticales 2.7 μm latae, fibulatae, leves, caulocystidia 8–54 × 5.5–13.5 μm, vulgo fusiformia, levia.

Foliicola.

Holotypus: A.A.R. de Meijer MA-3046 (No. 990.200–055; L); isotypus: MBM 188485.

Basidiomata scattered. Pileus 0.7–3.5 mm across, up to 3 mm high, hemispherical, with age centrally depressed, sulcate, translucent-striate, delicately pruinose, dry, pale greyish yellow (4B3) with yellowish white (4A2) centre. Context thin. Odour absent. Lamellae 11–14 reaching the stipe, tender, arcuate, up to 1.3 mm broad, decurrent, white, with concave, concolorous edge. Stipe 10–50 × 0.2–0.5 mm, hollow, fragile, equal, terete, dry, smooth, puberulous all over, dark red-brown (8E5 below, 8D4 higher up), pale ochraceous near the apex, insititious.

Basidia (none seen mature) c. 20 × 8–9 μm, clavate, 4-spored, clamped. Basidioles 22.5–23 × 5.5–8 μm, abundant, fusiform, clamped. Spores 8.2–9.6 × 3.8–4.5 μm (Q = 2.0), pip-shaped, smooth, amyloid. Cheilocystidia 14.5–30 × 7–12.5 μm, forming a sterile band (lamellar edge homogeneous), clavate, clamped, apically covered with comparatively few, unevenly spaced, coarse to very coarse, simple to furcate, cylindrical to somewhat inflated, obtuse excrescences, 4.5–8 × 2.7–4.5 μm. Pleurocystidia absent. Lamellar trama brownish vinescent in Melzer's reagent. Pileipellis a cutis of repent hyphae which are 1.8–3.5 μm wide, clamped, smooth, reticulately interconnected, embedded in gelatinous matter, with the uppermost hyphae pro-

*Etymology: adornatus, adorned, in reference to the ornamented pileocystidia.

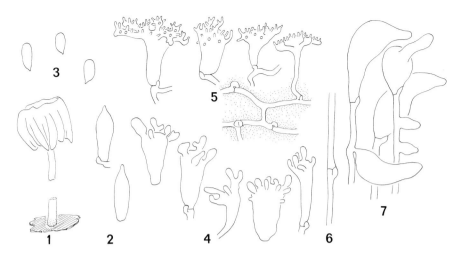

Fig. 53 (1–7) *Mycena adornata* (de Meijer MA-3046). – 1. Habitus and basal part of the stipe. – 2. Basidioles. – 3. Spores. – 4. Cheilocystidia. – 5. Hyphae of the pileipellis and pileocystidia. – 6. Hypha of the cortical layer of the stipe. – 7. Caulocystidia.
Fig. 1, × 5; all others, × 700.

ducing pileocystidia. Pileocystidia 14.5–36 × 7–15 μm, almost cylindrical to clavate, clamped, apically more or less pronouncedly flaring and branched, covered with simple, cylindrical excrescences 1.8–5.5 × 0.9–1.8 μm. Hyphae of the cortical layer of the stipe 2.7 μm wide, clamped, smooth, not embedded in gelatinous matter, the caulocystidia 8–54 × 5.5–13.5 μm, issuing terminally and laterally, generally fusiform, smooth.

On fallen leaves of a dicotyledonous tree in dense ombrophilous forest, 1200 m alt.

Holotype: '*Mycena adornata* Maas G. and de Meijer / 16 March 1995 / Paraná: Quatro Barras, Parque Marumbi, Morro Sete / A.A.R. de Meijer MA-3046' (No. 990.200–055; L); isotype: MBM 188485.

Several features of *Mycena adornata* call to mind those in some species of *Marasmius* Fr., such as the centrally depressed pileus; the insititious stipe which is dark red-brown below, much paler above; the great number of basidioles; the shape and ornamentation of the cheilocystidia (resembling those of *Marasmius curreyi* B. and Br.); the shape of the pileocystidia (resembling those in *Marasmius* section *Androsacei* Kühn.). However, the spores of *Marasmius* species are non-amyloid, there is no species of *Marasmius* which has its hyphae of the pileipellis reticulately interconnected and embedded in gelatinous matter, and the caulocystidia of *M. adornata* are definitely more mycenoid than marasmioid. On the other hand, *M. adornata* fits none of the sections of *Mycena* thus far described. It represents, in fact, a rather aberrant section.

The pileus of *Mycena adornata* appeared to be dry when collected, but given the fact that the hyphae of the pileipellis are embedded in gelatinous

142

matter, the possibility of the pileus turning glutinous or even viscid in wet weather cannot be excluded. This is why the species may be keyed out under both captions 'Pileus viscid' and 'Pileus dry'.

30. MYCENA sect. **Diversae** Maas G. and de Meijer, *sect. nov.*

Basidiomata statura media. Pileus glaber, siccus, griseobrunneus. Caro odore fungoideo. Lamellae molles, arcuatae, albae, margine concolores. Stipes fragilis, siccus, e albido griseobrunneus, fibrillis substrato affixus.

Basidia clavata, fibulata. Sporae inaequilateraliter ellipsoideae, leves, amyloideae. Cheilocystidia lageniformia, fibulata. Pleurocystidia nulla. Trama lamellarum iodi ope haud vinescens. Hyphae pileipellis fibulatae, leves. Hyphae stipitis corticales fibulatae, leves, caulocystidia diversiformia.

Ramulicola.

Species typica: *Mycena diversa.*

This section, along with section *Nodosae* Maas G. and de Meijer, should be placed near section *Exornatae* Maas G. (1982: 538).

Mycena diversa* Maas G. and de Meijer, *spec. nov.* – Fig. 54

Basidiomata dispersa vel gregaria. Pileus 5–27 mm latus, convexus, dein applanatus, striatus, glaber, siccus, hygrophanus, griseobrunneus. Caro pileo concolor, odore fungoideo. Lamellae 12–18 stipitem attingentes, molles, arcuatae, usque ad 3 mm latae, late adnatae, decurrentes, intervenosae, albae, margine concolores. Stipes 8–30 × 0.7–2 mm, cavus, fragilis, aequalis, cylindraceus, levis, apice pruinosus vel subfloccosus, primo albidus, basi pallide griseus, demum pallide griseobrunneus, basi obscurior, fibrillis albis substrato affixus.

Basidia c. 35 × 6–7 µm, clavata, 4-sporigera, fibulata. Sporae 8.1–9.8 × 3.6–4.5 µm, inaequilateraliter ellipsoideae, leves, amyloideae. Cheilocystidia 40–50 × 9–11.5 × 3.5–5.5 µm, lageniformia, fibulata. Pleurocystidia nulla. Trama lamellarum iodi ope haud vinescens. Hyphae pileipellis 1.8–2.5 µm latae, fibulatae, leves, parum gelatinosae. Hyphae stipitis corticales 1.8– 2.5 µm latae, fibulatae, leves, caulocystidia 24–55 × 4.5–10 µm, diversiformia.

Ramulicola.

Holotypus: A.A.R. de Meijer RSC-3130 (No. 991.343–793; L); isotypus: MBM 188512.

Basidiomata scattered to gregarious. Pileus 5–27 mm across, convex, flattening with age and with the margin involute or revolute, smooth to somewhat uneven, translucent-striate, glabrous, dry, hygrophanous, the centre and striae grey-brown (5D4–5E4), between the striae pale grey (4B2). Context concolorous with the pileus. Odour fungoid, taste mild. Lamellae 12–18 reaching the stipe, tender, arcuate, up to 3 mm broad, broadly adnate, somewhat decurrent to strongly decurrent, more or less pronouncedly intervenose, white, with concolorous edge. Stipe 8–30 × 0.7–2 mm, hollow, fragile, equal, terete, smooth or grooved on one side, pruinose to minutely floccose near the apex, glabrous farther down, dry, at first whitish, then pale yellowish grey to pale brownish grey (4B3–5B3) with darker grey-brown base (5C4–5E4), attached to the substratum by a densely bushy mass of very fine, pure white fibrils which turn brownish after drying.

Basidia c. 35 × 6–7 µm, clavate, 4-spored, clamped, with sterigmata

*Etymology: diversus, differently characterized, that is, different from all other *Mycena* species.

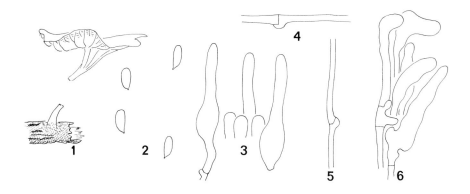

Fig. 54 (1–6) *Mycena diversa* (de Meijer RSC-3130). – 1. Habitus and basal part of the stipe. – 2. Spores. – 3. Cheilocystidia. – 4. Hypha of the pileipellis. – 5. Hypha of the cortical layer of the stipe. – 6. Terminal cells (caulocystidia).
Fig. 1, × 2; all others, × 700.

4.5 μm long. Spores 8.1–9.8 × 3.6–4.5 μm (Q = 2.4), narrowly pip-shaped to almost cylindrical, smooth, strongly amyloid. Cheilocystida 40–50 × 9–11.5 × 3.5–5.5 μm, occurring mixed with the basidia (lamellar edge hetero-geneous), not numerous, lageniform, clamped. Pleurocystidia absent. La-mellar trama not vinescent in Melzer's reagent. Pileipellis a cutis of one or two repent, radiately aligned hyphae which are 1.8–2.5 μm wide, clamped, smooth, slightly gelatinizing. Hypoderm made up of parallel hyphae with inflated cells up to c. 20 μm wide. Hyphae of the cortical layer of the stipe 1.8–2.5 μm wide, clamped, smooth, the caulocystidia 24–55 × 4.5–10 μm, frequently cespitose, variously shaped, thin-walled.

On fallen, decayed twigs (and, occasionally, leaves) of *Araucaria angusti-folia* in mixed ombrophilous forest, 900 m alt.

Holotype: '*Mycena diversa* Maas G. and de Meijer / 10 July 1995 / Paraná: Rio Branco do Sul, near cemetery / A.A.R. de Meijer RSC-3130' (No. 991.343–793; L); isotype: MBM 188512.

Strong amyloidity of the spores coupled with a negative reaction of the lamellar trama in Melzer's reagent is thus far known in yet another South American species – *Mycena radiata* (Dennis) Sing. ex Maas G. (1985: 415), the type species of section *Radiatae*. The two species differ from each other in the nature of the surface of the pileus (squamulose at the centre in *M. radiata*), in the disposition of the lamellae (free from the stipe in *M. radiata*), in the nature of the lamellar edge (lacking cheilocystidia in *M. radiata*). It is clear that *Mycena diversa* does not belong to section *Ra-diatae*. Because of its deviating reactions to Melzer's reagent, it cannot be a member of any other section of *Mycena* either, and this is reflected in the specific epithet *diversa*.

PART III

For the preparation of a flora of South American species of *Mycena*, a key to Singer's species is indispensable. In fact, Singer had intended to publish 'keys to the species of the genera treated . . . after the general treatment of the genus,' a task which if completed would have been a formidable accomplishment. As it is, however, only two instalments were published, covering the genera *Agrocybe* to *Clitopilus* (Singer, 1978 and 1979). Further keys were omitted from later editions of his '*Agaricales*' 'in spite of the fact that many mycologists would have liked to have them at their disposal' (1978: 192). It is these lines which have led to the decision to try to make a key to his Mycenas, even though already some work has been done by Raithelhuber (1995: 12).

The following attempt, of course, can never bear comparison with a key based on one's own investigation of Singer's type specimens. But, at least, it is something to begin with and it is here offered in the belief that it is doubtful whether there will ever be one person in the position to reexamine Singer's *Mycena* types scattered among six different herbaria.

Some of the characters described by Singer seem to be of an unstable nature, as e.g. in *M. abieticola* (1973: 37) 'Hyphis plerumque defibulatis,' or in *M. juaniicola* (1959: 390)' Spores . . . . varying from inamyloid to extremely feebly amyloid,' or pileus colours changing considerably with age. To take care of such varying possibilities, several species have to reappear in the key more than once.

Another point which needs explanation is that the keys, leaving out the sections, lead directly to the species. The reason is that (i) several of Singer's sections and stirpes to which the South American species have been assigned are unfamiliar to the first author; (ii) quite a few species have been described by Singer without a clue as to where they should be placed; (iii) several descriptions are unequal or (iv) sadly deficient.

Key 1.

1. Pileus white, whitish or pallid (with the centre somewhat darker or not): 2
1. Pileus differently coloured: .... Key 2
2. Spores globose to subglobose: 3
2. Spores pip-shaped to (almost) cylindrical: 4
3. Pileus c. 17 mm across, glabrous. Basidia 2-spored (Venezuela):
.... *M. dennisii* Sing. (1955: 394) (syn. *Corrugaria alba* Dennis, 1953: 497)
3. Pileus up to 5 mm across, pulverulent. Basidia 4-spored (Argentina):
.... *M. yalensis* Sing. (1973: 48)
4. Cheilocystidia (sometimes only apically) ornamented: 5
4. Cheilocystidia (although sometimes branched) not ornamented, or absent or unknown: . . 25
5. Pileus 0.5–10 mm across: 6
5. Pileus up to 30 mm across. Spores 2.3–2.8 μm broad. Hyphae of the pileipellis smooth
(Argentina): .... *M. aconquijensis* Sing. (1960: 382)

147

6. Stipe springing from a basal disc or from a basal patch of thin, radiating fibrils: 7
6. Stipe attached to the substratum in a different way: 15
7. Hyphae of the pileipellis or their terminal cells diverticulate: 8
7. Hyphae of the pileipellis smooth (Juan Fernandez Islands):
.... *M. austrocapillaris* Sing. (1959: 391)
8. Hyphae of the cortical layer of the stipe or their terminal cells diverticulate: 9
8. Hyphae of the cortical layer of the stipe smooth: 12
9. Pileus 4–7.5 mm across: 10
9. Pileus 1–2 mm across: 11
10. Lamellae adnate, decurrent with a tooth. Pileipellis not containing spherocysts (Chile):
.... *M. minutuliaffinis* Sing. (1969: 131)
10. Lamellae free. Pileipellis containing spherocysts (Bolivia): ...... *M. sotae* Sing. (1962: 62)
11. Growing on fruit of a broad-leaved tree (Brazil): .... *M. depilata* Sing. (1989: 72)
11. Growing on the rachis of *Dryopteris* sp. (Juan Fernandez Islands):
.... *M. dryopteridis* Sing. (1959: 388)
12(8). Pileus 6 mm across. Lamellae forming a collarium. Growing on fallen dicotyledonous
leaves (Brazil): .... *M. agloea* Sing. (1989: 69)
12. Pileus 0.5–2 mm across: 13
13. Growing on the rachis of *Dryopteris* sp. (Juan Fernandez Islands):
.... *M. dryopteridis* Sing. (1959: 388)
13. Growing on other substrata: 14
14. Spores 3.5–5.7 μm broad. Growing on fruit of a dicotyledonous tree (Brazil):
.... *M. depilata* Sing. (1989: 72)
14. Spores 2.5–4.2 μm broad. Growing on fallen dicotyledonous leaves (Brazil):
.... *M. semipilosa* Sing. (1989: 84)
15(6). Spores 2 μm broad, cylindrical. Hyphae of pileipellis and cortical layer of the stipe
diverticulate (Cuba): .... *M. petiolorum* (Berk. and Curt.) Dennis (1952: 402)
15. Spores 2.5–6.5 μm broad, pip-shaped: 16
16. Pileipellis containing spherocysts and acanthocysts (Brazil):
M. asterophora Sing. (1983: 114; a synonym of *M. heteracantha*, see Desjardin, 1995: 73)
16. Pileipellis different: 17
17. Hyphae of the pileipellis smooth (Ecuador): ....*M. debiliformis* Sing. (1978: 28)
17. Hyphae of the pileipellis or their terminal cells diverticulate: 18
18. Hyphae of the pileipellis embedded in gelatinous matter (Bolivia):
.... *M. ixoleuca* Sing. (1973: 41)
18. Hyphae of the pileipellis not embedded in gelatinous matter: 19
19. Pileus pruinose to finely granular: 20
19. Pileus glabrous: 23
20. Cheilocystidia 4.5–8 μm broad: 21
20. Cheilocystidia 8.7–16 μm broad: 22
21. Pileipellis a cutis made up of filamentose hyphae. Growing on fruit of a broad-leaved tree
(Brazil): .... *M. depilata* Sing. (1989: 72)
21. Pileipellis made up of globose cells. Growing on fallen leaves (Brazil):
.... *M. subtenerrima* Sing. (1989: 85)
22. Pileus 1–2 mm across. Stipe with 50–70 μm long, ampullaceous caulocystidia. Growing on
the rachis of *Dryopteris* sp. (Juan Fernandez Islands): .. *M. dryopteridis* Sing. (1959: 388)
22. Pileus 2.5–6 mm across. Stipe with 67–173 μm long, tapering hairs. Not growing on ferns
(Juan Fernandez Islands): .... *M. triplotricha* Sing. (1959: 386)
23(19). Lamellae narrowly adnexed. Basidia 12–13 μm long (Argentina):
.... *M. microleucoides* Sing. (1989: 80)
23. Lamellae broadly adnate to arcuate-decurrent. Basidia longer: 24
24. Pileus glabrous. Growing on diseased pods of *Theobroma cacao* (Brazil, Costa Rica, Grenada, Trinidad): .... *M. theobromicola* (Murrill) Dennis (Singer, 1987: 463)

24. Pileus covered with hairs 80–300 × 2–4 μm. Growing on fallen leaves (Brazil):
.... *M. microtrichialis* Sing. (1989: 82)

25(4). Stipe yellow-brown: 26

25. Stipe white: 27

26. Spores 5–6 μm broad. Pleurocystidia present (Argentina):
.... *M. micromphale* Sing. (1951: 236)

26. Spores 3–4 μm broad. Pleurocystidia absent (Chile): ..... *M. subulifera* Sing. (1969: 136)

27. Stipe springing from a basal disc or from a basal patch of thin, radiating fibrils: 28

27. Stipe differently attached to the substratum. Lamellae decurrent. Spores 7.5 × 4 μm. Cheilocystidia smooth (Argentina):
M. neotropicalis Sing. (1989: 82; syn. *Marasmiellus foliicola* Sing. apud Sing. and Digilio, 1951: 148. – *Mycena foliicola* (Sing.) Sing.; not *Mycena foliicola* Métrod, 1949: 131)

28. Growing on ferns (Colombia): .... *M. dumontii* Sing. (1989: 72)

28. Growing on other substrata: 29

29. Growing on diseased pods of *Theobroma cacao* (Brazil, Costa Rica, Grenada, Trinidad):
.... *M. theobromicola* (Murrill) Dennis (Singer, 1987: 463)

29. Growing mostly on fallen leaves or decaying wood: 30

30. Hyphae of the pileipellis gelatinized. Cheilocystidia absent (Argentina):
.... *M. piterbargii* Sing. (1969: 116)

30. Differently characterized: 31

31. Stipe glutinous. Pileus dry. Lamellae arcuate (Brazil):
.... *M. glutinocothurnata* Sing. (1989: 73)

31. Stipe dry: 32

32. Cheilocystidia 3.5–5.5 μm broad. Spores 2.5–3.7 μm broad (Argentina, Chile):
.... *M. microleuca* Sing. (1965: 157)

32. Cheilocystidia 5.5–12 μm broad: 33

33. Lamellae adnate and more or less decurrent with a tooth: 34

33. Lamellae not adnate. Pileus pulverulent, pileipellis containing acanthocyst-like cells (Brazil):
.... *M. biornata* Sing. (1973: 38)

34. Pleurocystidia present: 35

34. Pleurocystidia rare or absent:... 36

35. Spores amyloid (Chile):..................... *M. novissima* (Speg.) Sing. (1969: 128)

35. Spores inamyloid (Chile): .... *M. valdiviana* Sing. (1969: 118)

36. Pileus minutely pubescent. Caulocystidia present (Chile):
..................................*M. hyalinotricha* Sing. (1969: 124)

36. Pileus glabrous. Caulocystidia absent (Chile): .... *M. omniumsanctorum* Sing. (1969: 137)

Key 2.

37. Pileus red, pink or flesh-colour: 38

37. Pileus differently coloured: .... Key 3

38. Stipe glabrous: 39

38. Stipe pubescent, at least apically: 46

39. Lamellae yellow. Stipe orange-brown. Hyphae of the pileipellis diverticulate (Argentina):
.... *M. nothofagetorum* Sing. (1969: 114)

39. Lamellae not yellow: 40

40. Lamellae with some pink colour or purple: 41

40. Lamellae white, whitish or pale grey: 42

41. Cheilocystidia ornamented. Stipe purple (Ecuador): .... *M. piguicola* Sing. (1978: 32)

41. Cheilocystidia smooth. Stipe white (Argentina): .... *M. ribesina* Sing. (1969: 113)

42. Stipe white or whitish without any pink shade: 43

42. Stipe pinkish at the apex, or rosy-isabelline or lilaceous-livid: 44

43. Hyphae of the pileipellis diverticulate (Argentina): .... *M. heroica* Sing. (1960: 387)

43. Hyphae of the pileipellis smooth (Argentina): .... *M. ribesina* Sing. (1969: 113)
44. Pileus 20–30 mm across: 45
44. Pileus 7–8 mm across. Lamellae adnexed, pale grey. Spores 5.5–9 × 3 µm (Ecuador):
.... *M. aequatorialis* Sing. (1978: 27)
45. Spores 5–7 × 3–4 µm. Stipe c. 1 mm broad (Mexico):
.... *M. cuticolor* (Murrill) Sing. (1973: 39)
45. Spores 7.3–10 × 4–4.7 µm. Stipe 2–3.5 mm broad (Argentina):
.... *M. sosarum* Sing. (1960: 389)
46(38). Lamellae orange-yellow, with red edge. Cheilocystidia 24–28 µm broad (Brazil):
.... *M. kermesina* Sing. (1989: 77)
46. Lamellae pallid or grey, at times with dark edge. Cheilocystidia 2.5–7 µm broad (Brazil):
.... *M. longicrinita* Sing. (1989: 79)

Key 3

47. Pileus orange-red, orange, yellow or greenish: 48
47. Pileus differently coloured: .... Key 4
48. Pileus yellow-floccose or greenish-floccose. Lamellae and stipe white. Pileipellis containing
acanthocysts (Brazil): .... *M. chloroxantha* Sing. (1983: 114)
48. Differently characterized: 49
49. Cheilocystidia smooth: 50
49. Cheilocystidia ornamented: 59
50. Lamellae white, pallid or greyish: 51
50. Lamellae yellow or orange: 55
51. Spores globose to subglobose: 52
51. Spores pip-shaped: 53
52. Hyphae of the pileipellis smooth (Bolivia): .... *M. leucoxantha* Sing. (1973: 42)
52. Hyphae of the pileipellis diverticulate (Argentina): ..... *M. melinocephala* Sing. (1973: 43)
53. Pileus 8–9 mm across. Stipe yellow-brown, apically white. Hyphae of the pileipellis diverticulate (Colombia): .... *M. xanthocephala* Sing. (1973: 48)
53. Pileus 2.5–4.5 mm across: 54
54. Stipe orange. Basidia 32–33 µm long (Chile): .... *M. chusqueophila* Sing. (1965: 159)
54. Stipe brownish yellow or dark brown. Basidia 15–18 µm long (Brazil):
.... *M. poecila* Sing. (1989: 83)
55(50). Spores pip-shaped: 56
55. Spores globose, 4.7–6.5 × 4.3–6.2 µm. Hyphae of the pileipellis diverticulate (Brazil):
.... *M. icterinoides* Sing. (1989: 75)
56. Pileus 5–19 mm across: 57
56. Pileus 1–2 mm across. Six lamellae reaching the stipe (Brazil):
.... *M. microxantha* Sing. (1989: 82)
57. Spores 6.3–8.2 × 4–4.8 µm: 58
57. Spores 8.2–11.2 × 5–6 µm (Argentina): .... *M. nothofagetorum* Sing. (1969: 114)
58. Cheilocystidia 18–27 × 6.7–8.2 µm (Bolivia): .... *M. carminis* Sing. (1973: 39)
58. Cheilocystidia 40–45 × 9–18 µm (Venezuela):
.... *M. xanthopus* (Dennis, 1961: 86, as *Hemimycena*) Dennis (1970: 41)
59(49). Spores pip-shaped to almost cylindrical: 61
59. Spores globose to subglobose: 60
60. Pileus pale citrine. Hyphae of the pileipellis smooth (Bolivia):
.... *M. leucoxantha* Sing. (1973: 42)
60. Pileus honey-coloured. Hyphae of the pileipellis diverticulate (Argentina):
.... *M. melinocephala* Sing. (1973: 43)
61. Lamellae yellow to orange-yellow: 62

61. Lamellae white, eight reaching the stipe. Hyphae of the pileipellis embedded in gelatinous matter (Colombia): .... *M. ixoxantha* Sing. (1973: 42)
62. Spores 6–8.2 × 3.8–4.8 μm: 63
62. Spores 4.2–6 × 2.3–3.5 μm (Cuba, Guatemala, Costa Rica, Jamaica, Trinidad):
.... *M. citricolor* (Berk. and Curt.) Sacc. (Pegler, 1983: 262)
63. Pileus 6–19 mm across, orange-red. Spores amyloid (Bolivia):
.... *M. carminis* Sing. (1973: 39)
63. Pileus 2 mm across, cadmium-yellow. Spores non-amyloid (Argentina):
    M. tucumanensis Sing. (mentioned in Agar. modern Taxon: 414. 1986, but nomen nudum)

Key 4.

64. Pileus blue, greyish blue, lilaceous, violet or dark purple: 65
64. Pileus brown, yellowish brown, red-brown, purplish brown, dark brown, grey-brown, grey or almost black: .... Key 5
65. Pileus 1 mm across, umbilicate, purplish violet. Growing on fallen leaves (Brazil):
.... *M. microjonia* Sing. (1989: 80)
65. Not these characters combined: 66
66. Lamellae free: 67
66. Lamellae adnate to decurrent: 69
67. Lamellar edge concolorous with the sides. Spores 3.5–5 μm broad: 68
67. Lamellar edge darker coloured than the sides. Spores 6–8 μm broad (Chile):
    M. cyanocephala Sing. (1969: 112) [= *M. interrupta* (Berk.) Sacc., according to Horak, 1983: 10]
68. Pileus 5–9 mm across. Stipe without basal disc (Chile): *M. eucryphiarum* Sing. (1969: 111)
68. Pileus c. 3 mm across. Stipe springing from a basal disc (Chile):
.... *M. mostnyae* Sing. (1969: 108)
69. Stipe glabrous: 70
69. Stipe pubescent, at least below: 75
70. Lamellae white: 71
70. Lamellae not white: 72
71. Pileus blue or greyish blue. Stipe grey or greyish blue. Cheilocystidia 8–18 μm broad (Chile):
.... *M. cyanella* Sing. (1969: 110)
71. Pileus with pinkish or lilaceous shades. Stipe lilaceous livid. Cheilocystidia 6–8 μm broad (Argentina): .... *M. sosarum* Sing. (1960: 389)
72. Hyphae of the pileipellis diverticulate: 73
72. Hyphae of the pileipellis smooth: 74
73. Lamellar edge darker than the sides. Spores 5–7.5 × 3.2–4.2 μm (Argentina):
.... *M. austroavenacea* Sing. (1969: 115)
73. Lamellar edge concolorous with the sides. Spores (7–)7.5–10.5 × 4.5–6 μm (Brazil):
.... *M. porphyrocephala* Sing. (1989: 84)
74. Basidia 4-spored. Spores amyloid (Cuba, Martinique, Trinidad):
.... *M. holoporphyra* (Berk. and Curt.) Sing. (1962: 64); Pegler (1983: 257)
74. Basidia 2-spored. Spores inamyloid (Argentina, Brazil, Lesser Antilles):
.... *M. violacella* (Speg.) Sing. (1955: 235); Pegler (1983: 260)
75(69). Spores globose to subglobose. Cheilocystidia smooth (Costa Rica):
.... *M. cyanosyringea* Sing. (1982: 44)
75. Spores pip-shaped to cylindrical: 76
76. Spores 7–8.5 × 4.5–4.8 μm. Hyphae of the pileipellis smooth (Bolivia):
.... *M. griseorete* Sing. (1962: 64)
76. Spores 4–5.2 × 1.5–2.3 μm. Hyphae of the pileipellis diverticulate (Brazil):
.... *M. ionocephala* Sing. (1989: 77)

Key 5.

77. Spores non-amyloid: 78
77. Spores amyloid: 90
78. Hyphae of the pileipellis smooth: 79
78. Hyphae of the pileipellis diverticulate: 80
79. Pileus up to 5 mm across, convex or shallowly umbilicate: 81
79. Pileus 9–15 mm across, strongly umbilicate (Argentina): ... *M. februaria* Sing. (1960: 386)
80. Spores 5–6 × 4 μm. Pileus c. 5 mm across (Trinidad):
    .... *M. albostriata* Dennis (1970: 42; = *M. umbilicata* Dennis, 1951: 469)
80. Spores 7.5–9 × 6–7 μm. Pileus 2.5 mm across (Brazil): .... *M. pluvialis* Sing. (1989: 83)
81(78). Spores 2.3–3.3 μm broad: 82
81. Spores 4–6.5 μm broad: 83
82. Pileus grey to dark grey. Lamellae 4–6 reaching the stipe (Brazil):
    .... *M. igapoensis* Sing. (1989: 76)
82. Pileus pale brown. Lamellae 15 reaching the stipe (Argentina):
    .... *M. rubrimontana* Sing. (1969: 118)
83. Lamellae white, whitish or pallid, with concolorous edge: 84
83. Lamellae differently coloured or with darker edge: 88
84. Lamellae free: 85
84. Lamellae adnate to decurrent: 86
85. Stipe with the base broadened like a disc. Cheilocystidia 9–10 μm broad. Context inodorous
    (Brazil): .... *M. aosma* Sing. (1973: 37)
85. Stipe not broadened at the base. Cheilocystidia 10.7–21.5 μm broad. Odour distinctly of
    chlorine (Argentina): .... *M. austroalcalina* Sing. (1960: 384)
86. Pileus 5–7.5 mm across, without a papilla. Stipe dry: 87
86. Pileus c. 23 mm across, with striking papilla. Stipe viscid (Colombia):
    .... *M. idroboi* Sing. (1973: 41)
87. Stipe 20 mm long, apically fuliginous(Juan Fernandez Islands):
    .... *M. juaniicola* Sing. (1959: 390)
87. Stipe 5 mm long, apically white (Bolivia): .... *M. neospeirea* Sing. (1973: 44)
88(83). Lamellae yellow or brownish. Stipe 11–20 mm long: 89
88. Lamellae pallid with violaceous brown edge. Stipe 4–5 mm long (Costa Rica):
    .... *M. castaneostipitata* Sing. (1989: 70)
89. Lamellae yellowish with dark brown edge. Spores 6.5–7.5 μm long (Brazil):
    .... *M. castaneomarginata* Sing. (1989: 70)
89. Lamellae brownish without darker edge. Spores 10.7–12.7 μm long (Juan Fernandez
    Islands): .... *M. juaniicola* Sing. (1959: 390)
90(77). Spores globose or subglobose: 91
90. Spores pip-shaped to almost cylindrical: 96
91. Cheilocystidia ornamented: 92
91. Cheilocystidia smooth: 95
92. Pileus honey-yellow, yellow-brown or reddish brown: 93
92. Pileus dark grey. Stipe white (Costa Rica): .... *M. costaricensis* Sing. (1982: 41)
93. Stipe insititious, up to 5 mm long (or only little longer). Hyphae clampless (Argentina):
    .... *M. hypsizyga* Sing. (1969: 122)
93. Stipe not insititious, 15–22 mm long: 94
94. Basidia 2-spored. Spores 10.5–13.5 μm long. Hyphae predominantly clampless. Growing on
    Abies (Mexico): .... *M. abieticola* Sing. (1973: 37)
94. Basidia 4-spored. Spores 8–10.5 μm long. Hyphae clamped. Growing on wood in montane
    Alnetum (Argentina): .... *M. melinocephala* Sing. (1973: 43)
95(91). Cheilocystidia 6–8(–15) μm broad. Growing on the ground in a meadow (Uruguay):
    .... *M. pratensis* Sing. (1973: 46)
95. Cheilocystidia 14.5–18.7 μm broad. Growing on decayed wood (Juan Fernandez Islands):

153

155

REFERENCES

Berkeley, M.J. (apud Cooke) – Fungi of Java. Grevillea **18**: 54 (1890).

Corner, E.J.H. – Descriptions of two luminous tropical agarics (*Dictyopanus* and *Mycena*). Mycologia **42**: 423–431 (1950).

Corner, E.J.H. – Further descriptions of luminous agarics. Trans. Br. mycol. Soc. **37**: 256–271 (1954).

Corner, E.J.H. – A monograph of Cantharelloid fungi. Ann. Bot. Mem. **2** (1966).

Corner, E.J.H. – *Boletus* in Malaysia. Singapore (1972).

Corner, E.J.H. – The tropical complex of *Mycena pura*. Trans. bot. Soc. Edinburgh, **150**th Ann. Suppl.: 61–67 (1986).

Corner, E.J.H. – Agarics in Malaysia. I. Tricholomatoid, II. Mycenoid. Nova Hedwigia Beih. **109** (1994).

Dennis, R.W.G. – Some Agaricaceae of Trinidad and Venezuela. Leucosporae: Part 1. Trans. Br. mycol. Soc. **34**: 411–482 (1951).

Dennis, R.W.G. – Fungi venezuelani: IV. Kew Bull. **15**: 67–156 (1961).

Dennis, R.W.G. – Fungus flora of Venezuela and adjacent countries. Kew Bull. Addit. Ser. **3** (1970).

Desjardin, D.E. – A preliminary accounting of the worldwide members of *Mycena* sect. *Sacchariferae*. Bibl. mycol. **159**: 1–89 (1995).

Garrido, N. – Agaricales s.l. und ihre Mykorrhizen in den Nothofagus-Wäldern Mittelchiles (*Mycena*: pp. 210–216). Bibl. mycol. **120** (1988).

Grgurinovic, C. – *Mycena* in Australia: Section *Roridae*. Austr. syst. Bot. **8**: 537–547 (1995).

Hedger, J., D. Jean Lodge, G. Dickson, H. Gitay, T. Laessøe and R. Watling – The BMS expedition to Cuyabeno, Ecuador: An introduction. Mycologist **9**: 146–148 (1995).

Horak, E. – A contribution towards the revision of the Agaricales (Fungi) of New Zealand. New Zealand J. Bot. **9**: 403–462 (1971).

Horak, E. – *Mycena rorida* (Fr.) Quél. and related species from the Southern Hemisphere. Ber. schweiz. bot. Ges. **88**: 20–29 (1978).

Kühner, R. – Le genre *Mycena* (Fries). Encycl. mycol. **10** (1938).

Lodge, D. Jean – Three new *Mycena* species (Basidiomycota, Tricholomataceae) from Puerto Rico. Trans. Br. mycol. Soc. **91**: 109–116 (1988).

Maas Geesteranus, R.A. – Studies in Mycenas 9–14. Proc. K. Ned. Akad. Wet (C) **83**: 403–416 (1980).

Maas Geesteranus, R.A. – Studies in *Mycena*–15. A tentative subdivision of the genus *Mycena* in the northern Hemisphere. Persoonia **11**: 93–120 (1980).

Maas Geesteranus, R.A. – Studies in Mycenas 72. Berkeley's fungi referred to *Mycena*–2. Proc. K. Ned. Akad. Wet. (C) **85**: 527–539 (1982).

Maas Geesteranus, R.A. – Conspectus of the Mycenas of the Northern Hemisphere–1. Sections *Sacchariferae, Basipedes, Bulbosae, Clavulares, Exiguae*, and *Longisetae*. Proc. K. Ned. Akad. Wet. (C) **86**: 401–421 (1983).

Maas Geesteranus, R.A. – Conspectus of the Mycenas of the Northern Hemisphere–2. Sections *Viscipelles, Amictae*, and *Supinae*. Proc. K. Ned. Akad. Wet. (C) **87**: 131–147 (1984).

Maas Geesteranus, R.A. – Conspectus of the Mycenas of the Northern Hemisphere–3. Section *Filipedes*. Proc. K. Ned. Akad. Wet. (C) **87**: 413–447 (1984).

Maas Geesteranus, R.A. – Conspectus of the Mycenas of the Northern Hemisphere–4. Section *Mycena*. Proc. K. Ned. Akad. Wet. (C) **88**: 339–369 (1985).

Maas Geesteranus, R.A. – Studies in Mycenas 177. Section *Radiatae* remodelled. Proc. K. Ned. Akad. Wet. (C) **88**: 413–417 (1985).

Maas Geesteranus, R.A. – Conspectus of the Mycenas of the Northern Hemisphere–5. Sections *Luculentae, Pterigenae, Carolinenses*, and *Monticola*. Proc. K. Ned. Akad. Wet. (C) **89**: 83–100 (1986).

Maas Geesteranus, R.A. – Conspectus of the Mycenas of the Northern Hemisphere– 6. Sections *Polyadelphia* and *Saetulipedes*. Proc. K. Ned. Akad. Wet. (C) **89**: 159–182 (1986).

Maas Geesteranus, R.A. – Conspectus of the Mycenas of the Northern Hemisphere– 9. Section *Fragilipedes*, species A–G. Proc. K. Ned. Akad. Wet. (C) **91**: 43–83 (1988).

Maas Geesteranus, R.A. – Conspectus of the Mycenas of the Northern Hemisphere-10. Sections *Lactipedes, Sanguinolentae, Galactopoda*, and *Crocatae*. Proc. K. Ned. Akad. Wet. (C) **91**: 377–403 (1988).

Maas Geesteranus, R.A. – Conspectus of the Mycenas of the Northern Hemisphere-12. Sections *Fuliginellae, Insignes, Ingratae, Euspeireae*, and *Caespitosae*. Proc. K. Ned. Akad. Wet. (C) **92**: 331–365 (1989).

Maas Geesteranus, R.A. – Conspectus of the Mycenas of the Northern Hemisphere-13. Sections *Calamophilae* and *Calodontes*. Proc. K. Ned. Akad. Wet. (C) **92**: 477–504. (1989).

Maas Geesteranus, R.A. – Conspectus of the Mycenas of the Northern Hemisphere-14. Sections *Adonideae, Aciculae*, and *Oregonenses*. Proc. K. Ned. Akad. Wet. (C) **93**: 163–186 (1990).

Maas Geesteranus, R.A. – Conspectus of the Mycenas of the Northern Hemisphere-15. Sections *Hiemales* and *Exornatae*. Proc. K. Ned. Akad. Wet. **94**: 81–102 (1991).

Maas Geesteranus, R.A. – Studies in Mycenas. Additions and Corrections. Proc. K. Ned. Akad. Wet. **94**: 377–571 (1991).

Maas Geesteranus, R.A. – Two new Mycenas of section *Insignes* from the Netherlands. Proc. K. Ned. Akad. Wet. **95**: 469–472 (1992).

Maas Geesteranus, R.A. and A. Hausknecht – *Mycena pallescens*, a new species of section *Fragilipedes* from La Réunion (France, Africa). Öst. Z. Pilzk. **4**: 51–54 (1995).

Métrod, G. – Mycènes de Madagascar (*Mycena, Corrugaria, Pterospora*). Paris (1949).

Montagne, [J.F.]C. – *Cryptogamia guyanensis*. Annls Sci. nat. (Bot.) VI **1**: 94–144 (1854).

Montagne, [J.F.]C. – Septième centurie de plantes cellulaires nouvelles, tant indigènes qu'exotiques. Annls Sci. nat. (Bot.) IV **5**: 333–374 (1856).

Montagne, [J.F.]C. – Sylloge generum specierumque Cryptogamarum. Parisiis (1856).

Murrill, W.A. – *Prunulus*. North Amer. Flora **9**: 319–344 (1916)

Patouillard, N. – Quelques espèces nouvelles de champignons extraeuropéens. Rev. mycol. **13**: 135–138 (1891).

Patouillard, N. and A. Gaillard – Champignons du Vénézuela et principalement de la région du Haut-Orénoque, récoltés en 1887 par M.A. Gaillard. Bull. Soc. mycol. Fr. **4**: 7–46 (1888).

Pegler, D.N. – A preliminary agaric flora of East Africa. Kew Bull., Addit. Ser. **6** (1977).

Pegler, D.N. – Agaric flora of the Lesser Antilles. Kew Bull., Addit. Ser. **9** (1983).

Pegler, D.N. – A revision of the Agaricales of Cuba 1. Species described by Berkeley and Curtis. Kew Bull. **42**: 501–585 (1987).

Raithelhuber, J. – Neue oder wenig bekannte Tricholomataceae Argentiniens. Metrodiana, Sonderheft **1** (1972).

Raithelhuber, J. – Hongos argentinos I. Buenos Aires (1974).

Raithelhuber, J. – Der Arten- und Formenkreis um *Mycena pura*. Metrodiana **9**: 26–40 (1980).

Raithelhuber, J. – Die Gattung *Mycena* in Südamerika. Metrodiana **10**: 5–18 (1984).

Raithelhuber, J. – Die Gattung *Mycena* in Südamerika, 2. Teil. Metrodiana **10**: 24–34, 40–44 (1984).

Raithelhuber, J. – Die Gattung *Mycena* in Südamerika, 3. Teil. Metrodiana **11**: 2–20 (1984).

Raithelhuber, J. – Die Gattung *Mycena* in Südamerika, 4. Teil. Metrodiana **11**: 31–45 (1985).

Raithelhuber, J. – Die Gattung *Mycena* in Südamerika, 5. Teil. Metrodiana **12**: 3–10 (1985).

Raithelhuber, J. – Nomina nova. Metrodiana **14**: 22 (1986).

Raithelhuber, J. – Flora mycologica argentina. Hongos I. Stuttgart (1987).

Raithelhuber, J. – Flora mycologica argentina. Hongos III. Stuttgart (1987).

Raithelhuber, J. – Nomina et combin. nova. Metrodiana **16**: 79. (1988).

Raithelhuber, J. – Flora mycologica argentina. Hongos III. Stuttgart (1991).

Raithelhuber, J. – Agaric flora of South America (11). *Mycena*. Metrodiana **23**: 12–52 (1996).

Raithelhuber, J. – Agaric flora of South America (12). Metrodiana **23**: 124–152 (1996).

159

Rick, J. Contributio II ad monographiam Agaricinarum brasiliensium. Brotéria (Bot.) 17: 101–111 (1919).

Rick, J. – Contributio IV ad monographiam Agaricacearum brasiliensium. Brotéria (Bot.) 24: 97–118 (1930).

Rick, J. – Agarici riograndenses (Secund parte). Lilloa 2: 251–316 (1938).

Rick, J. – Agarici riograndenses. Index. Lilloa 5: 13–30 (1939).

Rick, J. – Basidiomycetes Eubasidii in Río Grande do Sul-Brasilia. Iheringia (Bot.) 8 (1961) (not seen).

Robich, G. – On a new species of *Mycena* from Spain. Persoonia 16: 245–248 (1996).

Ryvarden, L. and I. Johansen – A preliminary polypore flora of East Africa. Fungiflora. (1980).

Singer, R. – Notes sur quelques Basidiomycètes. IIIe Serie. Rev. Mycol. 2: 226–242 (1937).

Singer, R. – New species of Agaricales from Pernambuco. An. Soc. biol. Pernambuco 13: 225–233 (1955).

Singer, R. – Basidiomycetes from Masatierra (Juan Fernandez Islands, Chile). Ark. Bot. II 4: 371–400 (1959).

Singer, R. – New and interesting species of Basidiomycetes. VI. Mycologia 51: 375–400 (1960).

Singer, R. – Diagnoses fungorum novorum Agaricalium II. Sydowia 15: 45–83 (1962).

Singer, R. – Mycoflora australis. Beih. Nova Hedwigia 29: 1–392 (1969).

Singer, R. (apud N. Lazo) – Contribution à l'étude des Macromycètes du Chili. Lejeunia 61: 1–32 (1971).

Singer, R. – Diagnoses fungorum novorum Agaricalium III. Beih. Sydowia 7: 1–106 (1973).

Singer, R. – The Agaricales in modern taxonomy. 3rd ed., Vaduz (1975).

Singer, R. – Interesting and new species of Basidiomycetes from Ecuador II. Nova Hedwigia 29: 1–98 (1978).

Singer, R. – Keys for the identification of the species of Agaricales I. Sydowia 30: 192–279 (1978).

Singer, R. – Keys for the identification of the species of Agaricales II. Sydowia 31: 193–237 (1979).

Singer, R. – Acanthocytes in *Amparoina* and *Mycena*. Cryptogamie (Mycol.) 4: 111–115 (1983).

Singer, R. – The Agaricales in modern taxonomy. 4th ed., Koenigstein (1986).

Singer, R. – *Mycena theobromicola*, a fungus associated with cacao pod rot. Mycologia 79: 463–464 (1987).

Singer, R. New taxa and new combinations of Agaricales (Diagnoses fungorum novorum Agaricalium IV). Fieldiana (Botany) 21: 1–133 (1989).

Singer, R. and A.P.L. Digilio – Pródromo de la flora argentina. Lilloa 25: 5–461 (1951).

Singer, R. and L.D. Gomez P. – Basidiomycetes of Costa Rica 1. Brenesia 19–20: 31–47 (1982).

Singer, R. and M. Moser – Forest mycology and forest communities in South America. Mycopathol. Mycol. appl. 26: 129–191 (1965).

Smith, A.H. – North American species of *Mycena*. Univ. Mich. Stud., Scient. Ser. 17 (1947).

Spegazzini, C. – Fungi fuegiani. Bol. Acad. nac. Cienc. Córdoba 11: 135–308 (1887).

Spegazzini, C. – Algunos hongos chilenos. Rev. Chil. Hist. nat. 21: 117–126 (1917).

Spegazzini, C. – Algunos hongos chilenos. Rev. Chil. Hist. nat. 22: 95–104 (1918).

Spegazzini, C. – Mycetes chilenses. Bol. Acad. nac. Cienc. Córdoba 25: 1–124 (1921).

Spegazzini, C. – Cryptogamae nonnullae fuegianae. An. Soc. cient. Argent. 94: 59–85 (1922).

Spegazzini, C. – Observaciones y adiciones a la Micologia Argentina. Bol. Acad. nac. Cienc. Córdoba 28: 267–406 (1926).

UNESCO – International classification and mapping of vegetation. Ecology and Conservation 6. Paris (1973).

Veloso, H.P. and L. Goés-Filho – Fitogeografia brasileira, classificação fisionômico-ecológica da vegetação neotropical. Bol. Tècn. Proj. RADAM-BRASIL, Sér. veg. 1 (1982).

Watling, R. and N.M. Gregory – Census catalogue of World members of the *Bolbitiaceae*. Bibl. mycol. 82 (1981).

160

If not indicated otherwise, all specific epithets are those of members of *Mycena*. New names are in **bold-face** type. Subdivisions of genera are indicated by the sign §.

I D DAY